# SURVIVING SUDDEN
# ENVIRONMENTAL CHANGE

# SURVIVING SUDDEN ENVIRONMENTAL CHANGE

## UNDERSTANDING HAZARDS, MITIGATING IMPACTS, AVOIDING DISASTERS

*Edited by*
JAGO COOPER AND PAYSON SHEETS

*Authors*
David A. Abbott, John Marty Anderies, Jago Cooper, Andrew Dugmore, Ben Fitzhugh,
Michelle Hegmon, Scott E. Ingram, Keith W. Kintigh, Ann P. Kinzig, Timothy Kohler,
Stephanie Kulow, Emily McClung de Tapia, Thomas H. McGovern, Cathryn Meegan,
Ben A. Nelson, Margaret C. Nelson, Tate Paulette, Matthew A. Peeples,
Jeffrey Quilter, Charles L. Redman, Daniel H. Sandweiss, Payson Sheets,
Katherine A. Spielmann, Colleen A. Strawhacker, Orri Vésteinsson

UNIVERSITY PRESS OF COLORADO

© 2012 by the University Press of Colorado

Published by the University Press of Colorado
5589 Arapahoe Avenue, Suite 206C
Boulder, Colorado 80303

 The University Press of Colorado is a proud member of
the Association of American University Presses.

The University Press of Colorado is a cooperative publishing enterprise supported, in part, by Adams State College, Colorado State University, Fort Lewis College, Metropolitan State College of Denver, Regis University, University of Colorado, University of Northern Colorado, and Western State College of Colorado.

∞ The paper used in this publication meets the minimum requirements of the American National Standard for Information Sciences—Permanence of Paper for Printed Library Materials. ANSI Z39.48-1992

Library of Congress Cataloging-in-Publication Data

Surviving sudden environmental change : understanding hazards, mitigating impacts, avoiding disasters / editors, Jago Cooper and Payson Sheets ; authors, David A. Abbott ... [et al.].
    p. cm.
  Includes bibliographical references and index.
  ISBN 978-1-60732-167-5 (pbk. : alk. paper) — ISBN 978-1-60732-168-2 (ebook)  1. Environmental archaeology—Case studies. 2.  Social archaeology—Case studies. 3.  Natural disasters—Social aspects—History—To 1500. 4.  Climatic changes—Social aspects—History—To 1500. 5.  Human ecology—History—To 1500. 6.  Human beings—Effect of climate on—History—To 1500. 7.  Social evolution—History—To 1500. 8.  Social change—History—To 1500. I. Cooper, Jago. II. Sheets, Payson D. III. Abbott, David A.
  CC81.S87 2012
  930.1—dc23
                        2011045973

Text design by Daniel Pratt
Cover design by Zoë Noble and Daniel Pratt

21  20  19  18  17  16  15  14  13  12        10  9  8  7  6  5  4  3  2  1

# Contents

# Foreword

*Thomas H. McGovern*

It is a genuine pleasure to provide this foreword to what will certainly become a key volume for the integration of the long-term perspective (*longue durée*) with present and future efforts to cope with hazards to the environment and human welfare. As Payson Sheets and Jago Cooper emphasize in their introduction and overview chapter, this group of contributors draws upon an impressive range of disciplines and well-developed case studies from around the globe. They are united in a growing movement among archaeologists, environmental historians, and paleoecologists to make a well-understood past serve to create a more genuinely sustainable future and increase human resilience in the face of both gradual and sudden change (Constanza, Graumlich, and Steffen 2007; Crumley 1994; Dugmore et al. 2007; Fisher, Hill, and Feinman 2009; Hornberg, McNeill, and Martinez-Alier 2007; Kirch 1997, 2007; Kohler and van der Leeuw 2007; Marks 2007; McGovern et al 2007; Norberg et al. 2008; Redman et al. 2004; Rick and Erlandson 2008; Sabloff 1998).

## THE EAGLE HILL MEETING, OCTOBER 2009

The editors and contributors are also connected by their participation in the three-day Global Longterm Human Ecodynamics Conference hosted by the Humboldt Field Research Institute at its excellent facility in Eagle Hill,

Maine, on October 16–19, 2009 (http://www.eaglehill.us/). The conference was generously funded by a grant from the US National Science Foundation (NSF), Office of Polar Programs (OPP), Arctic Social Sciences Program, as part of President Barack Obama's American Recovery and Reinvestment Act. Our OPP grants officer, Dr. Anna Kerttula de Echave, played an invaluable and inspirational role before, during, and after what proved to be an incredibly energized and successful meeting. The Eagle Hill meeting grew out of discussions with the NSF about the desirability of harvesting fresh data and perspectives acquired by some of the large-scale projects funded under new cross-disciplinary initiatives, including the NSF Biocomplexity competition, the Human and Social Dimensions of Global Change program, and the International Polar Year (2007–2009), as well as various European interdisciplinary programs (BOREAS, Leverhulme Trust projects), to promote more effective interregional (especially north-south) communication and integration of teams, cases, and new ideas. In spring 2009 a team drawn from the North Atlantic Biocultural Organization (NABO) research and education cooperative (Andy Dugmore of the University of Edinburgh, Sophia Perdikaris and Tom McGovern of CUNY, and Astrid Ogilvie of the University of Colorado) was tasked with organizing a working conference that would connect teams and scholars active in diverse areas of human ecodynamics research and involve students participating in Sophia's Islands of Change Research Experience for Undergraduates (REU) program. The October Eagle Hill meeting eventually had seventy-one faculty and student active participants, representing a dozen disciplines and nations worldwide. Prior to the meeting, participants interacted through the NABO website maintained by Dr. Anthony Newton (University of Edinburgh), and this on-line collaboration and preparation proved critical to the success of the meeting (for a full report on the Eagle Hill meeting and a list of faculty participants, see http://www.nabohome.org/meetings/glthec2009.html).

As part of the pre-meeting preparation we grouped participants into working groups, each with at least two chairs charged with organizing their groups, leading discussions before and during the meeting, and preparing presentations by each working group for discussion by the entire group. The teams and chairs were:

- Methods, Data, and Tools (chairs Doug Price and Tina Thurston): New analytic tools allow transformation in our abilities to trace migration, reconstruct diet, and reconstruct settlement. Some specialties and approaches are very recent in origin (stable isotopes, aDNA), and others have recently been able to significantly upgrade their general utility through expanded data resources (archaeobotany, zooarchaeology, geoarchaeology).

- Who Cares Wins (Shari Gearheard and Christian Keller): Education, community involvement, policy connections, and interdisciplinary engagement. Moving beyond outreach to mobilize traditional environmental knowledge (TEK) and local knowledge and expertise for global science. Engaging underrepresented sources of innovation and expanding human resources. Connecting science to the public and providing diversity to policy makers.

- Hazards and Impacts (Payson Sheets and Jago Cooper): Recurring hazards, differential impacts, long-term lessons for vulnerability and resilience, successful and unsuccessful models of response and adaptation.
- Climate Change (Socorro Lozano and Lisa Kennedy): Climate change impacts, threshold crossings, adaptation versus resilience, past lessons for future impacts.
- Models and Visualization (Shripad Tuljapurkar and Tiffany Vance): Digital resources for education, data integration and dissemination, integrative modeling, and exploration of complex causality and complex self-organizing adaptive systems.
- Coping and Scale (Tate Paulette and Jeff Quilter): Societies of different scales have produced cases of both failure and long-term sustainability in balancing demands of specialization, short-term efficiency, and long-term flexibility in the face of discontinuous but often rapid changes in natural and social environments.
- Ecodynamics of Modernity (Steve Mozorowski and Jim Woollett): Past "world system" impacts since CE 1250, commoditization, repeated pandemic impacts, climate change, Columbian exchange, mass migration, cross-scale integration and linkage, maximum potential for integration of history, ethnography, archaeology, and multi-indicator environmental science.

All of these team presentations provoked intense and productive discussions (some of which lasted far into the night), but the Hazards and Impacts team led by Payson and Jago was a clear "star" session among many very strong contenders. In part, this reflected the dynamic of the conference, where all participants were deeply committed to using their expertise to make concrete and practical contributions to improving the lives of present and future residents in their research areas. As discussed fully in Jago and Payson's introductory chapter, hazards research provides a well-structured venue for the long-term perspective to have immediate and positive benefits, and this has attracted contributors from other Eagle Hill teams to what had been the Hazards and Impacts team project.

## THE GLOBAL HUMAN ECODYNAMICS ALLIANCE (GHEA)

The Eagle Hill meeting resulted in a strong consensus to continue and broaden discussions begun in Maine, drawing in more teams, disciplines, and world areas to achieve a genuinely global perspective that could take on projects such as this excellent volume, as well as sponsor field and laboratory collaborations, student training, public education, and engagement with global change science. This consensus led to a proposal to organize and launch a new Global Human Ecodynamics Alliance (GHEA). Ben Fitzhugh (University of Washington) generously agreed to take on the work of launching the group and a series of meetings in Arizona (hosted by Peggy Nelson and her team), Edinburgh (hosted by Andy Dugmore jointly with the Scottish Alliance for Geoscience, Environment, and Science [SAGES]), and St. Louis (organized by Ben at the Society for American Archaeology meetings). GHEA is now up and running with its new official website created by Anthony (www.gheahome.org).

GHEA is intended to be an open, loosely structured, and very flexible group (down low in the "r" area of the classic resilience metaphor loop) that will seek to build community and aid scholars, students, and members of the wider public in connecting across national and disciplinary boundaries. All are invited to participate and join through the website. GHEA is rapidly evolving in response to member interests, but some bullet points incorporated into GHEA from the Eagle Hill meeting may indicate shared interests:

- Productive Engagement with Global Change and Challenges of Sustainability
- Promoting Diversity of Knowledge Sources
- Integration of Policy, Education, Outreach, Community Participation in Global Science
- Spatial Patterning, Place-Based Learning, Longitudinal Research Programs
- Critical Times and Places: thresholds, tipping points, regime shifts.

This book is an early product of the Global Human Ecodynamics Alliance and sets a high standard for future GHEA collaborations.

## ACKNOWLEDGMENTS AND THANKS

We would like to thank our hosts in Eagle Hill, Maine, for a memorable conference venue, and we gratefully acknowledge the dedication and sleep deprivation of the CUNY REU team (Marissa Gamiliel, Reaksha Persaud, and Jessica Vobornik) and CUNY doctoral student Cory Look, who also handled many IT issues and logistics so competently. We also thank CUNY doctoral students Amanda Schreiner and George Hambrecht for heroic long-distance late night driving. We are all greatly indebted to Shari Gearheard, whose amazing recording and synthesizing skills preserved an excellent record of fast-moving and intense discussions. This conference was funded by an American Recovery and Reconstruction Act grant from the National Science Foundation, Office of Polar Programs, Arctic Social Sciences Program (NSF OPP ASSP #0947852), and supplements to the NABO International Polar Year Arctic Social Science Program grant (NSF OPP ASSP #0732327), for which we are profoundly grateful.

On a personal note, I particularly thank Payson and Jago for their incredible energy and dedication at every stage of this collaboration. From energizing their working group at the Eagle Hill conference through every phase of securing NSF subvention support for the book project to organizing the rapid and effective peer review through arranging the innovative and effective publication format in close collaboration with the University Press of Colorado, they have proved to be a remarkably talented and exceptionally capable team. Many thanks to the editors.

## REFERENCES

Constanza, Robert, Lisa J. Graumlich, and Will Steffen, eds.
2007    *Sustainability or Collapse? An Integrated History and Future of People on Earth.* MIT Press, Cambridge, MA.

Crumley, Carole, ed.
1994    *Historical Ecology.* School of American Research Press, Santa Fe, NM.

Dugmore, Andrew J., Douglas M. Borthwick, Mike J. Church, Alastair Dawson, Kevin J. Edwards, Christian Keller, Paul Mayewski, Thomas H. McGovern, Kerry-Anne Mairs, and Guðrún Sveinbjarnardóttir
2007    The Role of Climate in Settlement and Landscape Change in the North Atlantic Islands: An Assessment of Cumulative Deviations in High-Resolution Proxy Climate Records. *Human Ecology* 35: 169–178.

Fisher, Christopher T., J. Brett Hill, and Gary M. Feinman
2009    *The Archaeology of Environmental Change: Socionatural Legacies of Degradation and Resilience.* University of Arizona Press, Tucson.

Hornbprg, Alf, J. R. McNeill, and Joan Martinez-Alier, eds.
2007    *Rethinking Environmental History: World System History and Global Environmental Change.* Altamira, Lanham, MD.

Kirch, Patrick V.
1997    Microcosmic Histories: Island Perspectives on "Global" Change. *American Anthropologist* 99(1): 30–42.
2007    Hawaii as a Model System for Human Ecodynamics. *American Anthropologist* 109(1): 8–26.

Kohler, Timothy A., and Sander van der Leeuw, eds.
2007    *The Model-Based Archaeology of Socionatural Systems.* School of American Research Press, Santa Fe, NM.

Marks, Robert B.
2007    *The Origins of the Modern World: A Global and Ecological Narrative from the Fifteenth to the Twenty-First Century,* 2nd ed. Rowman and Littlefield, Toronto.

McGovern, Thomas H., Orri Vésteinsson, Adolf Fridriksson, Mike Church, Ian Lawson, Ian A. Simpson, Arni Einarsson, Andy Dugmore, Gordon Cook, Sophia Perdikaris, Kevin Edwards, Amanda M. Thomson, W. Paul Adderley, Anthony Newton, Gavin Lucas, and Oscar Aldred
    2007    Landscapes of Settlement in Northern Iceland: Historical Ecology of Human Impact and Climate Fluctuation on the Millennial Scale. *American Anthropologist* 109(1): 27–51.

Norberg, Jon, James Wilson, Brian Walker, and Elinor Ostrom
    2008    Diversity and Resilience of Social-Ecological Systems. In *Complexity Theory for a Sustainable Future*, ed. Jon Norberg and Graeme S. Cumming. Columbia University Press, New York, pp. 46–81.

Redman, Charles L., Steven R. James, Paul R. Fish, and J. Daniel Rogers, eds.
    2004    *The Archaeology of Global Change.* Smithsonian Institution Press, Washington, DC.

Rick, Torben C., and Jon M. Erlandson, eds.
    2008    *Human Impacts on Ancient Marine Ecosystems: A Global Perspective.* University of California Press, Berkeley.

Sabloff, Jeremy A.
    1998    Distinguished Lecture in Anthropology: Communication and the Future of American Archaeology. *American Anthropologist* (December): 869–875.

# Chapter Abstracts

## Chapter 1
## HAZARDS, IMPACTS, AND RESILIENCE AMONG HUNTER-GATHERERS OF THE KURIL ISLANDS

*Ben Fitzhugh*
University of Washington

In the anthropological and archaeological literature, hunter-gatherers are often treated as victims of short-term environmental catastrophe and longer-term environmental change, responding to extreme environmental perturbations through adaptation or local extinction/emigration. The Kuril Biocomplexity Project was designed in part to evaluate the extent to which the hunter-gatherer settlement history in the environmentally dynamic Kuril Islands was affected by catastrophic events and sustained climate changes. This chapter pulls together newly generated archaeological, geological, and paleoenvironmental evidence to consider the extent to which Kuril hunter-gatherers were vulnerable to extreme environmental hazards in combination with relatively high geographic insularity.

The chapter explicitly discusses the *key hazards* (volcanic eruptions, earthquakes and tsunamis, low biotic diversity, climate change, and their effects on sea ice distributions, storminess and marine productivity, and geographic-social insularity), evidence of *past impacts* (frequencies and intensities of volcanic eruptions, earthquakes, and tsunamis and significant changes in climate and marine productivity), and evidence for *human mitigation, vulnerabilities,* and *resilience* to these hazards (settlement displacement and hiatuses in occupation, evasive settlement placement, foraging selectivity, and development of selective exchange networks). A major conclusion of this case study is that hunter-gatherers were remarkably resilient to environmental calamities, which for the most part had limited impacts on settlement history. Explaining the discontinuous occupation history of the Kurils instead requires consideration of the effects of social networking in the context of relative insularity and the cultural implications of social, political, and economic developments in the more densely occupied "mainland" regions to the south and west. From this study we can begin to develop a generalized model concerning social scale and networks of social and economic interdependence that can help us better conceptualize *future risks* to human occupation of these and similar relatively insular environments.

## Chapter 2
## RESPONSES TO EXPLOSIVE VOLCANIC ERUPTIONS BY SMALL TO COMPLEX SOCIETIES IN ANCIENT MEXICO AND CENTRAL AMERICA

*Payson Sheets*
UNIVERSITY OF COLORADO, BOULDER

The full range of societal complexities, from small egalitarian villages to state-level civilizations, was impacted by explosive volcanic eruptions in ancient Central America and Mexico. Some societies were remarkably resilient and recovered from the volcanic disasters within decades. Others were vulnerable to sudden massive stresses and failed to recover. This chapter explores the factors that contribute to resilience or vulnerability, including societal complexity, demography and mobility, connectivity, magnitude of the eruption, social conflict, organization of the economy, loss of traditional environmental knowledge (TEK), and political organization. Each factor can be scaled regarding its contribution to vulnerability. As societies respond to disasters, not everyone suffers. There were winners and losers in the ancient past, as there are with contemporary disasters. People learn from disasters and modify their vulnerabilities. Therefore the creative aspects of hazard perception are also explored in this chapter.

Chapter 3
## BLACK SUN, HIGH FLAME, AND FLOOD: VOLCANIC HAZARDS IN ICELAND

*Andrew Dugmore and Orri Vésteinsson*
UNIVERSITY OF EDINBURGH AND UNIVERSITY OF ICELAND

People in Iceland have lived (and died) with volcanic hazards for over 1,150 years. These hazards can be broadly grouped into four types: those from volcanic fallout (ash fall and pyroclastic flows), floods (of water melted from glaciers or dammed in rivers and *lahars*), lava, and pollution (poisoning from carbon monoxide and fluorine). They occur at irregular intervals and often widely separated times—maybe once or twice a generation, maybe once a millennium. When volcanic hazards do occur, their scale may be comparatively limited—affecting a small region for a short time—or their effects may be persistent and felt both across the entire island and much farther afield. Long recurrence times have meant there may be little specific planning to cope with volcanic impact.

The potential human impacts of volcanic eruptions do not depend on the size and type of eruption alone; the environmental and social context is vital. Few volcanic eruptions have directly or indirectly killed people, but when bad synergies occur, death tolls can be great.

Historically, communal resilience in Iceland that developed to face other environmental challenges, such as extreme weather, has been the basis of effective response to volcanic hazards and the mitigation of their impacts. Today, volcanic emergency planning in Iceland has specific provisions based on detailed geological assessments. The modern science of volcanic hazard assessment faces a number of specific challenges over establishing the nature of possible events and their potential impacts. Some past volcanic events have left clear traces behind, such as a layer of volcanic ash or a characteristic flood deposit. Other hazards, such as fluorine poisoning of livestock, leave no direct evidence, and their occurrence has to be inferred indirectly through, for example, studies of magma composition (to infer the presence of a volatile element) or written records of deaths of livestock or people. Even when there is direct physical evidence, such as the landscape record of a flood, it may be ambiguous. Was it from a volcanic event? How big was the event?

Serendipitously, the volcanic events that create hazards in Iceland have also created a very effective means of assessing those hazards. Volcanic eruptions frequently create extensive layers of volcanic ash (tephra) that are rapidly spread across the landscape. These deposits form marker horizons that are incorporated into the rapidly aggrading aeolian soils. We can identify, correlate, and date these tephra deposits; reconstruct extensive synchronous horizons; and use them to gain precise knowledge of past hazards: their magnitude, extent, and impact. The tephras themselves may be the hazard; we can tell if this is so because precise mapping of individual deposits can tell us their size and environmental impact. In a similar way we can, for example, use tephras to show that scattered traces of flooding may all belong to the same event and have originated from a volcano. Crucially, we can also reconstruct details of the environments at the time of past volcanic events and thus gain key data on the context of past hazards. Precise dating (to the decade, year, season, and even the day) allows true interdisciplinary collaboration and effective discussion about common questions of hazard, mitigation, and disaster among historians, archaeologists, ecologists, geographers, geologists, planners, and policy makers. Deeper time (multi-millennia) perspectives can give insight on possible return times and alert us to events that can occur but that have not (yet) been experienced in historical time.

## Chapter 4
## FAIL TO PREPARE, THEN PREPARE TO FAIL: RETHINKING THREAT, VULNERABILITY, AND MITIGATION IN THE PRECOLUMBIAN CARIBBEAN

*Jago Cooper*
UNIVERSITY OF LEICESTER

For over 5,000 years, Precolumbian populations in the Caribbean lived with the hazards created by the impacts of climate change—in particular, a 6-m rise in relative sea levels, marked variation in annual rainfall, and periodic intensification of hurricane activity. In this chapter I evaluate the ways Precolumbian populations identified the risk of these potential hazards and consider how they mitigated the impacts over time to build resilient communities. This research exploits the time depth of cultural practice to provide archaeological lessons that can inform current responses to the impacts of sudden environmental change in the Caribbean. I explore the temporal and spatial scales at which cause and effect between archaeological and paleoenvironmental phenomena can be correlated, analyzed, and interpreted. Using a series of well-researched case studies from around the Caribbean, I correlate archaeological data with the identified impacts of sudden environmental change to provide key patterns in the changing nature of Precolumbian cultural practices. I argue that Precolumbian communities developed settlement locations, food procurement strategies, and household architecture designs well suited to living through the impacts of sudden environmental change. I discuss how these past communities developed resilient lifeways in the face of both short- and long-term hazards and consider whether modern populations in the Caribbean could develop coping strategies that utilize these Precolumbian lessons for living through the impacts of climate change.

## Chapter 5
## COLLATION, CORRELATION, AND CAUSATION IN
## THE PREHISTORY OF COASTAL PERU

*Daniel H. Sandweiss and Jeffrey Quilter*
UNIVERSITY OF MAINE AND HARVARD UNIVERSITY

The coast of Peru is subject to a multitude of hazards occurring at different temporal and spatial scales and often working synergistically to create major disasters for the region's human inhabitants. The best known of these hazards is El Niño, a recurring climatic perturbation that brings torrential rain, erosion of landscapes and infrastructure, loss of marine biomass, and plagues of diseases and insects. Earthquakes are also common and can prime the terrain with sediment that is set in motion by El Niño and cycled through the landscape by subsequent littoral and aeolian processes. The final round in the sediment cycle is sand swamping of agricultural systems, complementing the initial destruction from El Niño but on a longer timescale. All of the components of this system of synergistic hazards continue to operate today in the context of population growth and high-investment agrarian expansion. In this chapter we review several case studies involving El Niño, earthquakes, and sand, with attention to frequency and predictability, temporal and spatial scales, and human impacts. We conclude by considering the potential role of hazards across the long sweep of cultural development in ancient Peru and drawing lessons for the future.

## Chapter 6
## SILENT HAZARDS, INVISIBLE RISKS: PREHISPANIC EROSION
## IN THE TEOTIHUACAN VALLEY, CENTRAL MEXICO

*Emily McClung de Tapia*
UNIVERSIDAD NACIONAL AUTÓNOMA DE MÉXICO

This chapter provides a case study of risk and resilience from the Teotihuacan Valley in the northern Basin of Mexico. Between 100 BC and AD 600, the prehispanic city of Teotihuacan grew to occupy an area of roughly 20 km$^2$, with at least 100,000 inhabitants in the urban zone alone. The city had an enormous impact on the surrounding landscape, and the city's development was associated with adaptive strategies in which inhabitants modified the landscape to deal with the increased vulnerability to natural hazards created by rising population densities.

Results from recent geoarchaeological research in the Teotihuacan Valley suggest a complex history of landscape development closely associated with human impact. Clear evidence for alternating periods of landscape stability and instability is related to periodic erosion. Evidence for severe erosion and concomitant floods is directly related to the regional settlement history. Deforestation of surrounding slopes contributed to increased runoff that was partially controlled by terracing; the abandonment of terrace systems following population decline contributed to uncontrolled erosion and flooding. Historical documents describe similar events following the Spanish Conquest, which resulted in the relocation of at least one village and administrative center. These processes contributed to severe floods in Mexico City because the hydrological system of the Teotihuacan region drained into the lake system on which the Colonial city was constructed.

Erosion and floods are common today in the central highlands of Mexico; although the immediate causes may vary, inadequate management of slopes results in proportional risks for human lives and economic infrastructure. The transition from what was largely a rural agricultural economy to an urban-based service-oriented economy, together with a significant increase in population density, represents an enormous challenge to the sustainability of the Basin of Mexico. Archaeological settlement patterns and other kinds of archaeological and paleoecological evidence from the Teotihuacan Valley and elsewhere in the Basin of Mexico provide important lessons for modern-day communities. This case study suggests that urban communities integrated with productive rural hinterlands, rather than the current model of extensive industrial corridors and dense human settlements, contribute to greater resilience for human populations and sustainability for the environment.

## Chapter 7
## DOMINATION AND RESILIENCE IN BRONZE AGE MESOPOTAMIA
*Tate Paulette*
University of Chicago

Although Mesopotamia has long occupied a prominent position in the Western public imagination, recent events—in particular, the US-led occupation of Iraq and the large-scale looting of museums and archaeological sites—have drawn the Iraqi present and the Mesopotamian past vividly into the spotlight. Images of legendary ancient cities, now stranded in arid wastelands, and broken monuments to kings of vanished civilizations resonate powerfully with modern audiences, themselves increasingly uncertain about our collective future. For a world in which environmental disaster and economic collapse loom on the horizon, ancient Mesopotamia can provide both cautionary tales and success stories. Recurring hazards such as drought, disease, flooding, and river channel shifts were regularly planned for, counteracted, and endured in Mesopotamia. Several episodes of political and economic collapse, however, testify to the precarious balance that was sometimes struck between centralizing efforts and a capricious environment. The vigorous debates generated by these collapse episodes also exemplify the difficulty of pinning down and explaining the causal factors behind social and environmental transformations. The case studies presented here challenge the reader to tease apart the complicated interconnections that link human action and institutional management with processes of environmental degradation and climate change.

This chapter focuses on the Bronze Age (ca. 3000–1200 BC) in Mesopotamia. Following immediately on the heels of state formation and the so-called Urban Revolution, the Bronze Age was a time of demographic flux and intense political contestation. Cities dominated the landscape, and powerful urban institutions vied for control over the labor and resources of a heterogeneous population. During several brief episodes of political centralization, expansionist dynasties created regional-scale polities that eventually dissolved, leaving a recurring pattern of autonomous city-states. At the same time, occasional evidence for large groups of nomadic or semi-nomadic pastoralists hints at the existence of segments of the population that were able to operate, at least partially, beyond the bounds of institutional control.

The complexity and dynamism of the socio-political landscape in Bronze Age Mesopotamia must take center stage in any study of environmental hazards and their impact on human society. The inhabitants of Mesopotamia were confronted with a difficult and unpredictable environment, and many of them dealt directly with that environment on a daily basis as they plowed their fields, worked their gardens, or led their animals to pasture. For many, however, interaction with the environment was mediated by or filtered through institutional structures; the effects of institutional control were an ever-present fact of life, whether visible in the strict orchestration of daily tasks or, more indirectly, in the legacy of a heavily managed and modified agricultural landscape. This chapter provides an introduction to the range of hazards—both strictly "environmental" and human-induced—that threatened the livelihood of people and the survival of settlements and states in Bronze Age Mesopotamia. It also outlines the responses that were available and the short- and long-term impacts of different types of hazard. Throughout the discussion, emphasis is placed on the evolving role of institutional management and the shifting boundaries of institutional domination.

Chapter 8

## LONG-TERM VULNERABILITY AND RESILIENCE: THREE EXAMPLES FROM ARCHAEOLOGICAL STUDY IN THE SOUTHWESTERN UNITED STATES AND NORTHERN MEXICO

*Margaret C. Nelson, Michelle Hegmon, Keith W. Kintigh, Ann P. Kinzig, Ben A. Nelson, John M. Anderies, David A. Abbott, Katherine A. Spielmann, Scott E. Ingram, Matthew A. Peeples, Stephanie Kulow, Colleen A. Strawhacker, and Cathryn Meegan*

ARIZONA STATE UNIVERSITY
GRAND CANYON COLLEGE

Archaeology brings time depth to an array of issues, from migration and resettlement to climate change and environmental impacts of human actions. The long term does not provide predictions for future courses but it does provide examples, social-ecological experiments of sorts, by which we can come to better understand processes and relationships used to make contemporary decisions about managing for change versus managing for stability. In this chapter we describe a collaborative study of long-term relationships between ecosystems and social systems in the prehispanic and proto-historic southwestern United States and northern Mexico that examines key concepts employed by scholars and policy makers in the resilience community. This community's concern is with promotion of social and environmental policies that build resilient systems that can flexibly respond to uncertain future conditions and avoid catastrophic transformations. In this chapter we focus on three key concepts: rigidity, diversity, and tradeoffs.

Chapter 9

## SOCIAL EVOLUTION, HAZARDS, AND RESILIENCE: SOME CONCLUDING THOUGHTS

*Timothy A. Kohler*
WASHINGTON STATE UNIVERSITY

I briefly consider the history of social evolutionary models in anthropology and, even more briefly, in biology. I discuss the implications of the chapters in this book for these models, which as a group imply that such models must consider the types of risks and hazards a society faces, as well as the temporal and spatial structures of those risks. I outline what such a model would look like.

Chapter 10
## GLOBAL ENVIRONMENTAL CHANGE, RESILIENCE, AND SUSTAINABLE OUTCOMES
*Charles L. Redman*
ARIZONA STATE UNIVERSITY

Resilience of a system is often defined as the system's ability to maintain its basic structure and essential functions in the face of a stress or a shock. In many ways a socio-ecological system's response to the occurrence of a natural hazard is an excellent, although often extreme, case study of resilience. In examining these ecodynamics, we must differentiate between what we expect to be appropriate behavior based on our own implicitly justified normative views and what we actually observe in the past to be a sustainable situation. Many basic principles advocated in ecological versions of resilience theory—such as the value of redundancy, flexibility, stored capital, investment in mitigation, and maximum information flow—may in fact conflict with sustainable outcomes when applied to human-dominated systems. Moreover, a resilience approach is often predicated on the assumption that current conditions (natural in particular) are optimal and that change equates with degradation of the system and hence is negative. However, as we know from social systems, current conditions may not be desirable and may have feedbacks that strongly resist change (e.g., the poverty trap). Implementing a sustainability approach requires that we not only promote a system's adaptive capacity but also that we evaluate the desirability of the system as it now operates and develop measurable indicators that encode desirable, normatively held values. These indicators would include aspects of the biophysical functioning of the ecosystem but also equity and access to opportunities in the social system and how the two interact and ramify. In fact, most practitioners of sustainability find that the systems they study are not only less than optimal but also do not even meet minimal standards of sustainability. All of this becomes more complex in the face of potential, systems-transforming natural hazards.

**SURVIVING SUDDEN**
**ENVIRONMENTAL CHANGE**

# Learning to Live with the Dangers of Sudden Environmental Change

*Payson Sheets and Jago Cooper*

Human communities around the world are increasingly worried about the dangers of sudden environmental change. This book aims to illustrate how the full time depth of human experience can reveal the nature of these dangers and help build long-term sustainable societies. The diversity in human cultures across the past few thousand years is extraordinary, from small groups of hunter-gatherers to chiefdoms and states to empires with populations in the millions. The diversity of environments within which they lived is equally impressive, from deserts and oases through Arctic tundra to tropical rainforests with the greatest biomass and biodiversity of any terrestrial environment. Given this dual diversity, there are no recipes for evaluating how a culture should successfully adapt to its environment. But there is a phenomenon common to both cultures and environment, and that is change. Societies change as populations increase, for instance, and systems of authority emerge and strengthen as egalitarianism fades. In addition, societies affect their environments, sometimes for the better but often to the detriment of soils, flora, and fauna. Environments change on a short-term basis (weather and seasonality) and on a long-term basis (climate), and human societies of all kinds learn to adjust to those changes. Societies adjust to most environmental changes with little difficulty, as flexibility is built into adaptation. However, some changes are of such magnitude that societies are deeply affected by them, and the post-stress society is recognizably different or in some cases simply does not survive.

The most severe environmental changes, which massively impact societies, are often called "natural disasters." To find a truly and solely natural disaster, we would have to find an event that did not involve people, such as the K/T asteroid impact that killed off the dinosaurs 65 million years ago. Some studies of "natural disasters" emphasize the natural component and neglect the human social component, and, as discussed later, natural scientists and engineers receive most of the funding in disaster research. However, the authors in this book believe deeply that sociocultural factors are essential in understanding risk, impact, resilience, reactions, and recoveries from massive sudden environmental changes. Therefore we prefer the term *disaster* to *natural disaster* when people are involved.

Many disasters originate in the form of a force from nature, such as an earthquake, cyclone, tsunami, volcanic eruption, drought, or flood. But that is half of the story; people and their cultures are the rest of the story and must be as closely studied. How people distribute themselves across the landscape, how they feed themselves, how authority is structured, their perception of risk, their experience with earlier disasters, and the oral or written history of them are all crucial factors in how a society handles a disaster and how it recovers from it, or not.

The documented impacts of disasters have been huge in the past, and with worldwide populations increasing—often dramatically in hazardous zones—impacts are growing in the present and will continue to do so into the future. According to statistics gathered by the United Nations, every year about 200 million people are directly impacted by disasters (Mauch and Pfister 2009). That is seven times the number of people affected by wars per year.

Disasters are the stock-in-trade of many movies and TV shows and are becoming ever more horrendous with increasing special-effects sophistication. Of course, the popular media emphasize death and destruction, panic, looting, and personal suffering of physical and psychological natures. Some disasters are even credited with the end of civilizations. One would hope that the broadcast and print news media would deal with disasters in a more balanced manner, and occasionally they do. But a Central American journalist let one of us (PS) in on what he called international journalism's best-kept secret: journalists in any country greatly exaggerate the disasters in other countries, so no matter how bad living conditions are in their country, they appear worse elsewhere. Social science studies of disasters do record suffering, but the studies that go beyond the immediacy of the impact generally find remarkable resilience and recovery. In addition, disasters have a creative aspect in that people can learn from them and adjust their culture to be better prepared for them in the future. Oral histories and religious beliefs can incorporate the extreme phenomena, so the precursors can lead to evasive action.

## HAZARD-DISASTER RESEARCH

Using disasters as a means to explain major changes in people and their societies is common to many of the world's cultures. The biblical accounts of the flood and Noah's ark saving his family and fauna are known to all. Sumerian and Babylonian flood legends, also destroying evil and saving a few good people and animals, are older than the biblical flood, as they date back well over three millennia. Perhaps the traditional chasm between religion and science has inhibited many social scientists from serious study of disasters, combined with the overly dramatic popular media accounts.

Systematic study of disasters began with the work of Gilbert White (1945), a cultural geographer who studied the Johnstown, Pennsylvania, flood in terms of the physical phenomenon and how people and their culture affected their vulnerabilities. White began the comparative study of disasters in the social sciences, and he contributed an applied dimension of planning to reduce people's risks to future flooding. White's work clarified the distinction between disaster and hazard. The disaster is the actual catastrophic event, while a hazard is a disaster "waiting in the wings" and therefore subject to study, risk perception, and planning for mitigation of impact when the disaster actually occurs. White was the first to combine physical phenomena with cultural factors in an integrated fashion.

As cases grew, patterns were perceived, and as general interest in human ecology surged during the second half of the twentieth century, social scientists saw the need for theory building in the hazard/disaster field. A seminal volume by Ian Burton, Robert Kates, and Gilbert White (1978) contributed a framework for understanding and comparing relationships among people, societies, and sudden massive stresses. In it the authors relate external stresses to adjustments people make and identify three key thresholds. With a relatively minor stress, they suggest the minimal adjustment people make is Loss Absorption, which occurs after the first threshold of Awareness is crossed. Basically, people accept the losses, make minor changes, and get on with their lives. With greater stress the threshold of Direct Action is crossed, and Loss Reduction is the result. People deliberately do what they decide is necessary to deal with the significant changes in their natural and social environments. Still greater stress crosses the threshold of Intolerance, and people decide to take Radical Action. An example of Radical Action would be refugees deciding to migrate from the area of a disaster to a very different area, necessitating major changes in their society, their adaptation, or both.

Current social science research on hazards and disasters owes much to the early work of White and his associates. Their work has stimulated federal funding for hazard-disaster research, but ironically the predominance of support has favored the physical sciences and engineering. David Alexander (1995) surveyed the field and found that 95 percent of funding went to the physical and technological sciences, leaving only 5 percent for the social sciences. Alexander (1997) also explored the diversity of disciplines conducting disaster research and found a surprising total of thirty, ranging from the humanities through the social sciences to the physical sciences and engineering. The predominance of research focuses on the physical forcing mechanism, the immediacy of the disaster, and technological means of mitigating similar disasters in the future. Relatively rare are longer-term studies that trace the effects of a disaster and human responses to it. Some humanistic scholars in history have begun to do what they consider to be long-term studies of disasters, covering a decade or more (Mauch and Pfister 2009). Archaeologists can certainly expand on that time frame. And all disaster research fields can learn from the patterns and insights Mauch and Pfister provide.

## ARCHAEOLOGICAL CONTRIBUTIONS TO DISASTER STUDIES

As long as archaeologists have been excavating settlements and recording stratigraphy, they have encountered evidence of disasters. The evidence takes the form of a volcanic ash deposit, alluvium from flooding, walls collapsed from an earthquake, or loci abandoned because of drought. From the late nineteenth century until fairly recently, ash or flood deposits were viewed as temporal horizon markers or stratigraphic separators of cultural materials. Or in some cases they were examined as disasters, and some were ascribed causality in the decline or collapse of cultures or civilizations. Until recently they were described and interpreted as single cases and dealt with in atheoretical ways. A few surveys and assessments of the field of archaeological studies of disasters have been published, and they provide a means to understand the development of the field and explore ways in which future studies could be conducted.

The earliest survey of archaeological disaster studies was done in the late 1970s (Sheets 1980). That paper pointed out the above-mentioned shortcomings and emphasized the opportunities for archaeologists to do comparative analyses and take advantage of great time depths in studying disasters. It lamented the paucity of studies that combined natural and social science examinations of disasters and their aftermaths. Mary van Buren (2001: 129) conducted a survey of the field two decades later and noted that "archaeological research on disasters had increased substantially since Sheets' 1980 review of the topic." She noted the continued contributions by cultural geographers to disaster studies, in particular with the concept of vulnerability—that is, how people perceive hazards, deal with disasters, and recover from them. Vulnerability has economic, religious, political, social, and demographic aspects. These can become acute with the growth of populations as the disenfranchised lowest levels of societies are relegated to the most hazardous locations, in floodplains, for instance. She also noted that modern ecological concepts can contribute to future research but stated that a limiting factor is the persisting paucity of theory. Sheets (2008) has made some attempts in theory building, comparing three dozen cases of explosive volcanism affecting egalitarian to state-level societies in Middle America and beginning to see some patterns in factors that support resilience and other factors that increase vulnerability.

John Grattan and Robin Torrence (2007: 1) recently conducted a survey of the field and noted a "boom in archaeological research focused on the effects of ancient catastrophes on culture change." They listed six books published on the topic during the four-year period 1999–2002, and the publications have not diminished since their survey was completed. They note that social factors are handled in a more thorough manner in disaster studies than was the case in past decades. They suggest that disaster studies move beyond emphasizing the "gloom and doom" of the most dramatic immediate impacts. Disasters have creative aspects, as people learn from their experiences and adjust their adaptations. Unfortunately, modernization can lead to the loss of oral history and useful knowledge, an observation that resonates in the chapters that follow.

We take it as a salutary sign that the Geological Society of America is publishing some social science chapters in its geological volumes. For instance, six chapters by social scientists were published on volcanic-human interactions and social issues in the volume *Natural Hazards in El Salvador* (Rose et al. 2004).

## LIVING WITH THE DANGERS OF SUDDEN ENVIRONMENTAL CHANGE—ORIGINS OF THIS BOOK

As McGovern's foreword to this book suggests, the origins lie in a session on Hazards and Disasters at the Global Human Ecodynamics meeting in Eagle Hill, Maine, USA, in October 2009. Preparation for this session began with a month of on-line discussion among the eight contributors focused on three pre-defined themes of challenges, contributions, and future research that culminated in a combined group presentation to colleagues and government representatives at Eagle Hill. Each contributor brought together a combination of historical, archaeological, paleoclimatological, and environmental data from his or her selected case study to examine the role of societal context in the relative experience and varied impact of environmental hazards and disasters. This book maintains this group approach, which, we hope, can facilitate direct comparison between different case studies and enable an informed conceptual understanding of the different ways human communities have lived with the dangers of sudden environmental change. By utilizing the deep time perspectives of our interdisciplinary approaches, this book provides a rich temporal background to the human experience of environmental hazards and disasters.

The book provides eight separate case studies, each examining how one past human community has faced the impacts of sudden environmental change. Different cases of resilience and destruction are presented; as the book develops, it is hoped that key lessons for improved hazard and disaster management emerge.

Each of the case study chapters has a comparable structure and complementary thematic coverage that enables direct comparisons between the actions and reactions of the different human communities involved. The book provides well-researched case studies that cover a broad temporal and spatial spectrum. Research projects range from Arctic to equatorial regions, from deep prehistory to living memory, and from tropical rainforests to desert interiors. However, each chapter is united by the careful examination of how past peoples understood the hazards that threatened them, how they attempted to mitigate the potential impacts, and whether their survival strategies proved successful in avoiding disaster. Each chapter broadly follows the same four themes of key hazards, past impacts, mitigation, and future risks. In each case study, the *key hazards* that faced the past society or societies in question are identified, and the nature of the specific threats and the timescales at which they occurred are explored. The direct and indirect *past impacts* of these hazards are then examined, with particular attention focused on the possibility of both foreseeable and unforeseeable and positive and negative impacts on past societies. There is then a discussion of the ways human communities engaged with potential hazards, and evidence for *mitigation, vulnerability,* and *resilience* is revealed. These examples raise important topics for discussion surrounding the sophistication of ecological knowledge that cultures can develop over centuries or millennia, the intentionality of mitigation strategies, and the process of societal decision-making. The time depth of each case study provides an informed perspective for this wider discussion, as thresholds of change and cycles of renewal in the human ecodynamics of past societies are unraveled. Each chapter then looks toward *future risks,* considers the relevance of the past case studies for modern human communities, and assesses the relative threat of hazards and potential lessons from the past for the development of successful resilience strategies in the present.

## CONTRIBUTIONS TO HAZARD-DISASTER RESEARCH IN THIS BOOK

The chapters in this book are broadly ordered in relation to the nature of the hazards threatening past societies. The first chapters focus on the impacts of the geological hazards of earthquakes and volcanoes, while later chapters move toward the climatic hazards of extreme weather events and periods of weather variability.

*Chapter 1.* Fitzhugh's contribution takes us to the Kuril Islands in the Northwest Pacific and examines the impacts of volcanic eruptions, tsunamis, and climate variability on the human populations colonizing and occupying the different islands of this subarctic archipelago. The apparently marginal geographical, environmental, and climatic context of the Kurils provides an informative backdrop to what could be initially assumed to be a particularly exposed and highly vulnerable landscape for past human communities. However, Fitzhugh's research comparing the rich history of sudden environmental change in the region with detailed settlement history of the islands reevaluates these human communities' "vulnerability" to the impacts of local and regional hazards. The wide-ranging interdisciplinary data generated by the Kuril Biocomplexity Project help Fitzhugh provide an informed long-term picture of human ecodynamics on the islands where the past impacts of sudden environmental change can be better understood. The Kuril Islands are volcanically and tectonically highly active, and Fitzhugh provides a thorough examination of the major environmental hazards in the region, analyzing the likely past impacts of these hazards on the different people living on the islands through time. The Kuril Islands also highlight the potential importance of "social" hazards, as disruptions to inter-island networks of social interaction and fluctuating demographic trends can create increased vulnerability to the impacts of "natural" hazards. Furthermore, when Fitzhugh considers the terminal phase of Kuril Island occupation, it is the "social" hazards created by increased interregional interaction that push human populations to the tipping point of abandonment rather than the impact of a major volcanic eruption or tsunami in the region. Therefore this chapter uses a geographical region with a particularly large number of high-frequency environmental hazards to illustrate the complex nature of human vulnerability and show that it is only with an improved understanding of long-term social processes that the nature of human ecodynamics and the impacts of sudden environmental change can be fully understood.

*Chapter 2.* Sheets picks up on the theme of volcanic hazards raised by Fitzhugh and looks toward a 7,000-year regional picture of Mexico and Central America. Utilizing data gathered over many years of research, Sheets examines a series of case studies selected from a sample of thirty-six volcanic eruptions with known impacts on past societies in the region. Raising awareness of the need for more "social science" in hazard-disaster research, Sheets provides a persuasive argument for the use of these long-term perspectives that look beyond the immediate disaster event and evaluate the mid- to long-term positive and negative impacts on human communities. The case studies in this chapter highlight the potential benefits of capitalizing on past knowledge and integrating Precolumbian mitigation strategies, developed over centuries or millennia, into the strategic planning of the region's current disaster man-agement community. Sheets works with scaled vulnerabilities that contrast impacts from a natural science and social science perspective. This interplay between the quantifications of threat highlights the current gulf between geophysical stress and human agency in disaster-related research, and this has important implications for management practices. The high social impact on the Barrilles Precolumbian culture caused by the geologically minor Baru vol-canic eruption highlights the fact that vulnerability is always contingent on current social relations. The ongoing social conflicts at the time of the eruption stopped potential mitigation strategies, such as temporary migration, tradi-tionally employed by other communities facing larger eruptions elsewhere in the region. Another key lesson that emerges from this chapter is the advantage of a decentralized decision-making process in which local and vulnerable com-munities and villages have the local knowledge and authority to perceive haz-ards and mitigate disasters when they occur. This chapter ends with an intrigu-ing discussion regarding the link among hazard and disaster, preparation or failure, and the relative stability of social control—be it in the form of religious or social elites. This link among hazard, disaster, and social elites as mediators with direct or indirect responsibility for the impacts is thought-provoking. It seems clear from the case studies in this book that populations can be quick to apportion blame and can quickly change their allegiance should they feel failed by a social or religious elite in the face of an environmental hazard. This con-nection among hazard, disaster, and different elements of society is continued in the following chapters.

*Chapter 3.* Dugmore and Vésteinsson examine the impacts of volcanic eruptions on the Medieval occupation of Iceland, one of the most volcanically active countries in the world. This chapter begins by drawing an interesting comparison between the apparent ambivalence of the Medieval population to volcanic eruptions, based on the literature of the time, and modern-day overdependence on volcanoes as the reason behind periods of social change in Icelandic history. Therefore Dugmore and Vésteinsson investigate the truth behind the alleged impacts of volcanic activity through a more focused geo-graphical perspective that evaluates eruptions on a case-by-case basis. This chapter examines how the past impacts of Icelandic eruptions were shaped by the nature of Icelandic society itself and provides a close examination of the multiple hazards actually created by different volcanic eruptions. The relative threat of these contrasting hazards—including lava flows, ash clouds, fluorosis poisoning, volcanic gases, and volcanogenic floods—is considered in light of the settlement patterns and lifestyles of past communities. The biogeographi-cal contexts of different hazards are considered in careful detail, and concepts of marginality and the crossing of environmental thresholds are discussed. This chapter highlights some key features in human-environment relations and finishes with an interesting observation surrounding the apparent lack of planned mitigation strategies for volcanic eruptions in Iceland. This lack of preparation for volcanic eruptions is in contrast with the more established planning for the more common hazards created by periods of climatic variability. Therefore this research highlights the periodicity of disasters and the importance of potential parameters for predictability that enabled the development of successful mitigation strategies in Medieval Iceland. This focus on hazards arising from climate variability and periods of climate change is developed in the chapters that follow and provides interesting parallels with the themes of vulnerability, risk and mitigation, and the need for long-term studies of human ecodynamics.

*Chapter 4.* Cooper brings the theme of accessing past ecological knowledge to the islands of the Caribbean. Island populations in this region have always been vulnerable to the dangers of sudden environmental change, given the region's sensitivity to the highly variable climatic systems of the North Atlantic. This chapter reviews how 5,000 years of indigenous knowledge was effectively lost during the Colonial period, replaced primarily by European-influenced lifestyles that are not always well suited to environmental hazards in the region. Developing a regional interdisciplinary framework for the Caribbean, Cooper focuses on the impacts of cyclones, droughts, and floods caused by fluctuating climatic conditions and rising sea levels. By utilizing archaeological reconstructions of Precolumbian settlement locations, food procurement strategies, and household architecture designs, Cooper considers the relative resilience of Precolumbian lifeways that potentially provide useful mitigation strategies for the Caribbean today. Through a discussion of ethno-historical evidence for Precolumbian belief systems, it is possible to evaluate Precolumbian traditional ecological knowledge and a detailed awareness of the different stages of hazard impact. This research leads us to question how the concept of vulnerability should be applied. In the Caribbean the frequency of disasters highlights the importance of including the speed of reconstruction as part of a more comprehensive understanding of impact that looks beyond the event of the disaster itself and includes longer-term social and ecological processes. This chapter also discusses the potential implementation of improved disaster management strategies that employ past mitigation strategies using an example from an ongoing community project in northern Cuba.

*Chapter 5.* Sandweiss and Quilter draw our attention to the central Andean coastline of South America and the threat of key hazards in the region exacerbated by the impacts of El Niño Southern Oscillation cycles. The authors develop an innovative approach to the challenges of collecting, collating, and comparing interdisciplinary data that operate at different temporal and spatial scales. Building on case studies developed during fieldwork in the region, Sandweiss and Quilter show how their methodological approaches to interdisciplinary research can help highlight key issues of relative threat and vulnerability in past human communities and suggest key lessons for the development of resilient societies in the region. This study shows how humans living in "extreme environments" can live successfully through the impacts of climate variability and change. Furthermore, these studies highlight the complexity of studying the relationship between sudden environmental change and paleodemography, as past human communities in central and northern Peruvian coastlines thrived during periods of apparent climatic and environmental instability.

*Chapter 6.* McClung examines the relationship between this early city in the Americas and the impacts of sudden environmental change. Located in a closed hydrological basin, Teotihuacan had a precarious location within a landscape sensitive to variations in seasonal climate and precipitation change. McClung has led an interdisciplinary research project that includes a detailed paleoenvironmental reconstruction of the region. While showing the complexity involved in intensive landscape studies of this kind, the paleoenvironmental picture established in this chapter enables a clear understanding of how key hazards affected human populations living in the region and shows how they were often exacerbated by people. This chapter provides a fascinating early example of the parallels between urban development and increased vulnerability to climatic variability. McClung exposes the entwined relationship among deforestation, urban architecture, irrigation systems, and hazardous flooding that shows the increased risk of exposure created by this early American city. This theme, which parallels social development and changing vulnerabilities to environmental hazards, is developed further in chapter 7, which creates an interesting comparison between urbanization and risk in the New and Old Worlds.

*Chapter 7.* Paulette focuses his examination of urban development, political competition, and vulnerability to environmental hazards on the Bronze Age urban centers of Mesopotamia. Using case studies of archaeological sites from Northern and Southern Mesopotamia, Paulette bring together a range of interdisciplinary studies to examine the past impacts of key hazards such as droughts, severe winters, floods, soil degradation, and pestilence. Following a thoughtful consideration of the term *resilience*, this chapter develops a well-structured argument surrounding the relative resilience of Bronze Age Mesopotamian societies. Out of this study of urban development in the Near East arise some very interesting lessons for modern-day peoples living in the same area today. First and foremost, Paulette questions the resilience of centralized institutional hazard management systems that can often increase societal vulnerability to key hazards by implementing ill-conceived mitigation strategies focused on short-term solutions. In addition, Paulette observes a pattern in the increasing distribution of risk to different elements of society in tandem with growing social stratification and the emergence of an elite. Therefore Paulette raises key criticisms surrounding the themes of authority and social hierarchy in disaster management practice that echo some of the ideas Sheets developed around decentralized mitigation management even within state-level societies.

*Chapter 8.* Nelson and colleagues encourage us to consider aspects of resilience and vulnerability to environmental hazards using carefully selected case studies from the US Southwest and northern Mexico that provide examples of alternative human behavior in the face of similar environmental stress. The enormous body of archaeological data generated in this region is complemented by a uniquely detailed paleoclimatic reconstruction established by over 100 years of dendroclimatological research in the region. This interdisciplinary body of data provides a rare opportunity to look more closely at the cause and effect between social development and the problems created by environmental change. Using the ancestral communities in Mimbres, Hohokam, and Zuni regions of the United States and prehispanic communities around La Quemada in northern Mexico, Nelson and colleagues look at the relative success of different mitigation strategies in the face of precipitation variability over time. These case studies force us to think about the processes behind human decision-making and consider the medium- to long-term consequences of short-term solutions to the impacts of environmental hazards. This chapter provides key lessons for the implementation of mitigation strategies that clearly have direct relevance for modern-day populations living in the Southwest and facing very similar environmental hazards. These lessons from the past include the need to create carefully selected crop diversity that considers the climatic parameters of individual plants. The Hohokam case study also highlights the dangers of social isolation and the importance of maintaining regional interaction networks that enable resource procurement during times of need. Finally, this chapter makes us question whether absolute resilience to climatic variability is ever a realistic prospect for human communities; perhaps we should change the ultimate objective and work toward maximizing the adaptive capacity of human communities to identify and manage the inevitable challenges of environmental change.

*Chapter 9.* Kohler helps us consider the role of sudden environmental change within the wider framework of human social evolution. Providing an overview of key themes from the different chapters within the historical framework of archaeological thought and practice, Kohler enables the reader to consider the different chapters in this book from a global perspective. As Kohler points out, the paucity of the archaeological record should not negate the impact sudden environmental change might have had on deep prehistory, and the tendency to average past interpretations of population figures may well hide the boom-and-bust nature of human demography in the past. This overview suggests that perhaps the interactions among hazards, disasters, and human development should be more closely examined, with particular focus on the entwined relationship between "progress" and "vulnerability."

*Chapter 10.* Redman provides a global overview within which to consider all of the case studies with their varied spatial and temporal perspectives. This global comparison helps Redman to extract key messages from this book and bring the benefits of the long-term perspective on human-environment relations to the wider ongoing debates within the resilience community. This overview highlights the way different case studies in the book link the frequency of "natural disasters" and cultural ecological knowledge and enables an interesting approach to assessing the relative resilience of modern-day communities. Certainly, this summary suggests there are important lessons to learn from the past when considering the cause and effect between environmental stress and societal change and the paradoxical link between increased societal resilience and increased social vulnerability. Furthermore, Redman helps bring these lessons into a modern context by considering how climatic and environmental hazards differentially impact separate elements of societies over time.

### APPLIED ARCHAEOLOGY: HOW RESEARCH CAN AMELIORATE RISK

In this book, all of the contributors argue that the social sciences are crucial to the advancement of disaster studies and furthermore that it is only with the full time depth of human experience that concepts of hazard, risk, impact, and vulnerability can be truly understood. However, there is a benchmark that many in the disaster management community will hold us against, and that is whether there are actually any practical lessons from these studies of the past that can improve hazard management and disaster mitigation in the present. We argue that this book clearly shows that there are. In reading through the chapters, some clear practical lessons emerge regarding settlement location, household architecture, food procurement strategies, social networks, education, and disaster management planning.

The progressivist nature of many modern-day societies often precludes the use of "old-fashioned," "ancient," or even "stone age" ideas and technologies. This confidence in the "modern" even persuades many populations on the planet to live a way of life taken from regions with entirely different climates or environmental histories, solely because of recent geopolitical history or modern fashion. For example, the use of European river valley settlement locations in the Caribbean, adobe brick household architecture in Central America, or rice farming in the semiarid US Southwest can be hazardous transplants. As discussed earlier in this introduction, the importance of knowledge developed over the long term within contextual ecological settings is crucial to improve our understanding of human ecodynamics, and the case studies examined in this book show how this accumulated wealth of human experience can be accessed from deep time and applied to the present.

## Settlement Locations

People have always located their settlements in different parts of the land-scape. As many archaeologists will tell you, it is not always easy to explain why past communities chose a specific location. However, many chapters in this book highlight the way many prehistoric settlement locations are relatively protected from the past impacts of key hazards. The counterintuitive position-ing of settlements on the sides of volcanoes in Iceland is understood following a detailed analysis of different types of volcanic hazard from individual volca-noes that shows how some apparently similar locations in the landscape are in fact far less hazardous than others. Similar themes of potentially secure prehis-toric settlement locations are picked up in the Kuril Islands and the Caribbean. While it may not always be possible to simply move modern-day populations, it is interesting to understand why these past settlement locations were more resilient and consider adjusting modern landscapes to re-create past natural hazard defenses. It would be possible to start implementing this plan by simply including these data in current planning guidelines and include zoning restric-tions that can begin to decrease risk and improve living conditions in the study areas researched in this book.

## Household Architecture

Throughout this book the scaled temporality of past impacts helps to reevaluate the evolving impacts of different hazards. This is particularly impor-tant when considering household architecture, as the cost of reconstruction is often just as important as the building's resistance to an initial impact event. This is certainly the case in the Caribbean, where modern and Precolumbian household designs have distinctly contrasting approaches to hurricane pro-tection. Sheets finds similar evidence in Central America but also points out the difficulty in trying to persuade modern El Salvadorans to live in stilted wooden and thatched houses with mudded walls. Fortunately, the practicalities of implementing successful mechanisms of mitigation are not the key objective of this book, and the task of rebranding "Joya de Ceren architecture" for the first-time buyer/builder in central El Salvador is another person's job. However, using the different experiences of past human communities to develop the realities of vulnerability even a little can change the way the relative security of straw or brick houses is perceived.

## Food Procurement Strategies

Food procurement strategies are some of human societies' most vulnerable elements regarding the impacts of sudden environmental change. Minor variations in climatic conditions, such as late seasonal rains or an early frost, can have a profound impact on dependent human communities. A number of examples in this book highlight the benefits of diversifying resource and subsistence strategies and growing suitable crops within a wider range of likely climatic conditions. But perhaps one of the most important lessons surrounding food procurement strategies is the way human communities often increase medium- to long-term vulnerabilities by adopting short-term solutions to the immediate impacts of environmental hazards. Nelson and McClung provide excellent examples of how investments in food procurement technology to protect communities against the hazard of precipitation variability in fact reduce the longer-term availability of better potential mitigation strategies. This wider relationship among social development, urbanization, environmental degradation, and vulnerability to hazards is a fascinating topic that moves far beyond the scope of food procurement strategies and highlights the importance of linking social development, which relies on permanency in the landscape, with the parallel development of regional networks of social interaction.

## Reciprocal Social Networks

The chapters in this book highlight the importance of maintaining interregional social networks even, and perhaps especially, during times of plenty to help mitigate the dangers of sudden environmental change. It seems from the case studies in this book that to a certain extent the larger and more reliable the network of social interaction any past human community had, the greater the scale of impact that could be mitigated against. Parallels with modern global crises are important, as the relative availability of charitable relief and reconstruction following the 2004 tsunami in the Indian Ocean and the 2010 monsoon floods in South Asia were dependent on the strength of international relations and relative emotive, social, economic, and political indebtedness. Moving beyond this rather simplistic idea that it is good to have friends when in need, the different case studies in this book also show how important it is to decide which friends it is useful to have and, more specifically, the geographical region and environmental niche in which it would be most advantageous to have those friends following the impact of a known hazard. Therefore societies need to be careful not only to establish and maintain social networks with communities that are least likely to have been affected by the same hazard but also to consider which key resources will be required for the efficient and swift reconstruction of their community so that risks can be ameliorated.

## Education

Intrinsic to the aims of this book is that education is essential to successful disaster management and that the educational approach should be multidisciplinary, spanning the humanities, social sciences, and natural sciences. The importance of education in disaster management strategies is well established, but, unfortunately, so are the problems and limitations of trying to deliver national education policies and disaster management strategies through formal school curricula and radio, print, and television public announcements. This is particularly the case for hazards with low-frequency periodicity and intergenerational return rates that do not always resonate with people's fears and that enable people in San Francisco to sleep soundly at night. Therefore successful hazard mitigation requires that people have an innate hazard awareness enabling them to identify hazards before or as they are happening, understand the likely key impacts, and implement individual- and community-level mitigation strategies to avoid disaster (Crate 2008).

This knowledge base can be hard to establish and maintain, particularly when exacerbated by modern-day issues of demographic mobility and recent global diasporas. Perhaps this increasing distance among individuals, communities, and an understanding of the local environmental context is in fact one of the greatest modern hazards highlighted by this book, as people's ability to prepare for potential hazards has become increasingly difficult, particularly given sustained population increases. Therefore some chapters in this book show that informal knowledge systems—in the form of myth, folklore, ritual practice, and seasonal festivals—while considered unstructured and informal by modern pedagogical standards, actually provide a highly effective vehicle for intergenerational knowledge transfer that can facilitate hazard mitigation for hundreds or even thousands of years. Therefore, framing education within the context of local intergenerational knowledge transfer can help bring together the intergenerational geological timescales of some hazards with the multigenerational human timescales of individual lifetimes.

## Disaster Management Planning

This discontinuity between national education policy and local ecological knowledge flags the wider themes of responsibility, authority, and command-

and-control structures for effective hazard management. The Mesopotamian and Central American case studies in this book highlight the way impacts are socially contingent and locally variable, with the same forcing mechanism creating very different impacts in different locations. Therefore community responses to different hazards have to be equally variable to mitigate the specific impacts individuals and local communities face. This suggests that the very nature of a centralized national disaster management authority, as is most common around the world, is intrinsically unable to deal with local variation. Therefore the examples discussed in this book suggest that local nodes of authority (as Sheets phrases it) are the most effective management framework for avoiding disasters at the local level. Thus centralized national disaster management agencies perhaps should not be creating national policy but rather should be coordinating a network of locally organized, community-led hazard management cooperatives that are informed by local knowledge and comparative global case studies to create adjusted strategies targeted to the specific threats identified through long-term research into their local socio-environmental context.

## LONG-TERM PERSPECTIVES

This book highlights the ways an improved understanding of the human experience of hazards and disasters, and the timescales and geographical range at which impacts arrive, can improve disaster management planning. This deep time perspective also highlights how complex the process of introducing change into cultures can be, with case studies in this book showing how the introduction of successful short-term mitigation of environmental hazards can increase vulnerabilities over the long term. Therefore disaster planning requires a long-term perspective that considers the quality of life of both present and future generations. An archaeological time span can help create these responsible interventions, as case studies from the past, based on empirical evidence, can help predict the likely consequences of introduced cultural changes and improve disaster management planning over the long term. Sheets has seen how benign improvements in health, sanitation, and medicine in El Salvador, to which nobody would object, resulted in a 3 percent population growth rate. The birthrate was unchanged and the death rate declined consistently because of interventions. Populations doubled in twenty years and then again in another twenty years, with no increase in basic resources to sustain more people. With population control (family planning, contraception) discouraged by religious and political authorities, the result of the benign interventions in a few generations has been greater unemployment, underemployment, and malnutrition than there was in the beginning. Therefore, as well as offering practical suggestions for improved disaster management, we hope the case studies in this book help generate meaningful discussion of alternative viewpoints and provide a persuasive argument for communities and decision makers to reevaluate the reliance on the modern approach to the "natural" disaster and consider including the past as part of a "social" solution.

## FUTURE RESEARCH

All of the chapters in this book highlight the benefit of integrated interdisciplinary research that brings in comparative high-resolution data sets from human, climatic, and environmental perspectives. The case studies in this book show humans' varied response to different hazards and disasters and suggest that it is possible to evaluate relative risks and vulnerabilities correctly only when the entire timescale of potential impacts is taken into consideration. Therefore future research should focus on bringing together more long-term interdisciplinary studies that can help provide a fuller picture of the diversity and variability of global human ecodynamics.

We hope this book will provide a compelling and cohesive narrative that gives each reader both a rich understanding of key issues and a new perspective on how different human communities have dealt with the hazards and dangers of sudden environmental change. This book should allow people to consider for themselves the key lessons they wish to draw from the past. However, we argue that it is important to consider the scaled nature of impacts because short-, medium-, and long-term impacts often have very different effects on human communities and on different levels of society within those communities. Examples in this book suggest that changes to social networks and lifestyle choices often create the greatest vulnerabilities to environmental hazards over the medium to long term. Therefore it is essential to examine the dynamic interaction between societal development and environmental change and focus on the human experience of disaster. There is perhaps no better way to do this than by utilizing the time depth of human existence to create a worldwide social memory that reveals how different communities with divergent social systems and varied lifestyle choices have always lived with, and often through, the dangers of sudden environmental change.

## REFERENCES

Alexander, David
   1995    A Survey of the Field of Natural Hazards and Disaster Studies. In *Geographical Information Systems in Assessing Natural Hazards*, ed. Alberto Carrara and Fausto Guzetti. Kluwer, Dordrecht, pp. 1–19.
   1997    The Study of Natural Disasters, 1977–1997: Some Reflections on a Changing Field of Knowledge. *Disasters* 21: 284–304.

Burton, Ian, Robert Kates, and Gilbert White
1978     *The Environment as Hazard.* Oxford University Press, New York.

Crate, Susan
2008     Gone the Bull of Winter? Grappling with the Cultural Implications of and Anthropology's Role(s) in Global Climate Change. *Current Anthropology* 49: 569–595.

Grattan, John, and Robin Torrence, eds.
2007     *Living under the Shadow: Cultural Impacts of Volcanic Eruptions.* Left Coast Press, Walnut Creek, CA.

Mauch, Christof, and Cristian Pfister, eds.
2009     *Natural Disasters, Cultural Responses: Case Studies toward a Global Environmental History.* Lexington Books, Lanham, MD.

Rose, William, Julian Bommer, Dina Lopez, Michael Carr, and Jon Major
2004     *Natural Hazards in El Salvador.* Special Paper 375. Geological Society of America, Boulder, CO.

Sheets, Payson
1980     *Archaeological Studies of Disaster: Their Range and Value.* Paper 38. Institute of Behavioral Science, University of Colorado, Boulder.
2008     Armageddon to the Garden of Eden: Explosive Volcanic Eruptions and Societal Resilience in Ancient Middle America. In *El Niño, Catastrophism, and Culture Change in Ancient America,* ed. Daniel Sandweiss and Jeffrey Quilter. Dumbarton Oaks, Harvard University Press, Cambridge, MA, pp. 168–186.

van Buren, Mary
2001     The Archaeology of El Niño Events and Other "Natural" Disasters. *Journal of Archaeological Method and Theory* 8(2): 129–149.

White, Gilbert
1945     *Human Adjustment to Flood.* University of Chicago Press, Chicago.

# ONE

# Hazards, Impacts, and Resilience among Hunter-Gatherers of the Kuril Islands

*Ben Fitzhugh*

## ARCHAEOLOGICAL APPROACHES TO CATASTROPHIC EVENTS IN THE HUNTER-GATHERER CONTEXT

This chapter explores hunter-gatherer vulnerability in the context of relative isolation and a highly dynamic natural environment. The setting is the Kuril Islands of the Northwest Pacific, and the data set is a 4,000-year record of human settlement and environmental history generated by the Kuril Biocomplexity Project, a large, interdisciplinary, and international research effort fielded from 2006 to 2008. The presupposition entering this project was that this relatively isolated, volcanic, earthquake- and tsunami-prone subarctic region should be among the more difficult habitats for hunter-gatherer populations to occupy consistently and, as a result, that the archaeological record should reflect periodic abandonments, at least in the most isolated (and smallest) central islands. The results of this study speak less to this heuristic presupposition than to the idea of resilience in the face of ecological impoverishment, catastrophic events, and climate changes. The history we are uncovering highlights the importance of linked social, economic, and demographic processes in conditioning vulnerability and shaping people's resilience in the environment.

Hazards and disasters are the focus of increasing interest in natural and social science, stimulated by growing media attention to disasters around the world. Calls for improved prediction of catastrophic events have generated enhanced support for retrospective studies of historical pattern and periodicity in earthquakes, tsunamis, volcanic eruptions, floods, drought, climate change, and other natural hazards. Social science has entered this arena to better understand human responses to hazardous events and environmental change, most recently calling for more integrated research into the socio-natural dynamics of disasters (Blaikie et al. 1994; Oliver-Smith 1996; Oliver-Smith and Hoffman 2002; Sidle et al. 2004; Torrence and Grattan 2002). This latest turn recognizes that disasters are complex outcomes of linked social and environmental processes and that these histories often condition the severity of impacts on humans in the aftermath of extreme events.

Efforts to understand the socio-environmental dynamics of disasters have tended to focus on agricultural and industrial societies (but see Saltonstall and Carver 2002; Sheets 1999). From a comparative archaeological study of socio-ecological responses to explosive volcanic eruptions in Mesoamerica, Payson Sheets (1999) suggests that the impacts of such catastrophic events will scale with the degree of organizational complexity and investment in "built environment." He argues that small-scale egalitarian societies, at least in Central America, had the most organizational resilience. If Sheets is correct in this conclusion, we should expect to see similar degrees of resilience in other contexts in which small-scale societies were exposed to catastrophic events. The Kuril Islands offer another case for investigating the resilience of such societies.

## THE KURIL ISLANDS

The Kuril Islands provide a semi-controlled setting for investigating the historical impacts of volcanism, tsunamis, and climate change on maritime hunter-gatherers over the past 4,000 years. As a group of ecologically simple and geographically small volcanic islands stretched across 1,100 km of stormy, subarctic ocean, these islands would seem to epitomize an extremely vulnerable environment for human settlement. The relative isolation of the central Kurils may explain why they were left unoccupied until roughly 4,000 years ago, a barrier rather than a bridge between the Japanese archipelago and Kamchatka (figure 1.1).

In biogeographical terms, the Kuril Islands* are "stepping stone islands" between Hokkaido and the Kamchatka Peninsula—serving as both potential conduit and filter for the movement of plants, animals, and people between these larger landmasses. The islands serve largely as a filter to the expansion

---

* In this chapter "Kurils" refers to the "Greater Kuril" island chain linking Hokkaido to Kamchatka. A shorter string of islands, known as the "Lesser Kurils," stretches approximately 100 km northeast from Hokkaido's Nemura Peninsula. These islands are not discussed in this chapter.

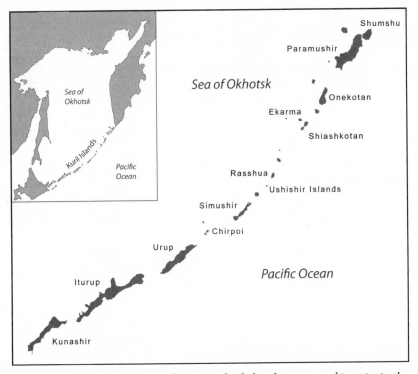

**1.1.** *The Kuril Islands. Illustration by Ben Fitzhugh, based on cartographic projection by Adam Freeburg.*

of land-based plant and animal taxa limited in their ability to disperse across wide channels with fast marine currents. As a result, the islands from Iturup northeast to Onekotan have relatively low terrestrial biodiversity and are dominated by tundra meadow and alpine ecosystems and a few terrestrial mammals uncharacteristically good at colonizing new lands, such as fox and vole. Birds, by contrast, are abundant and diverse in the absence of most predators, and the Kurils support dozens of species of resident seabirds and migratory waterfowl (Hacker 1951). Marine mammals are also well represented today around the shores and near-shore waters of many of the Kuril Islands. Sea lions, fur seals, and harbor seals are the most common species today, especially in the central islands, where they haul out in large numbers and raise pups in the summer. Sea otters are abundant in some areas—especially around the northern and southern islands—while absent in others. Their distribution seems to reflect the ecological differences in shellfish and fish productivity and diversity, which are also highest in the northern and southern ends of the chain compared to the center. The resulting ecological picture is one of higher taxonomic diversity in both terrestrial and marine resources in the southernmost and northernmost islands, which are also the largest and closest to "mainland" sources. The central islands—especially those from the Chirpoi Islands to Onekotan—have low biodiversity, and hunter-gatherers targeted marine mammals, birds (and their eggs), and limited varieties of fish. Archaeological evidence is consistent with a picture of reduced diversity in diets and more limited subsistence options in the central zone compared to the others (Fitzhugh et al. 2004).

The Kuril Biocomplexity Project (KBP) was designed to study the integrated history of humans, flora, fauna, geology, oceanography, and climate as part of a single, coordinated, interdisciplinary research effort. Following preliminary work in 1999 and 2000 (Fitzhugh et al. 2002; Pietsch et al. 2003), KBP started fieldwork in the summer of 2006 with an interdisciplinary team drawn from the United States, Russia, and Japan. The three summers from 2006 to 2008 were spent locating, mapping, and testing archaeological sites; sampling volcanic ash deposits, lake water, and rocks; studying coastal stratigraphy for tsunami deposits; measuring wave run-up elevations from recent and older tsunami deposits; coring lakes and peat bogs for pollens and other climate and ecosystem proxies; and studying modern crustal motion to better understand the dynamics of Kuril seismicity. In the process KBP identified and tested 70 archaeological sites from Kunashir to the Shumshu Islands. Resulting data include site and landscape maps; radiocarbon dates (286 archaeological dates and 17 purely geological dates, all by the AMS method); stone, pottery, and bone artifacts; stratigraphic descriptions of archaeological and geological sediments; physical and geochemical analyses of volcanic ash samples; lake cores from the north, central, and southern islands; and stratigraphically sequenced peat samples from almost every island. Project teams are working from these data to conclusions and combining forces to better understand the integrated Late Holocene history of the Kurils. It is in the context of this emerging synthesis that we seek to draw preliminary conclusions about the hazards affecting human settlement and lifestyle in the Kurils.

## KURIL ISLAND ARCHAEOLOGICAL HISTORY

The oldest dated archaeological site in the Kurils is located in central Iturup Island and dated to about 8,000 years ago (ca. 6000 BC)* (Vasilevsky and Shubina 2006; Yanshina and Kuzmin 2010; Zaitseva et. al 1993). It was occupied by a culture known as the Early Jomon. This one dated site and surface finds of Early and Middle Jomon pottery indicate the presence of people in the southern Kurils (closest to Hokkaido) during the Middle Holocene (ca. 6000

---

* Dates are given in calibrated calendar years BC or AD unless otherwise noted. Uncalibrated radiocarbon ages (raw dates) are designated as "rcybp."

to 2500 BC). The next oldest radiocarbon dates, also from southern islands, begin to appear around 2500 BC and correlate with apparent stabilization of the local climate and vegetation (Anderson et al. 2009).

Between 1900 and 1400 BC we start to see evidence for settlement on many of the central and northern islands. This expansion conceivably relates to the spread of a more effective seafaring technology into the Japanese archipelago that would have facilitated greater movement into the Kurils, as it apparently did in the previous millennium in Island Southeast Asia (Oppenheimer and Richards 2001). In this very early phase of Kuril occupation, it is possible that people from southern Kamchatka might have colonized the northernmost islands of Shumshu and Paramushir. In general, however, all diagnostic cultural traits (predominantly decorated pottery) in this time and during the rest of history suggest southern origins, either starting in or passing through Hokkaido to get to the Kurils.

Our radiocarbon database indicates an abrupt jump in Kuril occupation beginning around 500 BC. This surge represents the leading edge of almost 1,500 years of more or less continuous settlement during the Epi-Jomon period, with substantial pit-house villages established on many of the Kuril Islands. The Epi-Jomon were a maritime-oriented hunting and fishing people who lived in the Kurils in small pit houses roughly 3–5 m in diameter and left behind cord-marked pottery, a variety of stone tools, and—in rare, well-preserved deposits—distinctive bone and wood artifacts, including barbed and toggling harpoon heads. The Epi-Jomon represent the continuity of Jomon hunting-and-gathering lifeways in Hokkaido and the Kurils at a time when Yayoi rice farmers had assimilated and displaced Jomon lifestyles in more southerly Japan (Habu 2004; Hudson 1999; Imamura 1996).

In the mid-first millennium AD a new culture, known as the Okhotsk, swept the southern shores of the Okhotsk Sea from origins in the Lower Amur, Sakhalin Island, or both (Amano 1979; Ono 2008). The Okhotsk culture colonized the Kurils sometime around AD 800, more or less replacing a waning Epi-Jomon population. From about AD 800 to 1300 the Okhotsk dominated the Kurils from south to north. They used distinctive thick-walled pottery, lived in larger oval to pentagonal houses ranging from 5 to 15 m in diameter, and pursued a range of game, from fish and shellfish to birds and sea mammals.* During this interval, southern and central Hokkaido supported a culture known as Satsumon, derived from the assimilation of Hokkaido Epi-Jomon and immigrants from northern Honshu bearing a mixed hunting-gathering

---

\* Epi-Jomon populations likely ate a similar range of foods in the Kurils, but faunal remains dating prior to the Okhotsk period were hard to come by in the highly acidic volcanic soils of the Kurils.

and millet farming subsistence economy (Crawford 1992, 2008; Crawford and Takamiya 1990).

Curiously, archaeological evidence of human settlement in the Kurils disappears around AD 1300–1400, at least for 200 years or so. This gap in evidence for Kuril occupation corresponds to the emergence of cultural traditions recognized as precursors of modern Ainu ethnic culture. In Hokkaido the emergence of the Ainu is characterized by complete abandonment of pit-house dwellings and pottery in favor of aboveground structures and imported iron and lacquer containers. In the Kurils and southern Kamchatka, however, archaeologically identified Ainu material culture includes the continued use of pit houses and the construction of "Naiji" pottery with internal lug handles reminiscent of the iron pots in use to the south.

According to the ethno-historic records beginning at the start of the eighteenth century, the Kuril Ainu ("Kuriles" or "Koushi") lived throughout the northern, central, and southern Kuril Islands. They spoke distinctly northern and southern dialects of the Ainu language, different from those spoken in Hokkaido and southern Sakhalin. The Ainu suffix "-kotan" means village, suggesting that the islands of Onekotan, Kharimkotan, Shiashkotan, and Chirinkotan maintained Ainu villages. Stepan Krasheninnikov (1972) reports that the northern Kuril Ainu lived from Simushir to Shumshu and that the Simushir occupants traveled seasonally to Chirpoi Island to hunt birds and trade with southern Kuril Ainu coming from Urup. On Kunashir and Iturup, Igor Samarin and Olga Shubina (2007) have documented a number of *chasi*, or fortifications, they attribute to Ainu populations. The ethno-historical data therefore strongly suggest that Ainu lived in the Kurils prior to initial Russian contact in the early eighteenth century, while the archaeological evidence suggests they may not have been there more than a century earlier. Whatever the resolution of this discrepancy, we can clearly say that the Ainu did not maintain the substantial settlements in the Kurils (especially the central Kurils) that the earlier Epi-Jomon and Okhotsk settlers did. Something changed fundamentally in the nature of the human-environmental relationship at this time.

After contact with agents of expanding Russian and Japanese states, Kuril Ainu populations dwindled until the remaining residents were forcibly resettled on Shikotan Island in the Lesser Kurils in 1883. At the end of World War II the conquering Soviets sent the few surviving Kuril Ainu to Hokkaido, where it is believed the last member died in 1960 (Kaoru Tezuka, personal communication 2006). The rapidity of this depopulation in absence of evidence of significant genocide suggests fairly low population levels prior to contact.

Nineteenth- and twentieth-century occupation increasingly came to include Russian and Japanese outposts. These outposts were initially established to take advantage of the lucrative hunt for sea otter and fur seal pelts, but in the twentieth century they served the dual purposes of geopolitical military competition and commercial fisheries. Three towns are currently located in the islands on Kunashir, Iturup, and Paramushir. Remote military bases and outposts strung throughout the Kurils, many initially established by the Japanese combatants in World War II, were occupied by Soviet/Russian military personnel until the late 1990s. The end of the Cold War and the economic collapse of the Russian Federation led to the abandonment of most such outposts. Today, only three of four people live regularly between Urup Island and Onekotan (personal observation 2006–2008).

In summary, archaeological evidence shows that the Kurils were more or less continuously and substantially occupied from approximately 3,000 years ago until about 800 years ago. They were used by what appears to have been a much more limited population since that time. It is likely that the human population was concentrated in the northern and southern ends of the islands for the past 800 years, as it is currently. Hence the central islands once again represent a geographical gap in human settlement, as they appear to have done prior to 1900 BC.

## KEY HAZARDS, PAST IMPACTS, AND HUMAN RESPONSES

Geologically, the Kurils are the product of the tectonic collision of oceanic and continental plates at the Kuril-Kamchatka subduction zone. This ongoing process causes relatively frequent volcanic eruptions, earthquakes, and tsunamis that make life challenging for island residents. In addition, the islands are beset by fog much of the year, subject to dramatic storms, and variably packed with winter sea ice. Changes in climate have implications for the frequency of storms and the productivity of the marine ecosystem. Combined with relative isolation, these conditions make the Kurils hazardous for human occupation, especially when population density was low and social networks harder to maintain between isolated settlements (Fitzhugh, Phillips, and Gjesfjeld 2011). All of these factors make the Kurils (especially the remote and small central ones) seem as though they would be very risky places for anyone to live, especially hunter-gatherers depending on relatively unproductive ecosystems.

### Hazard 1: Volcanic Eruptions

There are currently thirty-two known active volcanoes that have erupted at least once in the past 300 years, twenty of them since the end of World War II. While most eruptions are small and disrupt only a limited part of an island, some do produce extensive landslides and pyroclastic flows (slurries of superheated rocks, mud, and other debris) that affect the nearby landscape and ecology. Volcanic ash deposits have less dramatic impacts but can be accompanied by hot and lethal gases that affect organisms living close to an erupting volcano.

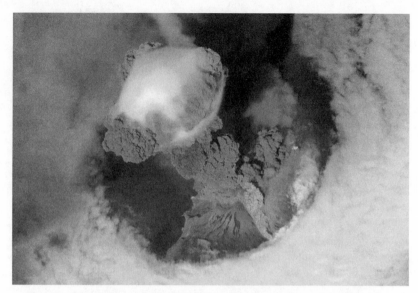

**1.2.** *Eruption of Sarychev Volcano on June 12, 2009, as photographed by the International Space Station. Image courtesy of Earth Sciences and Image Analysis Laboratory, NASA Johnson Space Center (ISS020-E-9048; http://eol.jsc.nasa.gov).*

Ash can then extend great distances, sometimes visibly layering the ground for tens of kilometers away from the eruption. Some ash deposits can be traced for more than 1,000 km through the Kuril chain as a result of favorable wind direction and sufficient volume of ejected matter. Ash can be mixed with toxic gases, and the sediment itself can be dangerous to inhale in large amounts. With sufficient deposition, volcanic ash will smother out plant growth and delay the return of vegetation cover until the ash itself has weathered into a viable soil (Griggs 1918).

One particularly impressive explosive eruption (VEI = 4) occurred during the period June 11–21, 2009, on Matua Island's Sarychev Peak. This eruption caught international attention because of the disruption it caused in flights between North America and East Asia. The eruption, documented by the International Space Station (figure 1.2), caused extensive pyroclastic flows and the partial collapse of the island's northwest face, leading to significant remodeling of coastal geometry. Because the ash plume went high into the atmosphere, ash had limited impact on the ground. Winds carried some of the sulfurous ash cloud east across much of the Pacific and some west across the Sea of Okhotsk, where it dusted parts of Sakhalin Island more than 600 km away. Interestingly, the southern flank of Sarychev Volcano and the adjacent coastal plane, including the location of a prehistoric archaeological site and an abandoned Soviet base, were minimally affected. A thin layer of ash and several dead voles and foxes observed in this otherwise unaffected southern part of the island in August 2009 provide indirect evidence of lethal toxic gas emissions accompanying the eruption. At the same time, sea mammals and seabirds remained or returned to the island less than a month following the eruption (Nadezhda Razzhegaeva, personal communication 2009).

The 2009 eruption was one of the two most explosive eruptions in a series of thirteen for Sarychev Peak since 1923. For much of the past century, the now unoccupied Matua Island supported an active military base. While the documented eruptions of Sarychev were oriented away from human settlements and thus did not result in human fatalities, the geological evidence of the southeastern portion of the island suggests different eruption patterns in the past. A minimum of eleven pyroclastic flows and thick tephra deposits have buried that landscape since people started living on the island 2,500 years ago (Fitzhugh et al 2002; Ishizuka 2001). In the more distant past, the entire low-elevation promontory that supported known human occupation, which makes up the southeastern third of the island, was created by one or more massive cone collapses and landslides. Thus the history of this volcanic island supports the conclusion that the area, direction, and degree of impact of any given eruption are variable and unpredictable.

Matua's volcanic history is mirrored on that of other islands throughout the chain. Past flows and landslides have remodeled sections of several islands. Landslides often formed the best low-elevation foundation for subsequent human occupations, demonstrated by archaeological settlements placed on features of former landslides on the smaller islands of Makanrushi, Kharimkotan, and Ekarma. Kharimkotan, for example, has two low-elevation landforms, one on each side, that were created by landslides in the past 2,000 years. Living on the flanks of an active volcano is always inherently hazardous, and most of the central Kurils are little more than volcanic cones with narrow coastal benches suitable for human occupation.

Ash deposits are less hazardous than lava flows and landslides, but they can extend over much greater areas and distances. Ash layers are ubiquitous throughout the Kurils and form one of the primary sources of sedimentary accumulation. Some of the more widespread tephras are sourced to caldera-forming eruptions in Kamchatka and Hokkaido. Two caldera eruptions occurred in the Kurils in the Late Holocene: the eruptions of Medvezhya on Iturup Island about 400 BC and the eruption of Ushishir, ca. 200 BC.

Regarding the past impacts and responses to volcanic eruptions of the Middle to Late Holocene, based on dated and chemically correlated tephra deposits sampled during the KBP, Mitsuhiro Nakagawa and colleagues (2009) report that eruption frequency and intensity in the Kurils was highly variable during the Holocene. The central Kurils appear to have consistently produced the greatest frequencies of eruptions in all time periods (they contain a greater proportion of the volcanoes in the chain), compared to the north and south. Major (but comparatively small) eruptions that left limited local ash deposits are found in relatively high frequencies. For example, for the last 2,000 years, Nakagawa and colleagues (2009: figure 7) document nine major eruptions between Kunashir and Chirpoi Islands (southern Kurils), nineteen between Simushir and Rasshua (central Kurils), and more than thirty from Chirinkotan/Shiaskotan to Shumshu (northern Kurils). Small eruptions that left limited local ash deposits are found in relatively high frequencies through time, though declining with age, probably as a result of soil formation processes that limit their identification in older strata. On the other hand, large (plinian- and caldera-forming) eruptions show distinct unevenness through time, with five such eruptions in the early Holocene (9500–6500 rcybp; ca. 8700–5400 BC), a hiatus in the Middle Holocene (6500–4000 rcybp; 5400–2500 BC), and eight in the Late Holocene (4000 rcybp/2500 BC to present). Four of the large eruptions in the Late Holocene occurred between 3,000 and 2,000 years ago during a time of rapid population growth in the Kurils. Population densities appear to have remained high in the Kurils throughout this interval of high volcanic activity, declining dramatically only approximately 800 years ago, long after the most intense volcanic interval had ceased. Thus, at the aggregate scale we conclude that volcanic eruptions posed minimal disruption to the human settlement history of the Kurils. These events might even have helped support human settlement by providing enhanced nutrients to the nearby marine system and stimulating increased biological productivity.

Archaeological evidence of direct volcanic impacts is difficult to confirm. Many archaeological deposits contain volcanic ash lenses preserved within archaeological layers, suggesting that small eruptions had minimal impact on occupation. In cases where archaeological deposits are capped by relatively thick volcanic layers, it is tempting to imagine a cataclysmic destruction of settlements and the abandonment of the location or death of the occupants (see Dumond 2004; Dumond and Knecht 2001). Geoarchaeologically, such conclusions are rarely warranted. Lacking significant agents of deposition other than volcanic eruptions and human activity, the termination of human deposits could have occurred decades or centuries prior to the formation of the volcanic layers that cap them.

This problem is exemplified at the site Rasshua 1 on southern Rasshua Island. Roughly 2,400 years ago, this site was heavily occupied by Epi-Jomon hunter-gatherers. About 2,200 years ago, Ushishir Volcano erupted 25 km to the south, leaving behind a sunken caldera that now constitutes Yankitcha Island. On Rasshua 1, there is an approximately 15-cm-thick layer of pumice-ash that was probably twice as thick before it compressed (figure 1.3). It is easy to imagine a Pompeii-like scene of people fleeing and becoming asphyxiated in the ash and gas, but in fact we do not know if people were even present on the

**1.3.** *Composite photo collage in which the outer/lower frames show the caldera rim of Ushishir Volcano with Rasshua Island in the distance. The central image shows the 20-cm-thick, 2,000-year-old Ushishir volcanic ash layer found in excavation on Rasshua Island sandwiched between Epi-Jomon archaeological strata (Rasshua 1, Test Pit 2). Ushishir photos by Volodimir Golubtsov; inset photo by Ben Fitzhugh.*

site at the time the eruption occurred. Cultural deposits are also superimposed above this thick tephra layer. Radiocarbon ages from above and below bracket the tephra between 1990 ± 30 rcybp (OS-67131) and 2430 ± 25 rcybp (OS-67086). Currently, we cannot say when the Ushishir tephra fell within this interval. If at the beginning, it could have been the event that forced an abandonment of the site. Additional radiocarbon dates may help reduce this interval. Unfortunately, the lack of precision of radiocarbon dating will continue to put limits on the certainty with which we can link archaeological and geological events based on these kinds of data. Only rarely are archaeologists fortunate enough to find direct and unequivocal evidence of volcanic impacts in the form of evidence of catastrophic mortality (e.g., Cooley 2003) or structural damage from ash deposition preserved in ash molds (Shimoyama 2002).

What we can conclude from the Kuril evidence so far is that the small-, medium-, and large-scale eruptions between 3,000 and 1,000 years ago deterred human occupation in the Kurils little, if at all. The islands may have been abandoned for intervals following major eruptions and ash deposition, but reoccupation proceeded apace within at most a few hundred years. Eco-systems were likely damaged locally by the larger eruptions, depending on the character of landscape modification and burial of surface vegetation, but the ecological effects beyond individual islands or even on different parts of the erupting volcano often remained minimal. On balance, volcanic ash deposits probably improved plant productivity on land and phytoplankton productivity in the water more often than not (Griggs 1918). There is no evidence that people exercised specific settlement strategies to minimize the risks of volcanic impacts. While it is likely that eruptions occasionally destroyed settlements and resulted in human deaths, these factors were insufficient to discourage or shape patterns of human settlement. Volcanic hazards were tolerated by mari-time hunter-gatherers throughout occupation history.

## Hazard 2: Earthquakes and Tsunamis

Earthquakes are most hazardous for people living in large, brittle, and tall buildings or dependent on a fixed infrastructure (Sheets, this volume). Prior to the mid-twentieth century, occupants of the Kurils lived in semi-subterranean pit houses or, in very recent times, single-story aboveground log structures, and the most direct hazard from earthquakes would have been localized landslides in locations where the lay of the land forced settlements up against steep hillsides. More significant, large subduction zone earthquakes often cause major tsunamis that affect coastal occupants and the ecosystems they depend on. In November 2006, four months after the completion of the first KBP field expedition, a major earthquake near the central Kurils sent tsunami waves onshore throughout the region, reaching as high as 20 m above normal high-tide level (MacInnes et al. 2009b). These waves inundated one of our (fortunately abandoned) 2006 summer outpost camps. A slightly smaller earthquake and tsunami followed in January 2007 in the same region. The combination of these events damaged much of the coastline, moved large rocks and concrete bunkers from World War II, and ripped up shallow sub-tidal and intertidal ecosystems.

The KBP research has shown that tsunamis of this magnitude occurred throughout the Middle to Late Holocene. Sand deposits sandwiched between peat and tephra layers at elevations above storm wave levels testify to these past events. Modeling and geological evidence suggest that the Pacific coasts facing the Kuril-Kamchatka trench were most prone to this hazard, as compared to the Okhotsk (western) coasts. Perhaps as a result, we found most archaeologi-cal sites on the Okhotsk sides of islands, though this could in part also reflect sampling bias, given greater opportunities to land and survey on the calmer Okhotsk Sea sides of islands. More significant, most archaeological sites were located on elevated landforms, between 20 and 40 m (and in one extreme case at 100 m) above sea level atop terraces fronted by steep banks. While archaeo-logical sites located closer to shore on beaches or low platforms near good land-ings could have been selectively lost to erosion, it seems likely that the high elevation of existing archaeological sites throughout the Kurils reflects a strat-egy for mitigating the hazards of tsunamis.

For mariners making a living from the sea, tsunamis also posed a hazard to boaters working in shallow water or at the shore at the time of a tsunami strike. As with volcanic events, people undoubtedly perished from tsunamis and, unless their wooden dugout vessels were carried to the tops of terraces, they sometimes lost their boats. Ecological damage as a result of tsunamis remains unquantified, but tsunamis probably have significant if not long-lasting impacts on the ecological productivity of littoral zones. On the other hand, tsunami disturbance on Pacific coasts combined with more protected "buffer" zones on Okhotsk Sea sides contributes resilience to the system at the scale of islands and larger regions. As long as populations did not get too large, these occasional impacts would have only required modest relocation, not island abandonment.

While our research has not provided any evidence of direct tsunami impacts on human settlements, the persistence of what appear to be substantial populations throughout the central islands during the Late Holocene in spite of evidence of major tsunamis on the order of once every 500–1,000 years sug-gests that tsunami events themselves caused little, if any, change in the course of human settlement history or culture. The one adaptive response evident in our data is placement of settlements on high terraces and in more protected locations.

## Hazard 3: Weather and Climate Change

Somewhat less catastrophic, but potentially no less hazardous, are unpre-dictable changes in weather and climate that could affect the ability to navigate the islands and potentially alter the productivity of the marine environment. Weather is used here to indicate daily to annual patterns of atmospheric con-ditions, especially as they interact with the sea surface and marine currents to produce changing fog, surf, and wave patterns, which are inherently hazardous in this oceanic landscape. The Kurils are statistically the foggiest place on earth, and it is rarely possible to see the horizon and often, in fact, little more than the boat in which one is sitting. Modern navigators, including KBP scientists, rely almost entirely on GPS and navigational charts to find their way through the Kurils. Earlier mariners had to learn the landscape more or less by feel and read clues in the waves and currents, birds, and marine organisms to move between and along islands. Fog is most prevalent in summer months when storms are less frequent and less severe.

Large storms pass through the Kurils year-round but with particular intensity between September and May. Winter storms are more violent and bring
hazardous sea ice and other debris into the Sea of Okhotsk and the southern
(and sometimes northern) Kurils. Boat landings in storms are particularly
perilous and would have been exceedingly challenging on many of the smaller
islands, with little or no protection from wind and swells. Storm waves and wind
can push large logs and ice high up the beach and onto low coastal benches or
terraces, creating hazards for beached boats and any residences placed too close
to sea level. Understanding how weather and currents interact to create dangerous conditions would have been a prerequisite to settling the central Kurils for
any past colonists.

Changes in the patterns, frequency, and intensity of weather over periods
ranging from decades to millennia constitute climate change. Changes at these
scales altered the dynamics of storminess, the hazardousness of travel, and productivity of the marine ecosystem in ways that should be reflected in human
adaptations and possibly in changes in the nature of settlement, as they affect
the sustainability of the food supply and the maintenance of social networks
through the islands (discussed later). In cold climates, the North Pacific low-
pressure system tends to intensify, causing strong northerly winds to accelerate
the Oyashio Current that brings nutrient-enriched cold Arctic waters south
from the Bering Sea to the Kurils (Qiu 2001).

This same mechanism intensifies the counterclockwise circulation of the
Sea of Okhotsk, bringing iron-enriched waters from the mouth of the Amur
River to eastern Hokkaido and the southern Kurils. In warmer climate periods
the Oyashio Current, including the Okhotsk gyre, weakens, and a more stratified surface layer limits the degree of nutrient enrichment available for photo-
synthesis and primary production (ibid.). The North Pacific low-pressure system is strongest in winter months when light is least available in the subarctic
waters of the Kurils and the Sea of Okhotsk. As a result, increased winter mix-
ing actually tends to reduce primary productivity by limiting the penetration
of available light into the water column, despite availability of nutrients. In
the south, off the east coast of Hokkaido and the southernmost Kurils, where
winter light is stronger, primary productivity correlates with Oyashio Current
strength (Chiba et al. 2008). While the mechanisms are still to be fully understood (e.g., Schneider and Miller 2001), primary productivity overall should
be enhanced in the southernmost Kurils/Hokkaido in cold periods, while in
the central and northern Kurils primarily, productivity is actually observed to
increase somewhat in warmer periods when spring light returns to the region
(Chiba et al. 2008; Heileman and Belkin 2008). Thus, in a general way we can
expect that cold climates would have enhanced the biomass available for maritime hunter-gatherers in the southern Kurils, while warmer climates could have
made these islands less attractive. On the other hand, warm climate declines in

productivity in the south could have drawn people farther north to the modestly productive central and northern islands.

A combination of climate proxies from Hokkaido (Tsukada 1988; Yamada et al. 2010), the mainland surrounding the Sea of Okhotsk (Korotky et al. 2000), and marine cores in the Sea of Okhotsk (Kawahata et al. 2003) leads us to believe that climate changes occurred on the order of every 600–1,200 years over the past 2,500 years. Records are not perfectly correlated between sources but generally show reversals of climate from warm to cold (ca. 400 BC) to warm (between AD 200 and 800) and then to cold (AD 1200), shifting to warm again in roughly AD 1800. These conditions should have translated into changes in the marine productivity of the Kurils, but these factors did not generate consistent responses in human settlement history.

According to the productivity expectations discussed earlier and assuming that food was the limiting factor in human population densities following colonization, during colder climate phases we would expect the southern Kurils to have been most densely populated during the intervals between 400 BC to AD 200–800 and between AD 1200 and 1800, while the central and northern islands should have seen population expansion in the warmer phases. In fact, the first major population explosion throughout the archipelago occurred during the major cold phase of 400 BC to AD 200 and continued through the following warm phase. On the other hand, the AD 1200–1800 cold phase corresponds to what appears to be a near abandonment of the central Kurils as discussed earlier, in contrast to expectations. Whether we expect population expansion into the central and northern Kurils to be driven by crowding in the south (because of high productivity there) or by the relative benefits of marginally better foraging to the north during warmer periods, the historical patterns are inconsistent with expectations. Clearly, climate change is an insufficient—though probably contributing—causal variable in the changes observed (cf. Hudson 1999).

## Hazard 4: Socioeconomic Isolation and Integration

In the context of the hazards already outlined, the more isolated Kuril Islands produce another kind of hazard for human settlers—that of social isolation and greater difficulties in maintaining vibrant networks for critical information flow, marriage alliances, and support in times when local conditions deteriorated in any part of the archipelago (Fitzhugh, Phillips, and Gjesfjeld 2011). Social networks are easier to maintain when population densities are higher and settlements are closer together. In the central Kurils, maintaining networks between small and distant islands required more costly expeditions, which were all the more essential given the hazards of isolation. These connections would have linked the Kurils economically and socially with the more densely populated regions of Hokkaido and Kamchatka. These links, then, also tied the Kurils to the broader socio-political and economic "world systems" of these larger regions (Hudson 2004). These links, in turn, provided useful materials (like obsidian: Phillips and Speakman 2009) and information. They also engaged the occupants of the Kurils in broader flows of economic and political relations. These connections, essential as they were for reducing the negative consequences of geographic isolation, also tied the islanders to the broader historical patterns of the region and made them potentially vulnerable to socioeconomic and political changes beyond the Kurils.

The more interesting dynamics in this context occurred to the south of the Kurils, where Hokkaido served as the last substantial enclave of the Jomon hunter-gatherer-fisher tradition after rice agriculturalists took over the rest of the Japanese archipelago. Despite the expansion of agricultural populations south of Hokkaido around 500 BC, there is little evidence that Kuril occupants were drawn into substantial long-distance economic interdependencies. In this regard, we consider the Kuril occupants of the Jomon and Epi-Jomon periods to have been largely self-sufficient, while relying on neighbors primarily for security in times of local hardships. This situation changed between AD 700 and 1000 with the Okhotsk settlement. Okhotsk people were connected by economic exchange with Manchuria and may even have been motivated to expand around the Sea of Okhotsk and into the Kurils by the desire to provide valuable furs to the East Asian markets (Hudson 1999). At the same time, Japanese markets stimulated the expansion of the northeastern frontier, gradually drawing northern Honshu and eventually Hokkaido into lucrative trade relations. As southern products such as iron pots, lacquer-ware bowls, and firearms were traded north, northern products such as seal furs, eagle feathers, and salmon were passed south. Political powerbrokers emerged to control this trade, eventually imposing stringent demands on indigenous hunters for increased production of tradable commodities. This development and a somewhat parallel process from the north ultimately led to Japanese and Russian competition for control of the Kurils and the ejection of Kuril Ainu from the archipelago (Walker 2001).

Social connectedness with Hokkaido and Kamchatka appears to have had different implications for Kuril occupants through time. In general, Kamchatka appears to have been a source of obsidian for central and northern Kuril islanders (Phillips and Speakman 2009), despite stronger cultural affiliations to the south. We currently have no evidence for adverse impacts resulting from these northern connections and indeed can speculate that connections with the north may have proved beneficial for Ainu during the interval AD 1200–1800, when increased pressure was mounting on the southern Kurils for commodity production. The dearth of Ainu settlements in the central Kurils could reflect a relocation to the north by Ainu eager to escape the political and economic pressures of ruthless traders to the south. In the southern Kurils and Hokkaido, pressure put on Ainu for commodity production eventually resulted in a number of revolts—most famously one on Kunashir in 1789 that was put down by Japanese military force, marking a turning point in direct Japanese interest in the Kuril Islands (Walker 2001).

It appears that the major impact to successful hunter-gatherer settlement in the Kurils is as much or more social as it is environmental. During Okhotsk settlement, the Kurils were at least marginally connected to an expanding mercantile system of exchange in marine products with mainland East Asian polities. The warmer and wetter climate may have encouraged expanding human populations and the exploitation of a productive niche for marine mammal hunting. Okhotsk people may have colonized the Kurils more as entrepreneurs capitalizing on a lucrative natural resource zone than as a "naturally" expanding population simply looking for new subsistence opportunities. Whether they pushed Epi-Jomon peoples out or assimilated them is yet unclear.

A colder climate—perhaps with lower productivity in the more remote and least ecologically diverse central islands—in combination with a growing political economy to the south, drawing Kuril populations into expanding economic ties with power centers in Hokkaido and mainland Japan, seems to have had the effect of precipitating the relative abandonment of most of the Kurils. In this context we can expect that the central and northern Kuril Ainu took advantage of the geographic characteristics of the Kurils to create isolation from undesirable networks to the south. Following Russian incursion into the northern islands, this process was exercised in reverse when a group of northern Ainu relocated to the central island of Rasshua to escape Russian taxation demands (V. O. Shubin, personal communication 2008).

## RESILIENCE AND VULNERABILITY

These comparisons lead us to broader considerations of human vulnerability and resilience in small-scale, mobile hunter-gatherer populations compared with larger and more densely packed, sedentary, territorial, and infrastructurally rooted populations such as those examined in the remainder of this volume. Several conclusions can be drawn from the Kuril case study.

First, it is becoming clear that natural hazards in the Kurils had relatively little impact on the viability of occupants, once they had developed the capacity to settle and make a living in the islands at all. This is consistent with Sheets's (1999) argument that small-scale societies tend to be most flexible in the face of environmental "catastrophe." While this conclusion is consistent with general expectations for mobile populations living in low population densities, it is somewhat surprising in an environment like the Kurils, which by all expectations should have held hunter-gatherer populations close to the edge of sustainable settlement. The evidence does not currently support a notion of the Kurils as marginal in this fashion, though we cannot yet explain why Epi-Jomon and Okhotsk populations abandoned the island chain 1,300 and 800 years ago, respectively—if in fact they did. Perhaps environmental crises played some role as catalysts in weakening resident populations' holds and opening up the islands for a change of occupants.

Second and perhaps more interesting, the Kuril case highlights the importance of *socio-ecological* dynamics in the history of human settlement. We are coming to see Kuril history, as in other parts of the world, as fundamentally reflecting a complex integration of social, political, and economic factors interacting with environmental and geographical ones. Hunter-fisher-gatherers in the Kurils were not "complex hunter-gatherers" in the organizational sense used to refer to ethnographic peoples of the North American Pacific Northwest (Ames and Maschner 1999), the Channel Islands off California (Arnold 1996), the Calusa of Florida (Marquardt 1988), or the Middle Jomon of northern Honshu (Habu 2004). They lived in smaller groups and worked out their subsistence needs and procured tradable commodities in an ecologically limited and geographically challenging oceanic environment, but they maintained social and economic contacts throughout and beyond the chain and came to use the island geography strategically and politically as it suited them. They suffered the consequences of localized natural disasters, but their lifestyles and persistence in the Kurils appear to have been highly resilient to such factors. From a settlement perspective, the vulnerability of Kuril occupation (though not necessarily of the occupants) therefore seems to lie more in Kuril occupants' social interdependence with the outside world and ultimately in the contingency of expanding political powers that took interest in controlling the Kurils' natural fur wealth through territorial acquisition.

## CONCLUSION

Vulnerability and resilience provide a framework for considering the ways small-scale hunter-gatherer populations may be affected by hazards in the natural environment. In this chapter I have shown that the occupants of the Kuril Islands of Northeast Asia were surprisingly resilient to natural events such as volcanic eruptions, earthquakes, tsunamis, and climate variability but less resilient ultimately to outside pressures from competing groups and expanding demand for Kuril commodities. The result is a richer and more nuanced story of socio-ecological dynamics only starting to emerge from the data produced by the Kuril Biocomplexity Project's years of interdisciplinary research.

The value of this emerging picture for contemporary hazard management is not that small and mobile societies are more resilient to natural hazards, though that is clearly one conclusion. Societies of the twenty-first century do not have the luxury of returning to states of such flexibility. The implication is rather that vulnerability is inherently a complex socio-ecological condition. Ironically, the near abandonment of the Kuril Islands and ultimate extinction of Kuril Ainu populations in recent centuries are products of the *increasingly* interconnected and global scale of socio-political and economic interaction. The Kurils are actively contested in international disputes between Russia and Japan, but on the ground they are a backwater of the civilized world, squeezed of their cultural, economic, and geopolitical vitality in times past by changes in the currents of global politics. Geologically and ecologically as active as ever, these islands sit largely abandoned, waiting for the next cycle of human interest and activity.

*Acknowledgments.* This research was supported by the Kuril Biocomplexity Project, an international, interdisciplinary research program funded by the US National Science Foundation (ARC-0508109; Ben Fitzhugh, PI). Additional support was provided by the University of Washington, Seattle, Washington, USA; the Hokkaido University Museum, Sapporo, Japan; the Historical Museum of Hokkaido, Sapporo, Japan; the Sakhalin Regional Museum, Yuzhno-Sakhalinsk, Russia; and the Far East Branch of the Russian Academy of Sciences (IMGG: Yuzhno-Sakhalinsk, IVS: Petropavlovsk-Kamchatskiy, NEISRI: Magadan, TIG: Vladivostok). This chapter was improved with the thoughtful comments and editorial assistance of Pat Anderson, Laada Bilaniuk, Cecelia Bitz, Andrew Dugmore, Erik Gjesfjeld, Bre MacInnes, and Colby Phillips. Of course, all errors are my responsibility alone.

## REFERENCES

Amano, T.
1979    Ohôtsuku bunka no tenkai to chi'ikisa [Development and Formation of Okhotsk Culture]. *Hoppô Bunka Kenkyû* 12: 75–92 (Japanese).

Ames, K., and H.D.G. Maschner
1999    *Peoples of the Northwest Coast: Their Archaeology and Prehistory.* Thames and Hudson, London.

Anderson, P. M., A. V. Lozhkin, P. S. Minyuk, A. Yu, A. Y. Pakhomov, and T. V. Solomatkina
2009    Pollen Records and Sediment Ages from Lakes of Kunashir and Iturup Islands (Southern Kuril Islands). In *Environment Development of East Asian Pleistocene-Holocene (Boundaries, Factors, Stages of Human Mastering),* Proceedings of the International Scientific Conference, September 14–18, 2009, Vladivostok, Russia. Dalnauka, Vladivostok, pp. 13–16.

Arnold, J. E.
1996    Archaeology of Complex Hunter-Gatherers. *Journal of Archaeological Method and Theory* 3 (2): 77–126.

Blaikie, P., T. Cannon, I. Davis, and B. Wisner
1994 *At Risk: Natural Hazards, People's Vulnerability, and Disasters.* Routledge, New York.

Chiba, S., M. N. Aita, K. Tadokoro, T. Saino, H. Sugisaki, and K. Nakata
2008 From Climate Regime Shift to Lower-Trophic Level Phenology: Synthesis of Recent Progress in Retrospective Studies of the Western North Pacific. *Progress in Oceanography* 77: 112–126.

Cooley, A.
2003 *Pompeii.* Duckworth, London.

Crawford, G. W.
1992 The Transitions to Agriculture in Japan. In *Transitions to Agriculture in Prehistory,* ed. A. B. Gebauer and T. D. Price. Prehistory Press, Madison, WI, pp. 117–132.

2008 The Jomon in Early Agriculture Discourse: Issues Arising from Matsui, Kanehara and Pearson. *World Archaeology* 40(4): 445–465.

Crawford, G. W., and H. Takamiya
1990 The Origins and Implications of Late Prehistoric Plant Husbandry in Northern Japan. *Journal of Archaeological Science* 64: 889–911.

Dumond, D. E.
2004 Volcanism and History on the Northern Alaska Peninsula. *Arctic Anthropology* 41(2): 112–125.

Dumond, D. E., and R. Knecht
2001 An Early Blade Site in the Eastern Aleutians. In *Archaeology in the Aleut Zone of Alaska,* ed. D. E. Dumond. Department of Anthropology and Museum of Natural History, University of Oregon, Eugene, pp. 9–34.

Fitzhugh, B., S. Moore, C. Lockwood, and C. Boone
2004 Archaeological Paleobiogeography in the Russian Far East: The Kuril Islands and Sakhalin in Comparative Perspective. *Asian Perspectives* 43(1): 92–121.

Fitzhugh, B., S. C. Phillips, and E. Gjesfjeld
2011 Modeling Hunter-Gatherer Information Networks: An Archaeological Case Study from the Kuril Islands. In *Information and Its Role in Hunter-Gatherer Bands,* ed. R. Whallon, W. A. Lovis, and R. K. Hitchcock. Cotson Institute of Archaeology Press, Los Angeles, pp. 85–115.

Fitzhugh, B., V. Shubin, K. Tezuka, Y. Ishizuka, and C.A.S. Mandryk
2002 Archaeology in the Kuril Islands: Advances in the Study of Human Paleobiogeography and Northwest Pacific Prehistory. *Arctic Anthropology* 39(1–2): 69–94.

Griggs, R. F.
1918 The Recovery of Vegetation at Kodiak. Part 1 in the series "Scientific Results of the Katmai Expeditions of the National Geographic Society." *Ohio Journal of Science* 19(1): 1–57.

Habu, J.
2004 *Ancient Jomon of Japan.* Cambridge University Press, Cambridge.

Hacker, W. R.
  1951    The Kuril and Ryukyu Islands. In *Geography of the Pacific,* ed. Otis W. Freeman. John Wiley and Sons, New York, pp. 495–521.

Heileman, S., and I. Belkin
  2008    Oyashio Current LME. In *The UNEP Large Marine Ecosystem Report: A Perspective on Changing Conditions in LMEs of the World's Regional Seas,* ed. K. Sherman and G. Hempel. UNEP Regional Seas Report and Studies 182. United Nations Environment Programme, Nairobi, Kenya, chapter 24.

Hudson, M. J.
  1999    *Ruins of Identity: Ethnogenesis in the Japanese Islands.* University of Hawaii Press, Honolulu.
  2004    The Perverse Realities of Change: World System Incorporation and the Okhotsk Culture of Hokkaido. *Journal of Anthropological Archaeology* 23: 290–308.

Imamura, K.
  1996    *Prehistoric Japan: New Perspectives on Insular East Asia.* University College London Press, London.

Ishizuka, Y.
  2001    Volcanic Activity and Recent Tephras in the Kuril Islands: Field Result during the International Kuril Island Project (IKIP) 2000. Report on file with the Ben Fitzhugh Project (PI), University of Washington, Seattle. Available at http://www.anthro.washington.edu/Archy/IKIP/Geology/volcanismindex.htm.

Kawahata, H., H. Oshima, C. Shimada, and T. Oba
  2003    Terrestrial-Oceanic Environmental Change in the Southern Okhotsk Sea during the Holocene. *Quaternary International* 108: 67–76.

Korotky, A., N. Razjigaeva, T. Grebennikova, L. Ganzey, L. Mokhova, V. Bazarova, L. Sulerzhitsky, and K. Lutaenko
  2000    Middle- and Late-Holocene Environments and Vegetation History of Kunashir Island, Kurile Islands, Northwestern Pacific. *The Holocene* 10: 311–331.

Krasheninnikov, S. P.
  1972    *Explorations of Kamchatka, 1735–1741.* Translation of the original 1955 Russian publication by E.A.P. Crownhart-Vaughan. Oregon Historical Society, Portland.

MacInnes, B. T., J. Bourgeois, T. K. Pinegina, and E. A. Kravchunovskaya
  2009a    Tsunami Geomorphology: Erosion and Deposition from the 15 November 2006 Kuril Island Tsunami. *Geology* 37(11): 995–998.

MacInnes, B. T., T. K. Pinegina, J. Bourgeois, N. G. Razhigaeva, V. M. Kaistrenko, and E. A. Kravchunovskaya
  2009b    Field Survey and Geological Effects of the 15 November 2006 Kuril Tsunami in the Middle Kuril Islands. *Pure and Applied Geophysics* 166(1–2): 9–36.

Marquardt, W. H.

    1988     Politics and Production among the Calusa of South Florida. In *Hunters and Gatherers 1: History, Evolution, and Social Change*, ed. T. Ingold, D. Riches, and J. Woodburn. Berg, London, pp. 161–188.

Nakagawa, M., Y. Ishizuka, T. Hasegawa, A. Baba, and A. Kosugi

    2009     Preliminary Report on Volcanological Research of KBP 2007–08 Cruise by Japanese Volcanology Group. Unpublished report on file with the author.

Oliver-Smith, A.

    1996     Anthropological Research on Hazards and Disasters. *Annual Reviews of Anthropology* 25: 303–328.

Oliver-Smith, A., and S. Hoffman, eds.

    2002     *Catastrophe and Culture: The Anthropology of Disaster.* School of American Research Advanced Seminar Series. School of American Research Press, Santa Fe, NM.

Ono, H.

    2008     *Differences in Environmental Adaptation between Northern and Eastern Okhotsk Cultures and Their Cultural Backgrounds.* Проблемы биологической и культурной адапта ции человеческих популяций. Том 1 Археол опияб, Адаптационные стратегии древнег о населения Северной Евразии: сырье при емы обработки. Санкт-Петербурк, Наука, С 186–196 (English with Russian abstract).

Oppenheimer, S., and M. Richards

    2001     Fast Trains, Slow Boats, and the Ancestry of the Polynesian Islanders. *Science Progress* 84(3): 157–181.

Phillips, S. C., and R. J. Speakman

    2009     Initial Source Evaluation of Archaeological Obsidian from the Kuril Islands of the Russian Far East Using Portable XRF. *Journal of Archaeological Science* 36(6): 1256–1263.

Pietsch, T. W., V. V. Bogatov, K. Amaoka, Y. N. Zhuravlev, V. Y. Barkalov, S. Gage, H. Takahashi, A. S. Lelej, S. Y. Storozhenko, N. Minakawa, D. J. Bennet, and T. R. Anderson

    2003     Biodiversity and Biogeography of the Islands of the Kuril Archipelago. *Journal of Biogeography* 30(9): 1297–1310.

Qiu, B.

    2001     Kuroshio and Oyashio Currents. In *Encyclopedia of Ocean Sciences,* ed. J. Steele, S. Thorpe, and K. Turekian. Academic Press, New York, pp. 1413–1425.

Saltonstall, P. G., and G. A. Carver

    2002     Earthquakes, Subsidence, Prehistoric Site Attrition and the Archaeological Record: A View from the Settlement Point Site, Kodiak Archipelago, Alaska. In *Natural Disasters and Cultural Change*, ed. R. Torrence and J. Grattan. Routledge, London, pp. 172–192.

Samarin, I. A., and O. A. Shubina

    2007     Fortified Settlements of the Chasi Type on Kunashir Island: Kurile Isles of the Russian Far East. *North Pacific Prehistory* 1: 235–236.

Schneider, N., and A. J. Miller
  2001    Predicting Western North Pacific Ocean Climate. *Journal of Climate* 14: 3997–4002.

Sheets, P.
  1999    The Effects of Explosive Volcanism on Ancient Egalitarian, Ranked, and Stratified Societies in Middle America. In *The Angry Earth: Disaster in Anthropological Perspective*, ed. A. Oliver-Smith and S. Hoffman. Routledge, New York, pp. 36–58.

Shimoyama, S.
  2002    Volcanic Disasters and Archaeological Sites in Southern Kyushu, Japan. In *Natural Disasters and Cultural Change*, ed. R. Torrence and J. Grattan. Routledge, New York, pp. 326–341.

Sidle, R. C., D. Taylor, X. X. Lu, W. N. Adger, D. J. Lowe, W. P. de Lange, R. M. Newnham, and J. R. Dodson
  2004    Interactions of Natural Hazards and Society in Austral-Asia: Evidence in Past and Recent Records. *Quaternary International* 118–119: 181–203.

Torrence, R., and J. Grattan
  2002    The Archaeology of Disasters: Past and Future Trends. In *Natural Disasters and Cultural Change*, ed. R. Torrence and J. Grattan. Routledge, New York, pp. 1–18.

Tsukada, M.
  1988    Japan. In *Vegetation History*, ed. B. Huntley and T. Webb III. Dordrecht, Boston, pp. 459–517.

Vasilevsky, A., and O. Shubina
  2006    Neolithic of the Sakhalin and Southern Kurile Islands. In *Archaeology of the Russian Far East: Essays in Stone Age Prehistory*, ed. S. M. Nelson, A. Derevianko, Y. Kuzmin, and R. Bland. BAR International Series 1540. Archaeopress, Oxford, England, pp. 151–166.

Walker, B.
  2001    *The Conquest of Ainu Lands: Ecology and Culture in Japanese Expansion, 1590–1800*. University of California Press, Berkeley.

Yamada, K., M. Kamite, M. Saito-Kato, M. Okuno, Y. Shinozuka, and Y. Yasuda
  2010    Late Holocene Monsoonal-Climate Change Inferred from Lakes Ni-no-Megata and San-no-Megata, Northeastern Japan. *Quaternary International* 220(1–2): 122–132.

Yanshina, O. V., and Y. V. Kuzmin
  2010    The Earliest Evidence of Human Settlement in the Kurile Islands (Russian Far East): The Yankito Site Cluster, Iturup Island. *Journal of Island and Coastal Archaeology* 5(1): 179–184.

Zaitseva, D. I., S. G. Popov, A. P. Krylov, Y. V. Knorozov, and A. B. Spevakovskiy
  1993    Radiocarbon Chronology of Archaeological Sites of the Kurile Islands. *Radiocarbon* 35: 507–510.

## UNDERSTANDING HAZARDS, MITIGATING IMPACTS, AVOIDING DISASTERS

### Statement for Policy Makers and the Disaster Management Community

Hazards exist everywhere, and in many cases it is impractical to avoid them. The question to ask is, how can lessons from the past help us see what succeeded and what did not? What worked in the Kurils was a deep historical knowledge about the frequency and potential extremes of hazardous events so people could live in the least vulnerable places, maintain capacities for flexible response to catastrophes when they occurred, and maintain resilient and redundant infrastructures. Extrapolating from the archaeological Kuril situation to modern communities, with their higher population densities, heavier infrastructural requirements, and critical dependencies on non-local resource distribution networks, we can conclude that hazard planning has to include capacity building for decentralized response systems. Families, households, and local communities need to have the ability to respond creatively, with decision decentralization supported by higher governmental institutions so responses can scale with capacity. This also requires systems for rapid and decentralized information sharing.

# Responses to Explosive Volcanic Eruptions by Small to Complex Societies in Ancient Mexico and Central America

*Payson Sheets*

> Solutions [to hazards and disasters] are not to be found primarily in new technologies or better use of existing ones. The difficulties ... stem from social factors. Social problems can only be dealt with socially; technological improvements can only address technological problems.
>
> QUARANTELLI 1991: 27

Gilbert White (1945), a cultural geographer, pioneered the initial serious social science studies of natural hazards, disasters, recoveries, and mitigation. The field of hazard-disaster studies has grown impressively since then (Alexander 1997; Burton, Kates, and White 1978). David Alexander (1995, 1997) surveyed the field and found thirty different disciplines studying hazards and disasters, from the social sciences through the natural sciences and engineering. Because hazard-disaster research began in the social sciences, one might expect, or hope, that it led the way to today and received the majority of research support. Ironically, the natural sciences and engineering now overwhelmingly dominate the social sciences in funding for research in the domain of natural hazards and disasters and in applied dimensions. In virtually all cases within the natural sciences and engineering and even including the social sciences, the focus of research is the immediacy of the hazard, the disaster, recovery, and mitigation. Rarely have long-term studies covering decades or centuries been conducted, and even less frequently have scholars looked into what sectors of a society, or which competing societies, benefit from a disaster over long time spans. In addition, rarely have the creative aspects of disasters been explored, such as where native peoples with centuries of experience develop housing that is resistant to massive stresses, is relatively non-hazardous if it fails, and is easy to reconstruct. As societies "modernize," they too often turn away from traditional and appropriate architecture as "backward" and thus increase the risk of injury and death when disaster occurs. Archaeology is uniquely positioned to explore these aspects of hazards and disasters. It is my hope that archaeologists, aided by other social and natural scientists, can explore the negative and creative-positive aspects of hazards and disasters over long time spans in all occupied areas of the globe and share their insights with people inside and outside their discipline.

Another under-researched and under-theorized domain is how non-literate societies convey disaster knowledge, hazard recognition, and proper behavior from one generation to the next, over very long time spans. Literate societies underestimate these accomplishments, often losing traditional extreme-environmental knowledge and thus putting themselves in danger. Kevin Krajick's article "Tracking Myth to Geological Reality" (2005) summarizes a few cases, such as Northwest Coast native peoples believing that earthquakes and tsunamis can result from battles between the powerful sky deity, the thunderbird, and the ocean deity, the whale, and thus that they need to avoid low-lying coastal areas. Geoscientists have documented periodicities of a few hundred years between major earthquakes and tsunamis in the Seattle area. Similarly, when the massive Indonesian earthquake occurred in 2004, native peoples with long oral traditions in Thailand took to the sea and easily rode out the ocean swell. In contrast, about a quarter million literate people without this oral history drowned in the tsunami. Non-literate societies can maintain hazard perception for many centuries or even millennia by embedding knowledge in religious belief and through frequent repetition of the stories orally and in public performances.

In this chapter I explore the complex relationships between human agency and nature, particularly when nature changes suddenly. I have found thirty-six cases where explosive volcanism impacted ancient societies in what are now Mexico and Central America (Sheets 1999, 2008). What at first glance might seem like a reasonable sample size is actually quite limited, particularly because so few cases are amply researched in social and natural science domains. Few cases have had extensive investigations by volcanologists and archaeologists and thus are difficult to understand broadly and to use comparatively. Comparing explosive volcanic eruptions is rather complex, with significant variables including magnitude, speed of onset, volume of tephra (or dense rock equivalent), and geochemistry. When cultural factors are also considered, very detailed studies are required to seriously explore vulnerability, impacts, recoveries, social organizations, political orders, religion, traditional knowledge, and other important themes. Therefore this chapter is exploratory, in recognition of the formidable array of significant variables spanning the humanities, social sciences, and natural sciences.

## SCALED VULNERABILITIES

A first step in examining these cases is to compare them volcanologically. Of course, natural scientists and engineers have emphasized the geophysical agency of a disaster—whether it be flood, earthquake, tsunami, hurricane, or volcanic eruption—and have documented the importance of the speed of onset, intensity, and magnitude as key factors. Scaling the magnitude of volcanic eruptions is a crucial component for comparisons, and the Volcanic Explosivity Index (VEI) developed by the Smithsonian Institution, Museum of Natural History, is used here (http://www.volcano.si.edu/). The VEI is an 8-point scale of increasing magnitudes, with anything over 4 being "cataclysmic" or worse, with more than 0.1 km³ of tephra volume emitted. For reference, the Mount Saint Helens eruption in 1980 consisted of 1 km³ of tephra. Underdeveloped in the literature are the social factors that render a society vulnerable to sudden massive stress, and each of them can be scaled. This chapter considers such social factors and provides a preliminary methodological framework to examine them. Thus I define five broad categories of social factors that affect a culture's vulnerability to geophysical disasters. I also propose a scale with which to assess each domain of social vulnerability on a 5-point range: very low, low, moderate, high, and very high.

### Societal Complexity/Political Organization

Societal complexity ranges from small bands of egalitarian hunter-gatherers through egalitarian villagers; to moderate-sized ranked societies, often called chiefdoms; to large, complex societies, often called states, with highly differentiated classes or castes. In political organization, societies range from egalitarian groups that make decisions by consensus to highly structured societies with centralized authority at the top and strong institutions of enforcement, with limited but extant power of commoners to effect changes. Societal complexity and political organization parallel each other sufficiently to be combined here.

Within the sample of three dozen cases where explosive eruptions affected ancient Mexican–Central American cultures, I have found that the most resilient were the egalitarian villagers of the Arenal area, Costa Rica (Sheets 2001, 2008) (figure 2.1). The ten ancient eruptions of Arenal Volcano documented by our project (Sheets 1994) have been given VEI magnitudes of 4 (0.1 to 0.9

**2.1.** *Map of Mexico and Central America, with archaeological sites and volcanoes indicated. Map by Payson Sheets.*

km³ of tephra) and were thus evaluated as "cataclysmic." Volcanologists have documented many more eruptions of Arenal Volcano, and a total of thirty-two eruptions are listed by the Smithsonian, beginning 7,000 years ago and ending with the present ongoing eruption (figure 2.2). Some of them were from the adjoining cone of Cerro Chato. Cerro Chato and Arenal share the same magma chamber and for our purposes here can be considered the same source.

Of those thirty-two eruptions, twenty-three occurred during Precolumbian times. Presumably, the reason over half of them were not found in the archaeological record is that they were not of sufficient magnitude to deposit thick tephra layers at distances of 15 to 35 km eastward from the source, and they survived turbation and soil formation processes to preserve to today. The smaller of these eruptions surely caused less social and ecological disruption, but all of them served as reminders of the hazards the volcano posed and must have reinforced traditional knowledge, hazard awareness, disaster experience, and belief.

Presumably because Arenal egalitarian decision-making rested at the village or often at the household level, responses to an emergency could be rapid. Given the average periodicity of a big eruption every four centuries (and smaller

**2.2.** *Stratigraphy of air-fall volcanic ash deposits from Arenal Volcano, and soils developed on them, with Tom Sever for scale. Unit 65 is the soil that existed prior to Arenal erupting. Units 61, 55, 50, 40, and 20 were major eruptions that preserved even at this distance, 23 km away. Other ash falls have been incorporated into soils and are not visible. The thin Unit 10 is barely visible below the "U" and is the remains of the recent 1968 eruption. By Payson Sheets.*

ones more often), maintaining knowledge within an oral tradition would have been well within their capabilities. R. J. Blong (1982) discovered that Papua New Guinea natives passed extraordinarily detailed information about an eruption by oral history for a few centuries. Krajick (2005) documents the Klamath natives of Oregon maintaining generally accurate information about the eruption of Mount Mazama by oral tradition for 7,000 years. I scale the vulnerability of these Arenal villagers to the ten big eruptions of Arenal Volcano, in terms of social and political organization and adaptation, as very low.

Southeast Maya civilization and the early–fifth-century Ilopango eruption in El Salvador (Dull, Southon, and Sheets 2001) occupy the other end of the cultural and volcanological spectrum (figure 2.3). The eruption was so great it received a VEI of 6+ (71 km$^3$ of tephra emitted), evaluated as "paroxysmal," and thus was one of the greatest Central American eruptions in the past million years. The complex and hierarchical Miraflores branch of Maya civilization never recovered from the eruption (Sheets 2008). Not only was the society highly vulnerable because of hierarchical social stratification and a complex redistributive economy (ibid.), but the sheer magnitude of the eruption and its sialic (acidic, slow-weathering) chemistry stifled recovery in the central to eastern areas affected. While the eruption was devastating to local inhabitants,

**2.3.** *Ilopango volcanic ash 7 m deep burying a soil marked "S" that also contained a settlement before the eruption. This location, Ciudad Credisa, is ca. 12 km from the source. Mike Foster provides scale. Profile cleaned for recording. The Ilopango eruption was the greatest in Central America in the past 84,000 years. Photo by Payson Sheets.*

the magnitude of physical impact was lessened at more distant areas, such as Kaminaljuyu. However, the cultural effects at those distant locations were considerable, with a dramatic decline in population, abandonment of all ten previously occupied mound complexes, and intrusive Teotihuacan-style architecture (Michels 1979: 296)—which I suggest indicates outsiders taking advantage of local societal weakening. At even more distant localities, such as the Peten of northern Guatemala, a thin dusting of tephra could have been beneficial by adding porosity to tropical lowland soils, adding nutrients, and inhibiting insect pests. Crops in areas of eastern Washington State benefited from thin deposits of volcanic ash from the 1980 Mount Saint Helens eruption adding a mulch layer and killing insect pests by inhibiting their breathing.

Following the Ilopango eruption, natural processes of weathering, soil formation, plant succession, and animal reoccupation ensued. We estimate it took at least a half century for people to reoccupy the Zapotitan Valley, and the Ceren site is one of the earliest known settlements in that reoccupation (Sheets 2004) (figure 2.4). Ceren, a Maya village of commoners, thrived for almost another century until it was entombed by tephra from the Loma Caldera eruption shortly after AD 600. Loma Caldera is only 600 m north of the village, and the eruption occurred when magma moving upward came in contact with water of the Rio Sucio. Two warnings of the eruption occurred, the first of which was an earthquake of about magnitude 4 on the Richter scale, as evidenced by round-bottomed pots remaining on elevated surfaces and minor ground cracking in the eastern part of the site. But in a very tectonically active

**2.4.** *Structure 1 at the Ceren site, Zapotitan Valley, El Salvador. The valley and most of El Salvador were abandoned because of the fall of the Ilopango tephra ("I") and were reoccupied after a juvenile soil formed. Ceren residents lived and thrived for a few decades before being buried by 5 m of volcanic ash from the nearby Loma Caldera volcanic vent. Photo by Payson Sheets.*

area such as El Salvador, an earthquake of that magnitude would not cause alarm. The second warning would have caught people's attention, though, as this kind of eruption, a phreatomagmatic eruption, begins with a shrieking noise of steam. That sound is probably why we have found nobody in the village killed by the eruption, as everyone likely headed south in an emergency evacuation.

The Loma Caldera eruption was disastrous for Ceren and nearby settlements, but only within a diameter of 2–3 km from the epicenter. Most people living in the valley were not adversely affected by the eruption itself. But based on an estimated 30 km² area that would have had to have been evacuated and estimated population densities at about 200 per km² (Black 1983), around 6,000 people would have had to have resettled in other areas, which must have created strains on an already densely settled landscape. The stratigraphy at Ceren reveals two later explosive eruptions, both of which had greater regional impacts than did Loma Caldera. San Salvador (Boqueron) Volcano erupted (VEI 4) probably in the 900s, depositing a thick pasty wet tephra all across the valley but particularly thick in the southern and eastern portions. Those areas were abandoned for a generation or longer by an estimated 21,000 to 54,000 people (Sheets 2004: 116). The Boqueron eruption was more than an order of magnitude greater in impact than Loma Caldera but vastly smaller than Ilopango.

The most recent (uppermost) tephra layer at Ceren began falling on November 4, 1658, from the Playon eruption (VEI 3). Playon lava and tephra were devastating to Spanish Colonial agriculture, ranching, and indigo growing and processing (Sheets 2004) and to the natives' communal lands. Following the Spanish Conquest in the 1530s, native populations underwent severe depopulation as well as circumscription of their lands. The legal and adaptive hassles suffered by native Pipil Indians who were displaced by the Playon tephra and lava are described in detail by David Browning (1971). Prior to the eruption, the Pipiles utilized the shrinking lands around their town of Nexapa under the principle of communal property, but Spanish colonials operated under the principle of individual landownership. When both groups had their land taken away by the eruption, the Spanish administration discriminated against the Pipiles by denying them any land for almost eighty years but finally granted them legal title to a narrow strip of land up the slope of San Salvador Volcano. Colonial authorities looked after the economic well-being of the displaced Spanish cattle ranchers and indigo farmers promptly after the eruption because they were participants in the national economy and culture, to the detriment of the original occupants. Politically and economically disenfranchised groups are the easiest to ignore at times of stress or emergency by those in positions of authority, an unfortunate but almost universal phenomenon.

**2.5.** *Panama's Baru Volcano in the background and "no-man's land" in the middle
ground. The petroglyphs on the boulder in the foreground mark the boundary of the
Barriles chiefdom. Bruce Dahlin is excavating around the periphery of the boulder.
The "V" shape at the top of the volcano resulted from the lake breaching the edge of
the crater and scouring the side, creating large flood deposits below (not visible in
this view). Photo by Payson Sheets.*

## Societal Conflict

In the cases I have examined, the effects of the eruption of Volcan Baru in
western Panama at about AD 700 best illustrate the effects societal conflict can
have on increasing vulnerability to sudden great stress (figure 2.5). I assess this
factor as high in this case. The tephra deposited at the Barriles chiefdoms was
thin (Linares and Ranere 1980: 291), I am estimating about a half meter originally, weathered and compacted to ca. 10 cm at present. It did not receive a
Smithsonian VEI rating, perhaps because it was so small. Deposits comparable
to this in the Arenal area, at a good distance from the source, caused temporary
abandonment because of damage to flora and fauna. Full cultural recovery with
reoccupation at Arenal occurred fairly soon, probably within a few decades at
most. In contrast to Arenal, this Baru eruption caused abandonment of the
Barriles chiefdoms up and down the Rio Chiriqui and migrations over the
continental divide into the humid Caribbean lowlands, requiring fundamental
adaptive and cultural changes (Linares and Ranere 1980).

The Barriles society never recovered or reoccupied the area. Rather, a different culture group moved into the area following ecological recovery. Why were the effects on Barriles so severe from such a relatively small eruption? The apparent reason for such a drastic effect is that the chiefdoms were engaged in chronic warfare with each other (Sheets 2001) in a densely packed alluvial valley and thus were severely limited in areas in which to seek refuge. The Baru eruption and the Barrilles chiefdoms provide a case study that illustrates how societal conflict greatly increases vulnerability to even a relatively small unanticipated stress.

## Demography and Mobility

The above-mentioned Barriles chiefdoms also highlight another major category of social factors that directly affect a group's susceptibility to geophysical stress. The chiefdoms had demographically filled in the valley along the Rio Chiriqui, exploiting the productive alluvial soils but hemmed in by the weak soils on the surrounding hills (Linares and Ranere 1980). Such dense populations could be sustained under usual conditions but perhaps barely, as population increase may have been pushing the threshold of sustainability. But when Baru erupted in a minor way, the additional stress it caused was sufficient to overload the system. Because of the densely occupied landscape in western Panama, other nearby river valleys offered no refuge, so the impacted chiefdoms were forced to move to a distant and very different environment (ibid.). In contrast, the villagers in the sparsely populated Arenal area moved easily to nearby locales beyond the tephra blankets until ecological recovery had occurred. It is possible that Arenal refugees revisited their abandoned villages to walk the prescribed paths to and from their cemeteries, even before they could actually reoccupy the villages themselves (Sheets and Sever 2007). Population densities in Mesoamerica were far greater than those in Panama or Costa Rica, thereby providing few or no under-populated areas to which immigrants could relocate and maintain their cultural traditions. Thus we can see a range of demographically caused vulnerabilities, from very low (Arenal) to high (Barriles) to very high (Mesoamerica).

## Economy and Adaptation

Large, explosive volcanic eruptions that impact societies with complex redistributive economies and intensive agricultural systems with high degrees of vulnerability in Mesoamerica provide instructive contrasts to lower Central America. Claus Siebe (2000: 61) dates a "cataclysmic" eruption of Popocatepetl to slightly more than 2,000 years ago and ascribes a VEI of 6, thus approaching the Ilopango eruption in magnitude. His prediction of devastation of pro-

**2.6.** *Cholula, Puebla, Mexico. The talud-tablero architecture of a one-tier platform was buried by a deep* lahar *from Popocatepetl Volcano. The* lahar *is labeled in the middle ground. Photo by Payson Sheets.*

ductive lands in Puebla has been verified by excavations of the communities around Tetimpa by Patricia Plunket and Gabriela Uruñuela (Evans 2008: 250). Surely many immigrants headed downhill farther east to the big city of Cholula (ibid.: 251) and may have moved into that metropolis, likely at the lowest level of the social strata. The fact that talud-tablero architecture had been practiced for many decades in Tetimpa and then suddenly showed up in Teotihuacan at about the same time as the eruption suggests that many refugees may have fled from Puebla to that great Basin of Mexico city and perhaps introduced talud-tablero architecture there. Many of them may have become local construction workers. But this is curious, as one would not expect refugees to introduce an architectural style into their host settlement that became the religious form henceforth. Following ecological recovery, some farmers apparently traveled back up to their land at Tetimpa for agricultural purposes and then returned to safer locations below. But the later eruption of Popocatepetl, during the ninth century, again devastated the slopes around Tetimpa (Plunket and Uruñuela 1998, 2002). I believe Cholula was devastated by a massive *lahar*, that is, a huge mudflow of largely wet volcanic ash (Sheets 2008: 180), following that second eruption (figure 2.6).

In the middle and Late Formative, prior to Teotihuacan becoming a large city, Cuicuilco was the first community in the Basin of Mexico to develop

**2.7.** *Cuicuilco, highland central Mexico. The main pyramid is on the left and was partially buried by the lava from Xitle Volcano, on the right. The lava was excavated away from the base of the pyramid, down to the pre-eruption ground surface. Photo by Payson Sheets.*

a civic-ceremonial center with a large pyramid and perhaps 20,000 people (Evans 2008: 210). The eruption of Xitle Volcano (VEI 3) about 2,000 years ago deposited thick layers of tephra and lava, devastating and depopulating the southern basin for centuries (figure 2.7). Soils on top of the lavas have yet to recover, but they provide a scenic landscape for the modern Pedregal subdivision. Teotihuacan's rapid growth must have been, at least in part, a result of absorbing refugees from Cuicuilco and surrounding areas, in addition to those from Puebla. I suspect the refugees from both areas were absorbed into increasingly hierarchical Teotihuacan at the lowest level of society, as agricultural or construction workers or even as slaves.

The eruptions of Popocatepetl (Siebe et al. 1996), which affected Puebla (Tetimpa and Cholula); Xitle, which impacted Cuicuilco; and Ilopango, which affected the Miraflores Maya, impacted societies with complex redistributive economies and intensive agricultural systems. These societies relied on long-distance trade networks, centralized authority with occupational specialists, and markets for exchanges. A highly structured top-down economy is subject to disruption when a significant portion of that system is devastated. The agricultural system of all these societies was maize-based, supplemented by beans and squash, and likely manioc with the Maya. In these cases the economies and agricultural systems were highly developed, stretched somewhere close to their limits, and therefore I would rate their vulnerabilities to unanticipated sudden stresses as high. In all cases the impacted societies struggled to recover; in two of these cases they never did recover.

## Differential Impacts of Disasters: Of Course There Were Losers, but There Were Also Winners

The huge explosive eruption of Ilopango Volcano thoroughly eliminated the early vibrant Miraflores branch of Maya civilization in the southeast highlands in the fifth century AD (Dull, Southon, and Sheets 2001) or possibly the early sixth century, and it never recovered. However, at greater distances where a few centimeters of tephra fell, the benefits of increasing soil porosity—acting as mulch—and stifling of noxious insects would have been beneficial. For instance, the tephra should have had salutary edaphic effects on tropical soils in the Peten of Guatemala, including Tikal.

Tikal and other Maya sites in the tropical lowlands must have been impacted greatly by the worldwide atmospheric event of AD 536, which dramatically lowered temperatures for sixteen years and caused years without summers, crop failures, starvation, and political instabilities in Europe, Africa, and China (Gunn 2000). Hubert Robichaux (2000) argues that the event's dramatic dimming of sunlight and climatic effects must have caused agricultural difficulties for Tikal, leading to its weakening. Tikal showed no evidence of changing its adaptation and continued its reliance on exalted divine kingship. That weakening was exploited by Caracol, in alliance with Calakmul, to conquer Tikal in AD 562. Caracol, only 70 km away, would have been similarly impacted by the AD 536 phenomenon. However, Caracol developed extraordinarily extensive terracing systems that protected soils and maximized rainfall moisture retention, which buffered the effects of the event (Chase and Chase 2000). Also, Caracol was more heterarchical than Tikal, with more widespread distribution of preciosities and dispersed settlements of all social classes, integrated by a system of roadways. Then, 120 years later, Tikal revolted, defeated Caracol, and reestablished its independence.

The collapse of Classic Maya civilization in the ninth century, only in the Southern Maya Lowlands, was caused largely by anthropogenic factors of overpopulation, deforestation, soil damage, and nutritional difficulties (Webster, Freter, and Gonlin 2000), accelerated by drought (Curtis, Hodell, and Brenner 1996). Those who benefited from the collapse lived north and south of the depopulated area and benefited at least in part by seizing control of trade routes that used to go through the Peten. Thus sites in the Maya highlands prospered and even attracted immigrants such as the Pipil from central Mexico (Fowler 1989). The Putun (Chontal) Maya thrived after the Maya collapse, as they already had established trade routes linking central Mexico with coastal communities around the Yucatan Peninsula from their heartland in the southern Gulf Coast. By about AD 850 they were robustly expanding and took on a major political-economic role in Chichen Itza (Evans 2008: 386–390).

I believe it is important to explore the antecedents of the collapse of the Classic Maya civilization from the different perspectives of humanities and sciences. If we look at Tikal from a humanistic perspective, the apex of artistic achievement occurred during the reign of Jasaw Chan K'awiil I, from AD 682 to 734 (Martin and Grube 2008: 44), when Temples 1 and 2 were constructed, magnificent stela and lintel carving was done, and large twin-pyramid complexes were built every twenty years on a katun cycle. In contrast, a scientist exploring land use, subsistence, diet, population, and other infrastructure factors involved with sustainability would perceive an apex about two centuries earlier. In spite of crossing the threshold of sustainability, the arts and architecture thrived for perhaps a couple of hundred years until the collapse process began in earnest. William Haviland's analyses (1967) of human burials at Tikal revealed the dramatic decline in stature—an indication of poor nutrition—of elites and commoners from the Early to the Late Classic. In fact, the stature of both classes in the Late Classic was inferior to that even of the Preclassic period.

Tikal was not alone in experiencing an apex of humanistic accomplishment well after the threshold of sustainability had been crossed. At Copan the apex of art and architecture was reached under the thirteenth ruler, Waxaklajuun Ubaah K'awiil, AD 695–738 (Martin and Grube 2008: 203). As patron of the arts, more stelae were carved for him than for any other ruler, and they are in magnificently high relief. He began the Hieroglyphic Stairway, as well as numerous pyramids and temples, and built one of the largest and most elaborate ball courts of any in the Maya area during the Classic period. Webster and his colleagues (2000) document the deforestation, soil erosion, and other infrastructure difficulties of the Late Classic. Perhaps the construction of "Rosalila" around AD 550 (Martin and Grube 2008: 198) as the last building to use abundant stucco decoration, requiring huge amounts of firewood, marks the crossing of the threshold of sustainability.

## SUMMARY AND CONCLUSIONS

The "ceremonial centers" of complex societies were the loci of centralized political, economic, and religious authority. Where authority was highly centralized and severely impacted or destroyed by explosive volcanism, recovery of that culture did not occur, as exemplified by the Miraflores Maya and Cuicuilco and perhaps the Tetimpa area of Puebla (Plunket and Uruñuela 1998, 2002). Refugees were often absorbed at the lowest social level of receiving societies and had to adapt to their servitude. Where the magnitude of the eruption was not as great, complex societies have shown impressive resilience in the long run, such as San Andres and surrounding settlements impacted by the ninth- to tenth-century eruption of Boqueron (VEI 4) and the Loma Caldera eruption in the fifth or sixth century (VEI 3), both in El Salvador (Sheets 2002, 2008).

Decentralized egalitarian societies, such as those in the Arenal area, could react particularly rapidly to an emergency. Most decision-making occurred at the household level, presumably in the context of traditional oral knowledge, and evacuations could be effected at a moment's notice. Because only a tiny fraction of the diet came from domesticated foods and regional population densities were very low, refuge areas beyond the devastation could readily support refugees. Repopulating the disaster areas were the descendants of the pre-eruption villagers (Sheets and Sever 2007), and no culture changes could be attributed to any of the eruptions and dislocations. Of course, I am not recommending that worldwide populations change their cultures and adaptations to emulate Arenal villagers, as the time when that could be done was passed many millennia ago. However, there is a clear lesson for present-day complex societies to instill nodes of authority dispersed among populations inhabiting hazardous areas. The thousands of stranded Katrina victims in New Orleans standing still and looking upward at TV cameras in helicopters, passively waiting for government assistance, provide a compelling case. They did not know what to do and waited for top-down authority. Unfortunately for them, the authority was as woefully unprepared as they were.

Along with centralized authority in complex societies go redistributive economies. States are characterized as having high degrees of occupational specialization, and the products made by those specialists require elaborate systems to redistribute them. Such complex systems can function well under usual conditions but are subject to failure under unanticipated stresses. Further development of this topic could be done by modeling network structures with nodes and links, but that is beyond the scope of this chapter.

One of the smallest eruptions in the sample, the eighth-century eruption of Baru in Panama, had surprisingly severe consequences on the Barriles ranked societies (chiefdoms). They had to completely abandon the area, and they never reoccupied it even after full ecological recovery. Rather, they had to migrate over the divide and down into the much more humid tropical rainforest on the Caribbean side and fundamentally change their adaptation, settlement pattern, and other culture elements. I believe this is primarily because the chiefdoms were in a state of chronic warfare and thus made themselves vulnerable to a sudden unanticipated stress, even a very small one when compared with the other eruptions under consideration here.

Earlier in this chapter I gave some thought to encoding hazard and disaster information into myth and religion. That encoding can give societies templates for behavior and can often save lives, such as the traditional peoples heading out to sea after they felt the large 2004 Sumatra earthquake and the tide receded (Krajick 2005). Many lives were saved through recognition of the early warnings of a tsunami. Similarly, Northwest Coast societies encoded earthquakes and tsunamis into beliefs about battles between the thunderbird and the whale, both powerful deities, and would therefore head to high ground (ibid.). Where disasters were not similarly encoded and thus exceeded ideological understandings, explanation fails, and people can severely question their beliefs.

Another aspect of the relationships between disasters and religion is under-theorized and under-researched. Today we are comfortable explaining the origins of disasters in terms of plate tectonics, evacuating magma chambers, releases of stresses along fault planes, or other geophysical or climatic factors. However, cultures around the world consistently ascribed the sources of disasters to the supernatural domain prior to the development of Western empirical science in the past few centuries. Commonly, the elites in non-Western societies were primarily responsible for interceding between their people and the deities. Under usual conditions the elites could demonstrate their successes in communicating with the supernatural domain, thus strengthening their religious authority. But a truly great disaster must call into question religious belief as well as confidence in elite religious efficacy. Archaeologists would do well to explore the relationship between mega-disasters and significant change in religious belief and practice. Long-term worldwide suffering caused by an atmospheric phenomenon—probably a high altitude dust layer—in AD 536 was documented in many areas (Gunn 2000), such as about 75 percent of the people in a northern Chinese kingdom dying (Houston 2000). Margaret Houston (ibid.) suggests that the 536 impact could have contributed to the collapse of the Wei Empire and the loss of the mandate of heaven and facilitated the shift toward Buddhism. A disaster of this magnitude could have undermined confidence in religion, thus facilitating the emergence of a new religious order.

The AD 536 phenomenon was recorded in Europe and the Near East. In Italy the Roman senator Cassiodorus wrote that for a year the sun was so dimmed it cast no shadow at noon, and crops were not maturing because of perpetual frost and drought, causing famine (Young 2000: 36). The Byzantine historian Procopius reported similar conditions at Carthage, North Africa, as did historians in Mesopotamia and Constantinople (ibid.: 37). Bailey Young argues that the event contributed to the end of classical civilizations and the beginning of the Middle Ages. Although the event was not recorded as precisely in Britain, Elizabeth Jones (2000) believes it caused political chaos and spiritual disillusionment and perhaps contributed to epidemics in England, Europe, and the Near East.

The prophet Muhammad lived and developed Islam a few decades later than the phenomenon, and conversion spread astoundingly rapidly. The inexplicable climatic stresses and the disenchantment with extant belief systems may have facilitated that spread. Considerable research needs to be done before this could be considered compellingly demonstrated.

Demographic factors, of course, are major components in people making themselves less or more vulnerable to disasters. The single most important element is the spectacular population explosion of recent centuries, so it is not surprising that the tolls in deaths and destruction increase annually. Obviously needed are population control and zoning to restrict habitation in known hazardous areas. Within this study sample there is only one area where population did not increase dramatically to near carrying capacity, and that was the Arenal area. In spite of carefully examining the cultural inventory (artifacts, features, architecture, subsistence, economy, political organization, and pattern of settlement) for any evidence of volcanically induced change, we could find none. And that was not because of a paucity of eruptions. In our archaeological-volcanological research we documented ten large eruptions (VEI 4) in almost 400 years, and the Smithsonian website documents evidence of many other eruptions over a longer time period. Arenal peoples must have generated considerable traditional knowledge about eruptions, societal responses, and reoccupations, in spite of—or more likely because of—their frequency.

Are there lessons from the past that could inform us today? Native peoples in so many areas of the world, over centuries or millennia, developed architecture that was appropriate to the perceived hazards and experienced disasters. Pole-and-thatch structures or those of bajareque (wattle and daub) withstand strong winds and major earthquakes. Such bajareque structures can be quite sizable and ample, with two stories and easily 2,000 to 3,000 square feet (186–279 m²) in floor area. Even when the stress leads to strain that cannot be withstood and the walls shed the mudding, it causes little harm to inhabitants. However, with modernization, traditional architecture acquires an aura of backwardness, and people shift to unreinforced adobe or cinderblock architecture. Under usual conditions it survives and looks fine, but when it fails under earthquake stress it causes great injury and death. The reintroduction of traditional architecture under the guise of a new label with mystique, such as "Ceren architecture," can provide protection. Such reintroduction into El Salvador has begun.

We cannot encourage more than 6 billion people to revert to hunting and gathering or an Arenal-style sedentism and adaptation so they can maintain mobility in the face of disaster. But with the perspective furnished by archaeology, it appears to me that some of the great tragedies of the human experience in the past millennium are unfettered population explosion, loss of traditional environmental knowledge, and authorities' irresponsibility. Packing more and more people onto the earth's surface inevitably increases the tolls of death and destruction when disasters occur, in part by reducing the available options for successful mitigation. The need for birth control is patently obvious but tragically ignored. Given today's dense populations, at a minimum land-use planning to decrease residence in known hazardous areas needs to become policy throughout the world, and it needs to be done in concert with family planning so future generations are not squeezed back into those dangerous zones. Dispersed nodes of experience and authority for decision-making need to be created in hierarchically organized societies. Thus when the centralized authority is either incapacitated or unable to assist, local groups can take over in disaster assistance and recovery.

*Acknowledgments.* A robust expression of gratitude is appropriate for my colleagues who met in October 2009 at Eagle Hill, Maine, for a memorable working conference on global human ecodynamics. The discussions and presentations by Jago Cooper, Ben Fitzhugh, Dan Sandweis, Peggy Nelson, and Emily McClung de Tapia were particularly educational and stimulating for me. The conference was organized by Tom McGovern and supported by Anna Kertulla, Arctic Social Science Program, National Science Foundation. Anna's support is warmly appreciated, and her willingness to work toward publication subvention is heartily acknowledged.

The Volcanic Explosivity Indices used here to compare magnitudes of explosive eruptions are from the Global Volcanism Program of the Smithsonian National Museum of Natural History (http://www.volcano.si.edu/). Their compilations are greatly appreciated.

Christine Dixon, Jago Cooper, and Ben Fitzhugh kindly gave an earlier version of this chapter a careful reading and provided numerous suggestions to clarify some otherwise rather opaque text.

## REFERENCES

Alexander, David
> 1995    A Survey of the Field of Natural Hazards and Disaster Studies. In *Geographical Information Systems in Assessing Natural Hazards*, ed. Alberto Carrara and Fausto Guzetti. Kluwer, Dordrecht, pp. 1–19.
> 1997    The Study of Natural Disasters, 1977–1997: Some Reflections on a Changing Field of Knowledge. *Disasters* 21: 284–304.

Black, Kevin
> 1983    The Zapotitan Valley Archaeological Survey. In *Archeology and Volcanism in Central America: The Zapotitan Valley of El Salvador*, ed. Payson Sheets. University of Texas Press, Austin, pp. 62–97.

Blong, R. J.
> 1982    *The Time of Darkness: Local Legends and Volcanic Reality in Papua New Guinea*. University of Washington Press, Seattle.

Browning, David
1971    *El Salvador: Landscape and Society*. Clarendon, Oxford.

Burton, Ian, Robert Kates, and Gilbert White
1978    *The Environment as Hazard*. Oxford University Press, New York.

Chase, Arlen, and Diane Chase
2000    Sixth and Seventh Century Variability in the Southern Maya Lowlands: Centralization and Integration at Caracol, Belize. In *The Years without Summer: Tracing AD 536 and Its Aftermath*, ed. Joel D. Gunn. BAR International Series 872. Archaeopress, Oxford, England, pp. 55–66.

Curtis, Jason, David Hodell, and Mark Brenner
1996    Climate Variability on the Yucatan Peninsula (Mexico) during the Past 3500 Years, and Implications for Maya Cultural Evolution. *Quaternary Research* 46: 37–47.

Dull, Robert, John Southon, and Payson Sheets
2001    Volcanism, Ecology, and Culture: A Reassessment of the Volcan Ilopango TBJ Eruption in the Southern Maya Realm. *Latin American Antiquity* 12: 25–44.

Evans, Susan
2008    *Ancient Mexico and Central America*. Thames and Hudson, London.

Fowler, William
1989    *The Cultural Evolution of Ancient Nahua Civilizations: The Pipil-Nicarao of Central America*. University of Oklahoma Press, Norman.

Gunn, Joel, ed.
2000    *The Years without Summer: Tracing AD 536 and Its Aftermath*. BAR International Series 872. Archaeopress, Oxford, England.

Haviland, William
1967    Stature at Tikal, Guatemala: Implications for Ancient Maya Demography and Social Organization. *American Antiquity* 32: 316–325.

Houston, Margaret
2000    Chinese Climate, History, and State Stability in AD 536. In *The Years without Summer: Tracing AD 536 and Its Aftermath*, ed. Joel D. Gunn. BAR International Series 872. Archaeopress, Oxford, England, pp. 71–77.

Jones, Elizabeth
2000    Climate, Archaeology, History, and the Arthurian Tradition: A Multiple-Source Study of Two Dark-Age Puzzles. In *The Years without Summer: Tracing AD 536 and Its Aftermath*, ed. Joel D. Gunn. BAR International Series 872. Archaeopress, Oxford, England, pp. 25–34.

Krajick, Kevin
2005    Tracking Myth to Geological Reality. *Science* 310: 762–764.

Linares, Olga, and Anthony Ranere, eds.
1980    *Adaptive Radiations in Prehistoric Panama*. Peabody Museum, Harvard University, Cambridge, MA.

Martin, Simon, and Nikolai Grube
2008    *Chronicle of the Maya Kings and Queens*. Thames and Hudson, London.

Michels, Joe
    1979    A History of Settlement at Kaminaljuyu. In *Settlement Pattern Excavations at Kaminaljuyu, Guatemala*, ed. Joe Michels. Penn State University Press, University Park, pp. 277–304.

Plunket, Patricia, and Gabriela Uruñuela
    1998    Appeasing the Volcano Gods: Ancient Altars Attest a 2000-Year-Old Veneration of Mexico's Smoldering Popocatepetl. *Archaeology* 51(4): 36–43.
    2002    To Leave or Not to Leave: Human Responses to Popocatepetl's Eruptions in the Tetimpa Region of Puebla, Mexico. Paper presented at the 67th Annual Meeting of the Society for American Archaeology, Denver, March 21.

Quarantelli, Eugene
    1991    More and Worse Disasters in the Future: The Social Factors Involved. Preliminary Paper 173. Disaster Research Center, Newark, DE.

Robichaux, Hubert
    2000    The Maya Hiatus and the AD 536 Atmospheric Event. In *The Years without Summer: Tracing AD 536 and Its Aftermath*, ed. Joel D. Gunn. BAR International Series 872. Archaeopress, Oxford, England, pp. 45–54.

Sheets, Payson
    1994    Summary and Conclusions. In *Archaeology, Volcanism, and Remote Sensing in the Arenal Region, Costa Rica*, ed. Payson Sheets and Brian McKee. University of Texas Press, Austin, pp. 312–326.
    1999    The Effects of Explosive Volcanism on Ancient Egalitarian, Ranked, and Stratified Societies in Middle America. In *The Angry Earth: Disaster in Anthropological Perspective*, ed. Anthony Oliver-Smith and Susanna Hoffman. Routledge, New York, pp. 36–58.
    2001    The Effects of Explosive Volcanism on Simple to Complex Societies in Ancient Central America. In *Interhemispheric Climate Linkages*, ed. Vera Markgraf. Academic Press, San Diego, pp. 73–86.
    2004    Apocalypse Then: Social Science Approaches to Volcanism, People, and Cultures in the Zapotitan Valley, El Salvador. In *Natural Hazards in El Salvador*, ed. William Rose, Julian Bommer, Dina Lopez, Michael Carr, and Jon Major. Special Paper 375. Geological Society of America, Boulder, CO, pp. 109–120.
    2008    Armageddon to the Garden of Eden: Explosive Volcanic Eruptions and Societal Resilience in Ancient Middle America. In *El Niño, Catastrophism, and Culture Change in Ancient America*, ed. Dan Sandweiss and Jeffrey Quilter. Dumbarton Oaks, Harvard University Press, Cambridge, MA, pp. 167–186.

Sheets, Payson, ed.
    2002    *Before the Volcano Erupted: The Ancient Ceren Village in Central America.* University of Texas Press, Austin.

Sheets, Payson, and Thomas Sever
    2007    Creating and Perpetuating Social Memory across the Ancient Costa Rican Landscape. In *Remote Sensing in Archaeology*, ed. James Wiseman and Farouk El-Baz. Springer, New York, pp. 161–184.

Siebe, Claus
    2000    Age and Archaeological Implications of Xitle Volcano, Southwestern Basin of Mexico-City. *Journal of Volcanology and Geothermal Research* 104: 45–64.

Siebe, Claus, Michael Abrams, Jose Luis Macias, and Johannes Obenholzer
    1996    Repeated Volcanic Disasters in Prehispanic Time at Popocatepetl, Central Mexico: Past Key to the Future? *Geology* 24: 399–402.

Webster, David, Anncorinne Freter, and Nancy Gonlin
    2000    *Copan: The Rise and Fall of an Ancient Maya Kingdom*. Harcourt, Fort Worth.

White, Gilbert
    1945    *Human Adjustment to Flood*. University of Chicago Press, Chicago.

Young, Bailey K.
    2000    Climate and Crisis in Sixth-Century Italy and Gaul. In *The Years without Summer: Tracing AD 536 and Its Aftermath*, ed. Joel D. Gunn. BAR International Series 872. Archaeopress, Oxford, England, pp. 35–42.

## UNDERSTANDING HAZARDS, MITIGATING IMPACTS, AVOIDING DISASTERS

### Statement for Policy Makers and the Disaster Management Community

Hazards from volcanic eruptions, especially explosive eruptions, abound in Mexico and in every Central American country. Explosive eruptions can be damaging to vegetation, animals, and people, as the fine volcanic ash falling from the air can cause significant damage and, in large amounts, death.

Volcanologists can detect the early signs that a volcano is building toward an eruption with a moderate degree of accuracy. They can perceive when a warning needs to be issued and thus when people with their animals and prized possessions need to evacuate the hazard zone. They pay particular attention to earthquakes, which indicate that magma sources are moving close to the surface as well as an increase in sulfur gases being emitted. Warnings should be initiated by well-trained experts because a premature or inaccurate warning that leads to an unnecessary evacuation makes evacuees less likely to heed the next order to evacuate.

I suggest that planning and educational programs in schools and for adults be initiated in known hazardous areas so people know what to do in an emergency. Local nodes of decision-making need to be established so people are not waiting for information from the central government in the country's capital.

For example, Costa Rica's Arenal Volcano has been very active in ancient, historic, and recent times and continues to emit lava, volcanic ash, and sulfur gas today. Pyroclastic flows (huge clouds of volcanic ash, gases that kill everything in their paths because they have temperatures in the range of hundreds of degrees Celsius) have rushed down the north side of the volcano in recent decades. Against volcanologists' recommendations, resort lodges with hot spring pools have been built in those areas, and the only suggestion that acknowledges risk is for everyone to park their cars pointing outward toward the highway. This proposal is not smart, for if everyone rushed for their cars they would create a traffic jam, and the death rate would be extremely high. Rather, if people were told to simply climb the sides of the valley, most of them could reach relative safety within a few minutes.

In this chapter volcanic eruptions that have been encountered in archaeological sites are documented in Costa Rica and other countries. Because of the nature of preservation, only the largest eruptions, those that caused the deepest burial and greatest consequences for both nature and people, are found. Our work around Arenal Volcano found ten large eruptions during the past 4,000 years, an average of one per 400 years. It would be a mistake to think that figure is an accurate representation of how often eruptions occur. I suggest that anyone interested in Arenal's eruptions and thus risks to nearby people today should consult the easily accessed website of the Smithsonian Institution's Global Volcanism Program at http://www.volcano.si.edu/world, where they can find a more complete record of eruptions for individual volcanoes as well as eruptions by region. The more complete eruptive history of Arenal documents twenty-eight separate eruptions, almost three times as many as we found doing archaeological work.

As earthquakes routinely accompany volcanic eruptions, a note on earthquake hazards and mitigations is appropriate here. Millennia of experience with earthquakes by natives living in Mexico and Central America have led to the development of an architecture appropriate to seismically active areas. Called "wattle and daub," or "bajareque" in Central America, this architecture consists of a series of vertical poles firmly anchored into buildings' foundations—creating reinforcement for the walls—and tied tightly to the roof beams. The lower portions of walls are mudded, plastered, or both to provide privacy and solidity but not to the point that the structure lacks flexibility. Homes can be substantial, of two stories, and large. Any structure has limits, though, and if an extremely strong earthquake causes damage, the wall fails in small pieces that at most cause bruising and minor cuts. In contrast, the Spanish introduced unreinforced adobe brick architecture, and when a wall fails, it often kills people. Unfortunately, bajareque architecture gained a sense of being backward, so we renamed it "Ceren architecture" because the importance of that site to the Salvadoran people gave it prestige. People are now adopting Ceren architecture in the area.

# THREE

# Black Sun, High Flame, and Flood: Volcanic Hazards in Iceland

*Andrew Dugmore and Orri Vésteinsson*

Sól tér sortna, sígur fold í mar,
hverfa af himni heiðar stjörnur.
Geisar eimi við aldurnara,
leikur hár hiti við himin sjálfan.

The sun turns black, earth sinks into the sea,
the bright stars vanish from the sky;
steam rises up in the conflagration,
a high flame plays against heaven itself.

"VÖLUSPÁ" (THE WISE WOMAN'S PROPHECY), CA. AD 1270
LARRINGTON 1996: 11

Iceland is one of the most volcanically active areas on earth, but were it not for the description of the end of the world in the poem "Völuspá," one might think volcanic activity made little impression on Medieval Icelanders. Volcanic eruptions are duly recorded in annals from the early twelfth century onward, but as a rule they are noted with terse one-line accounts such as "1158: second fire in Hekla" (Storm 1888: 116) or at most with minimal amplifications like "such great darkness that the sun was blocked" (ibid.: 134). The most detailed surviving description is given for events in AD 1362:

> Fire erupted in four places in the South and lasted from early June until
> autumn with such enormities that the whole of Litlahérað was deserted, and

much of Hornafjörður and Lónshverfi. It devastated a nearly 200 km stretch [along the coast]. In addition Knappafell glacier burst forth into the sea with falling rocks, mud and dirt so that there was flat sand where before the sea had been 50 m deep. Two parishes were completely destroyed, those of Hof and Rauðalækr. The sand stood at mid-leg on flat land but was driven into dunes so that the houses could hardly be seen. Ash was blown to the North so that steps could be traced in the fallout. Also pumice was seen drifting on the sea off the Vestfjords, so dense that ships could hardly sail through. (ibid.: 226)

With the possible exception of the pre-literate period Eldgjá eruption in AD 934–938, the events of AD 1362 were by all accounts the greatest volcanic calamity in Iceland in the Middle Ages (Thórarinsson 1958). Several other major volcanic eruptions occurred during the twelfth and thirteenth centuries AD, a period when Icelandic scholars wrote copiously about both recent history and contemporary developments, but it seems that even if they had an appreciable impact on the environment and the economy, the eruptions were not considered significant enough for comment. Nature, let alone volcanic eruptions, is firmly in the background of these writings: there is not a single unequivocal reference to a volcanic eruption in the entire corpus of Icelandic Family Sagas (Falk 2007).

In contrast, modern writers have been eager to make the most of volcanic impacts on Icelandic history. Volcanism is routinely seen as one of the principal causes for the lack of development of Icelandic society by early modern times, while politicians like to claim that the perceived spirit and endurance of the Icelandic people was shaped on an anvil of ice and fire.

In this chapter we argue that neither the Medieval indifference nor the modern hyperbole is a useful guide to understand how volcanic hazards affected preindustrial Icelandic society. We suggest that each volcanic event has to be understood within its landscape and historical context. Most volcanic eruptions occurred far from settled regions and had limited or no effect on society. In particular regions, volcanism was one element in a complex of environmental processes that could have negative impacts on land use and settlement, in both the short and long term. These regions represent a small proportion of settled areas in Iceland, and in the national context their degradation had negligible repercussions. Dramatic case histories of Icelandic volcanic eruptions are well-known, indeed iconic, yet they can only be truly understood in the context of the society and environment at the time, as well as their antecedents, trajectories of change, and complex interactions with each other.

Occasionally, major eruptions and unlucky circumstances have contributed to nationwide calamities, depression, and famine. We stress that it was not the size or type of volcanic eruption alone that decided this outcome but rather the time of year it took place and the coincidence of other negative factors such as bad weather, failing fish stocks, or disease (in humans or animals)—factors that in combination could produce catastrophic shocks to the economic system. It is clear that Icelandic society dealt with such shocks on a routine basis. Some were exacerbated by volcanic eruptions and some were not, but in all cases the socioeconomic system recovered. This suggests that human suffering on a massive scale is not necessarily a measure of system resilience (or failure); societies can absorb enormous and inhuman pain and suffering without failing.

Volcanic activity has occurred within thirty active volcanic systems that collectively make up the volcanic zones that cover about one-third of Iceland (figure 3.1). Comparatively little of this area is settled. Eruptions are common, and there is geological evidence or written accounts (or both) for around 205 eruptions since the settlement of Iceland in the late ninth century AD (Thordarson and Larsen 2007). The exact number will never be known; but since two-thirds of the records come from the latter half of the settlement period (post–ca. AD 1500), when all sources of evidence are more abundant and clear, the total is probably closer to 300 than to 200 events.

## VOLCANIC HAZARDS

Volcanic activity in Iceland is varied and includes nearly all of the types of volcanoes and styles of eruptions known on earth (Thórarinsson 1981; Thórarinsson and Saemundsson 1979). Eruptions range from the explosive (in which over 95% of the volcanic products are tephra) to the effusive (where over 95% of the products are lava). Scales have varied by over 10 orders of magnitude, from the tiny (ca. 1 m³ Dense Rock Equivalent [DRE] erupted through a geothermal borehole) to the substantial (ca. 20 km³ DRE flood lava eruptions of Eldgjá in AD 934–938 and Laki in AD 1783–1784; Thordarson and Larsen 2007). Settings are also varied, with some fissures in dry locations and others in areas affected by high groundwaters, beneath glacier ice, or in the sea. The presence of water or ice has major implications, as it can turn potentially effusive activity explosive, create both floods and debris flows, and thus be a major determinant of hazard.

Potential volcanic hazards can be broadly grouped into those from lava, floods (of water melted from glaciers or dammed in rivers and *lahars*), fallout (ash fall and pyroclastic flows), pollution (such as fluorine poisoning), and climatic perturbation (Gudmundsson et al. 2008). These hazards have very different constraints and may occur at irregular intervals ranging from decades to millennia. Potential impacts are variable depending on environmental and social contexts and are best viewed alongside other natural hazards, from disease to extreme weather. The scale of volcanic hazards can be comparatively

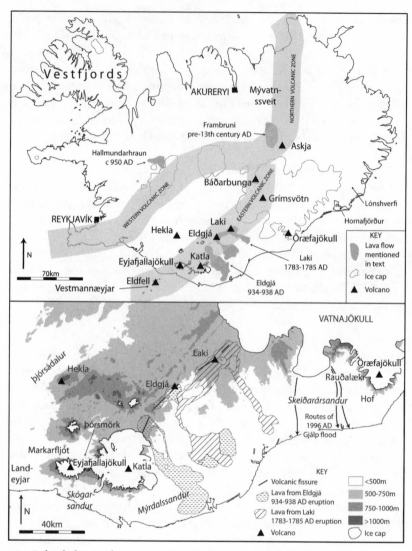

**3.1.** *Iceland, showing features named in the text. Cartography by Richard Streeter.*

limited; they can affect a small region, or the hazards can be felt across the entire island and much farther afield (Grattan, Durand, and Taylor 2003; Grattan et al. 2003; Witham and Oppenheimer 2004). It is notable that despite over 200 volcanic events that could have led to a disaster, few have killed people either directly or indirectly. Laki in AD 1783 indirectly led to the deaths of thousands of Icelanders because out-gassing from the eruption created a toxic haze that caused the deaths of many livestock and contributed to the ensuing famine. The major eruptions of Hekla in AD 1300 and Öræfajökull in AD 1362 may have also caused fatalities, but there is no direct evidence for this (Gudmundsson et al. 2008). The impacts of the eruption of Hekla in AD 1104 (which produced ca. 2 km³ of tephra) and Eldgjá in AD 934 (the largest eruption in historical times) are unknown. While the Katla eruption in AD 1755 may have only directly killed one person, famine resulting from exceptional and unrelated cold weather in the mid-1750s reduced Iceland's population by 5,800 (Karlsson 2000).

The human consequences of volcanic hazards have been shaped by the nature of Icelandic society. Historically, subsistence in Iceland has been based on pastoralism (primarily sheep and cattle) supplemented by utilizing wild resources, fishing from fresh waters and the sea, hunting marine mammals, wildfowling, and collecting eggs and shellfish (McGovern et al. 2007). Some cereal was grown during the first six centuries, but the practice died out in the sixteenth century AD. The slack was picked up by small-scale imports, but significant imports of foodstuffs did not begin until the late nineteenth century (Karlsson 2000). Icelandic society was self-reliant in its subsistence, a self-reliance based on flexible strategies of farming and wildlife exploitation. It is possible, however, that this flexibility came at the cost of economic development, which at best was sluggish until the end of the nineteenth century. The Icelandic system was designed to deal with setbacks, among which natural hazards were prominent, although disease and unfavorable weather had the most profound and persistent impacts. Modifying or abandoning the ability to deal with setbacks in favor of economic development did not seem like an acceptable strategy until modern times.

There tends to be little settlement in the immediate neighborhood of active volcanoes on the Icelandic mainland, in part because of the dispersed nature of pre-modern settlement in Iceland and in part because volcanoes form higher ground that has a less favorable climate. In addition, recent volcanic activity has been related to limited soil and vegetation cover. Notable exceptions can be found in Mývatnssveit, where settlement exists within the northern volcanic zone and along the southern coast.

Lavas create the most localized direct hazards, and within the volcanic zones they have flowed over farms built in the neighborhood of fissures. Ögmundarhraun, for example, is a lava on the Reykjanes Peninsula southwest of Reykjavik that overran the Krísuvík farm in the mid-twelfth century (Jóhannesson and Einarsson 1988). It has been argued that lava from the 1389 eruption of Hekla completely overran two or three farms (Thórarinsson 1968: 62–72), and in the north of Iceland the Mývatn fires of AD 1724–1729 produced lavas that extended over 34 km², including two farms and the farmhouses of the Reykjahlíð parsonage (Sæmundsson 1991). The church of Reykjahlíð, sited on higher ground, was left intact but was surrounded by the lava.

71

The only recent flows that extended outside the volcanic zones were the four very extensive flood lava eruptions of historical times: Eldgjá, AD 934–938; Hallmundarhraun, ca. AD 950; Frambruni, prior to the thirteenth century AD; and Laki, AD 1783–1784 (Thordarson and Larsen 2007). New lava has an enduring effect on landscape—reshaping topography, altering drainage routes, and creating bare rock surfaces that take centuries to reestablish vegetation communities and soil (Cutler, Belyea, and Dugmore 2008). Because of their nature, location, limited extent, and comparatively slow propagation, the flows of molten rock in and of themselves represent the most easily avoided yet locally destructive hazard. In 1973 major destruction (but limited death) was caused by the eruption of Eldfell on Heimaey, a small island off the south coast of Iceland. The absolute scale of the Eldfell eruption was small, but the fissure opened up on the edge of the town of Vestmannaeyjar and the lava destroyed 200 houses, with more damaged by tephra fall (Thórarinsson 1979). The town had grown up on the mostly submarine volcano system of Vestmannaeyjar because its summits form an island with a fine natural harbor off a mainland coast devoid of safe anchorages. Unusual for Iceland, major settlement was (and still is) in the heart of a volcanic system, and the result was that virtually any volcanic activity produced a real and present danger to the people of Heimaey and Vestmannaeyjar. Fortunately, in 1973 the fissure opened up 200 m outside the town rather than within the built-up area.

As with lavas, volcanogenic floods in Iceland may affect significant areas both within and outside the volcanically active areas; unlike lavas, they propagate at speeds that cannot be outrun on foot (Gudmundsson et al. 2008). Floods are a particular hazard because a number of highly active volcanoes are ice-covered. For example, there have been approximately eighty-five sub-glacial eruptions from the Grímsvötn and Bárdarbunga central volcanoes, and every one of the twenty-one Katla eruptions in historical times has resulted in floods, the largest having a peak discharge of 300,000 $m^3$/s and flooding up to 400 $km^2$ (Tómasson 1996). The areas affected by floods in historical times did, however, follow the course of established glacier meltwater routes and were generally subjected to repeated volcanogenic floods that helped create outwash or sandur plains with very limited settlement.

In these areas today, far greater impacts can happen as a result of twentieth-century developments that brought power lines, roads, bridges, and summerhouses to areas previously lacking infrastructure. The 1996 Gjálp eruption caused a flood that claimed no lives but cost 25 million euros in infrastructural damage (Gudmundsson, Sigmundsson, and Björnsson 1997; Gudmundsson et al. 2008). A notable exception to the general lack of settlement in potential *jökulhlaup* (glacial flood) routes is Landeyjar in southern Iceland. Here, on the delta of the Markarfljót, stable "land islands" mantled with deep soils developed between the distributaries of the main river (Haraldsson 1981).

Both grazing and fodder production are very good in Landeyjar, and prosperous farms have been established across the floodplain. Despite the Markarfljót draining the ice cap that overlies the volcano Katla, no historically recorded Katla eruptions have led to flooding of the area. Such flooding is possible, however, and it is potentially a real hazard because it has not occurred in the last millennium (Gudmundsson et al. 2008). In this respect Landeyjar today is not dissimilar to the parishes of Hof and Rauðalækr in Öræfajökull prior to AD 1362. They were prosperous, and local experiences since first settlement gave no indication of what was to come. In Lágeyjarhverfi and Álftaver on the edge of Mýrdalssandur, the abandonment of several settlements has been attributed to the effects of repeated flooding (Sveinsson 1947) but in this area the effects seem to have been gradual rather than catastrophic, with floods eroding the farmlands rather than directly threatening the settlements themselves.

The landscape impacts of floods may linger for generations, from the localized decadal endurance and slow melt of buried glacier ice within flood debris to the longer periods it may take for soils and vegetation to reestablish across the affected areas. Colonization is inhibited by the free-draining nature of flood deposits composed of pumice gravels. At the large scale, for example, the major sandur plains of Skeiðarársandur and Mýrdalssandur have little vegetation because of repeated historical inundations. At the small scale a limited (ca. 6 km$^2$) fan of pumice gravels formed on Skógasandur by a sixth-century AD flood from Katla (and not subsequently modified) remained vegetation-free until the late twentieth century AD, when a planting program introduced the Nootka lupin (*Lupinus nootkatensis* Donn ex Sims) to mitigate the hazard of blowing sand for road traffic crossing the area (Dugmore et al. 2000).

Tephra falls have affected much larger areas than either floods or lava flows; in contrast to the all-or-nothing effects of lavas or floods, their impacts grade in severity across the landscape depending on both the scale of fallout and the sensitivity of the affected zone (figure 3.2). They can have both negative and positive effects on the landscape. As the fallout decreases in thickness, the persistence of the impact also tends to be reduced. Very thick (m-scale) tephras will effectively act like flood deposits in terms of impact longevity; as the fallout decreases, so generally does the direct physical impact on the landscape. Deeper layers of tephra bury grazing; when they become mobile they can abrade vegetation and block watercourses, and it may take many seasons for the sediment to stabilize. Sigurdur Thórarinsson (1979) noted that following the AD 1693 eruption of Hekla, farms (which at that time in Iceland were all pastorally based) affected by more than 25 cm of freshly fallen tephra were never resettled; farms affected by 10–15 cm were abandoned for between one and four years, while fallout less than 10 cm deep caused extensive damage but did not lead directly to abandonment. Similar effects were caused by the AD 1875 eruption of Askja and seem to have also resulted from the AD 1104

**3.2.** *Tephra fall from the 2010 eruption of Eyjafjallajökull covering vegetation at about 600 m above sea level on the northwest flank of the volcano. When this picture was taken in early August 2010, rainfall was redistributing the tephra layer; the undisturbed parts of the fallout were having a selective impact on the low mountain vegetation, smothering some of it but not all. Photo by Andrew Dugmore.*

eruption of Hekla, although in AD 1104 the affected area coincided with the upland margins of settlement, and change may have been driven by unrelated factors (Thórarinsson 1967, 1979). Centimeter-scale tephra layers that allow vegetation (particularly grasses) to grow rapidly may have a positive medium-term impact. Mosses can be smothered, and the decay of vegetation buried by the ash can generate a nutrient pulse for the surviving vegetation. Furthermore, if the tephra is basic (not silicic) in composition, weathering of the ash itself can generate another fertilizing effect. In addition, dark tephras may warm the surface because of their lower albedo. This is good for vegetation because cold is often the key constraint on plant growth in Iceland.

Running counter to these trends of impact duration and type proportional to depth, a fine dusting of ash associated with adsorbed toxins and dry weather can result in the deaths of many grazing animals, most notably as a result of fluorosis poisoning: pollution can persist at high levels when there is no rain to flush it away. Hekla has erupted twenty-three times since AD 1104 (Thordarson and Larsen 2007), and on almost all occasions for which there are accurate records livestock has been poisoned by toxic fallout (Gudmundsson et al. 2008). This represents a significant hazard to a community dependent on pastoralism.

Volcanic gases can have similarly widespread and spatially variable impacts. The most profound historical impact of volcanic gases occurred in AD 1783–1784 as a result of emissions from the Laki flood lavas. These emissions created a persistent toxic haze across most of Iceland (Thordarson and Self 2003). Fluorosis poisoning of livestock and the related famine resulted in the loss of around 9,000 people, about a quarter of the population (Grattan 1998; Karlsson 2000). The haze spread through Europe, where it arguably resulted in the deaths of many more people than it did in Iceland. The haze and persistent high pressure over the British Isles and northwest Europe resulted in very poor air quality. The impact of this pollution is shown in "excess deaths"—higher mortality rates than would otherwise be expected. Mortality data through the eighteenth century AD establish trends of expected deaths season by season, and in AD 1783 summertime deaths were significantly higher than the established range and were closely associated with the haze. The heightened death toll in England probably claimed an additional 20,000 people (Grattan, Durand, and Taylor 2003; Grattan et al. 2003; Witham and Oppenheimer 2005), and the effects may not have stopped there because increased mortality can also be identified in Scotland. The Laki eruption likely affected climate, but in Iceland and northwest Europe this hazard may have been of limited impact compared with the direct effects of the volcanic gases.

The longevity of hazards as well as their scale depends on a range of factors that may vary in importance. First is the scale of the volcanic eruption itself, which is perhaps the most obvious factor but not necessarily the most important. The potential hazard from an eruption is fundamentally shaped by the setting and context of the event. Very similar underground movements of magma may become very different eruptions depending on the surface environment; high groundwaters may turn a potentially effusive (lava-producing) eruption into an explosive one. The presence of glacier ice over the vent may lead to flooding, and steep gradients leading away from the eruption site may propagate flooding more swiftly and over a larger area. Abundant overlying ice, plus a potential for the flood to "pond" and build up before release, may result in a large volume of floodwater and high peak flows. Proximity to plains can create the potential for extensive inundations. Wind direction and strength will determine the concentration or dispersal of both pollution and tephra-fall. Rain can mitigate the effects of volatile pollution and speed the process of ecological recovery. Most significant of all are the patterns and status of settlement. Are people in harm's way, and, if so, how able are they to cope?

Lava and floods, while locally catastrophic, have produced few fatalities because of their clearly defined extent and limited direct effect on settlement.

In contrast, fallout and pollution can impact very large areas, and both direct and indirect effects can be particularly severe.

Long recurrence times and their varied nature have meant that prior to the twentieth century AD there was little specific planning to cope with volcanic impact. However, communal resilience in Iceland that developed to face other environmental challenges, such as extreme or unpredictable weather, has been the basis of effective response to volcanic hazards and the mitigation of their impacts. In the absence of outside assistance, the ability to cope within Iceland has been largely determined by the ability (or otherwise) to utilize support from unaffected or less affected areas and to switch between alternative forms of subsistence, in particular between farming (terrestrial) and hunting (wild) resources. Extreme weather is far more frequent than volcanic eruptions and can produce similar stresses to ash falls. Domestic animals die; access to grazing, pasture productivity, and fodder production are all impacted; and access to wild resources such as fish may be compromised. The synergistic effects of volcanic hazards, including economic constraints, disease, and bad weather, have had some of the greatest effects on the Icelandic population.

The impact of the AD 1783–1784 "Haze Famine" was probably exacerbated by circumstances at the time—cold weather, the constraints imposed on eighteenth-century Icelandic society, an ineffectual response by the distant government, and a major earthquake in 1784 (Karlsson 2000). In 1755 Katla erupted, flooded large areas of Mýrdalssandur, and spread fallout through districts to the east of the volcano. It is debatable, however, whether any people died directly as a result. In contrast to the later Laki eruption, increased mortality at the time resulted from a range of other, non-volcanic hazards. The 1750s were a period of very unfavorable weather for the pastoralism that was the basis for subsistence. Pack ice appeared and persisted around the coast of Iceland. This sea ice interfered with subsistence fishing and locally intensified cold weather that impacted both rangeland grazing and fodder production. In 1755 pack ice remained off the northern coast of Iceland all summer, and in the autumn Katla erupted, adding to the misery of the people of southern Iceland. In 1756 the pack ice spread along the south coast. The cumulative effects of bad weather and social and economic constraints resulted in Iceland's population being reduced by around 5,800 people, two-thirds of total Icelandic mortality in the aftermath of Laki (ibid.). If less was known about the climate, as well as the social and economic contexts, of 1755–1756, the impact of the Katla eruption could be assumed to be far greater than it probably was. Perhaps the most remarkable aspect of the disasters of both the 1750s and 1783–1784 is the way the Icelandic population recovered. Although environmental impacts were exacerbated by synergistic effects, Icelandic society proved remarkably able to cope with multiple stressors (Vasey 1996).

## TEPHROCHRONOLOGY: DATING PAST HAZARDS
## THROUGH THE USE OF VOLCANIC ASH LAYERS

Serendipitously, the volcanic events that create hazards in Iceland have also created a highly effective means of assessing those hazards. Tephrochronology is a dating technique based on the identification and correlation of tephra layers that was pioneered in Iceland by Sigurdur Thórarinsson in the mid-twentieth century (e.g., Thórarinsson 1944, 1967) and that now has worldwide application (e.g., Self and Sparks 1981; Shane 2000). Tephra layers have distinctive characteristics that can be used to identify and correlate separate deposits of the same tephra layer, which can then define time marker horizons, or isochrones, that have great utility. Tephras exhibit a range of macroscopic features that reflect major differences in chemical composition, eruption mechanism, total tephra volume, principal directions of fallout, and depositional environments. In Iceland tephra layers can vary from millimeters to meters in thickness and are primarily composed of vesicular glass shards. The colors of layers as a whole vary from white through yellows, reds, browns, and grays to black. Tephra layers may be uniform in color or composed of characteristic mixes of different-colored pumices, crystals, or lithic fragments. Particle sizes range from cobble and coarse gravel grade to silt; particle shapes include a range of vesicularities and both rounded and elongated grains.

The analysis of many stratigraphic sections has led to the accurate mapping of individual tephra layers that clearly shows their geographical origin, the scale and nature of the eruption, and contemporary weather patterns (e.g., Larsen and Thórarinsson 1977; Larsen et al. 2001; Thórarinsson 1967). The ages of tephra layers have been determined in a variety of ways. Thórarinsson's groundbreaking work in Iceland showed that precise historical dates can be ascribed to tephra layers through a careful analysis of written records. For the earliest times of settlement in Iceland, when no contemporary written records exist, other approaches have to be used. Radiocarbon dating can give excellent results, especially if the dating is conducted within a Bayesian framework (Church et al. 2007); extrapolations can be made from securely dated layers using well-understood sediment accumulation patterns (e.g., Halflidason, Larsen, and Ólafsson 1992); and correlations can be made with the Greenland ice core records (e.g., Grönvold et al. 1995). A securely dated tephra layer can be used to define a landscape at a moment in time; with the identification of multiple in situ layers of primary fallout, intervals of time can be defined and changes tracked through both time and space (figure 3.3). Sometimes tephras within a stratigraphy may be moved on small scales (e.g., by soil movement) or large scales (e.g., by transport in glacier ice), or they may become incorporated in sediments of a different age by reworking and redeposition. In both of these situations the movement of the tephra represents an opportunity to gain more environmental data, as it allows movement to be traced through time.

**3.3.** *In areas downwind of volcanic eruptions, tephra layers can accumulate in aggrading soil profiles. In this soil section in southern Iceland, yellow-brown layers of aeolian sediment separate dark layers of volcanic ash. The 30-cm steel rule marks deposits formed around the time of Norse settlement: at the top of the ruler is black tephra from Eldgjá, AD 934–938; below that is the black tephra from Katla, around AD 920; and below that (in the middle of the rule) is the gray-brown "Landnám" tephra layer formed by Veiðivötn, AD 871 ± 2. Photo by Andrew Dugmore.*

Rapid aeolian sediment accumulation across Iceland means that different tephra layers falling across the same region are clearly separated, even if the tephra deposition was only separated by a period as short as one decade. The highest-resolution, best-dated sequences occur where there is a combination of high background aeolian sedimentation and the deposition of several tephra layers each century that are thick enough to form discrete horizons but shallow enough to allow vegetation to grow through the layer and stabilize the deposit. In Iceland this generally means a layer more than ¼ cm thick but less deep than the contemporary vegetation cover. A deep sward and heath may stabilize layers 5–10 cm thick, but centimeter-scale thicknesses of tephra rarely stabilize on well-grazed slopes because the vegetation needs to project through the tephra in order to survive and stabilize the surface.

Precise dating (to the decade, year, season, and even the day) allows true interdisciplinary collaboration and effective discussions about common questions of hazard, mitigation, and disaster among historians, archaeologists, ecologists, geographers, geologists, planners, and policy makers.

## INDIRECT HAZARDS FROM VOLCANIC ACTIVITY

Deeper (multi-millennia) time perspectives can reveal patterns of activity and give some indication of possible return times between events. Knowledge of volcanic activity over long timescales (for people but not volcanoes, which may be active over hundreds of thousands of years) can alert us to events that can occur but have not (yet) been experienced in historical time. Landscape provides a record of the sum total of these past events that is sometimes complete but most often fragmentary; much evidence is lost—destroyed by subsequent changes—and some processes leave little, if any, physical trace. What does remain, though, is still rich and diverse, with strong spatial patterns that are often the key to interpretation. Crucially, as the landscape is formed by the interplay of human and natural systems, it provides one way in which we can seek evidence of past hazards and also vulnerabilities that may otherwise leave little trace.

Various possible explanations exist for differing impacts of similar volcanic hazards. Different outcomes may occur as a result of variations in environmental sensitivity, as some places may experience threshold-crossing events because of the inherent status of their ecology, soils, location, or climate. This idea underpins the concept of *the over-optimistic pioneer fringe*: areas that are occupied but simply too marginal or vulnerable for long-term settlement and where environmental degradation and local settlement failure are inevitable consequences (Dugmore et al. 2006). Alternatively, areas that are not environmentally marginal or vulnerable to hazards at the time of initial settlement may become so. Stochastic variables (such as season or wind direction during an eruption) could be vital, although other natural events such as climate change may also be significant.

The settlement of Iceland (or *landnám*) led to extensive environmental changes that affected the potential impacts of volcanic hazards in general and of tephra fall in particular (e.g., Arnalds et al. 2001; Einarsson 1963; Hallsdóttir 1987). Wholesale environmental changes were inevitable for two main reasons. First, *landnám* was a large-scale colonization involving thousands of settlers who relied on a pastoralist subsistence base (Vésteinsson, McGovern, and Keller 2002); this led to the clearance of large areas of woodland to create both fields for fodder production and extensive grasslands for grazing. Second, the lack of indigenous grazing mammals led to the large-scale introduction of a domesticated biota (cattle, sheep, goats, pigs, horses, and dogs) hitherto absent from the island.

The consequences of people in Iceland drawing false analogies from similar-looking landscapes in the British Isles and western Norway may be one explanation for the considerable variation in local impacts produced by settlement and in the vulnerability to volcanic hazards. In the inland valleys of Thórsmörk in southern Iceland, for example, there is both an early onset of soil erosion and an early abandonment of five settlements that may have been either summer farms or permanently occupied sites (Dugmore et al. 2006). Climate reconstructions indicate that this settlement change is unlikely to have been caused by either fundamentally unfavorable local weather or systematic climate change (Casely and Dugmore 2007). Evidence for one possible factor can be seen in surviving soil profiles; several thick tephra layers would have been close to the surface at the time of settlement, so even minor disturbance of the vegetation would have exposed unstable pumice to erosion by wind and rain. In addition, the Katla eruption in approximately AD 920, which spread fallout as far as Reykjavik, would have fallen thickly in this area; soil erosion would have been enhanced as deep, unstable deposits of tephra killed underlying vegetation in gullies and hollows and at the foot of slopes.

We conclude that two quite different aspects of volcanic hazard contributed to environmental degradation in Thórsmörk: first, the enhanced landscape sensitivity caused by the presence of tephra layers close to the surface of the soil, and second, the direct impacts of the fallout from the 920 eruption of Katla.

The presence of volcanic impact and the coincidence of environmental degradation and settlement change, while notable, do not in and of themselves provide a satisfactory explanation of human-environment interaction because elsewhere they do not coincide, emphasizing that simplistic associations may be misleading. In the case of Thórsmörk, woodland management provides an alternative explanation of settlement change (Dugmore et al. 2006). The area contains one of the few surviving woods in the region and has a long history of providing charcoal to lowland farms. Woodland clearance occurred very rapidly around newly established settlement sites, and through the first 500 years of settlement woodland was gradually cleared from low-lying areas; pollen diagrams and the remains of charcoal production sites have enabled woodland clearance to be tracked up-valley. By the fourteenth century AD it is apparent that naturally wooded areas were much reduced, and it is about this time that settlement change occurred in the last wooded areas of Thórsmörk. Woodland was conserved, and seven centuries later it was still providing a key resource to an extensive network of lowland farms. While localized environmental degradation as a result of soil erosion (and the legacy of past volcanic eruptions), plus impacts of later volcanic eruptions, may have marginalized the Thórsmörk settlements, socio-political factors seem to be more important in the timing of settlement change. It is notable that a similar process of woodland conservation may have contributed to settlement change in the Thjórsardalur region close to Hekla (Dugmore et al. 2007).

## USING THE PAST TO IDENTIFY FUTURE HAZARDS

Today, volcanic emergency planning in Iceland has its own specific provisions based on detailed geological assessments (e.g., Gudmundsson et al. 2008).

The modern science of volcanic hazard assessment faces a number of specific challenges over establishing the nature of possible events and their potential impacts. Some past volcanic events leave clear traces behind, such as a layer of volcanic ash or a characteristic flood deposit. Others hazards, such as fluorine poisoning of livestock, may leave no direct physical evidence. Their occurrence has to be inferred indirectly through, for example, written records of impacts or studies of magma composition (to infer the presence of volatiles). Even when there is physical evidence, such as the landscape record of a flood, it may be ambiguous; was this caused by a volcanic event? How big was it?

Tephrochronology aids the understanding of past human-environment interactions by providing precise dating control and landscape-wide correlations. When combined with interdisciplinary approaches, this has helped the development of a more detailed, complex, and nuanced understanding of change. Just as the significance of past volcanic hazards for past human populations has benefited from the application of tephrochronology, so has tephrochronology aided understanding of what hazards are possible, even if people have not yet experienced them.

For example, Kate Smith (Smith 2004; Smith and Haraldsson 2005) has shown that floods from Katla have flowed eastward into areas unaffected by similar floods in recorded history (Larsen 2000). Future activity may not follow the pattern set by Katla's twenty-one historic eruptions. Indeed, geomorphological and stratigraphic mapping dated with tephrochronology shows that prehistoric floods from Katla did follow different routes and that they provide crucial data for contemporary emergency planning.

Immediately to the west of Katla, Eyjafjallajökull (1,666 m) is one of the largest volcanoes in Iceland (and Europe), capped by an ice cap of the same name. In March 2010 sub-aerial flank activity began that led to the formation of cinder cones and a small lava flow. This was followed by activity in the central crater that generated a comparatively limited volume of fine-grained tephra and international impacts out of all proportion to its scale (figures 3.4, 3.5, and 3.6). Context was again key; the generation of fine ash and the prevailing weather conditions led to its persistent dispersal over airports and across European and trans-Atlantic flight routes. Prior to 2010, only small-scale volcanic activity in the summit region and limited flooding were known from written sources, but geomorphological data constrained by tephrochronology have also identified flank activity in the late presettlement period and early tenth century AD. These eruptions produced extensive flooding over hill slopes to the northwest and southwest of the ice cap; if repeated, they could pose a serious hazard to local communities.

The identification of Late Holocene flank activity was a challenge because the channel erosion and "scabland" formations its floods created lie in zones also affected by glaciation and the seasonal melting of snow and ice. Recognition

**3.4.** *The pro-glacial area of Gígjökull in southern Iceland pictured three years before the 2010 eruption of Eyjafjallajökull. Gígjökull flows out of the northern breach of the summit crater of Eyjafjallajökull; glacier retreat since the late 1990s had created parts of the lake visible here. Photo by Andrew Dugmore.*

of volcanogenic flooding rested on chronology and the ability to tie extensive areas of erosion or deposition to a single time and event. In this case (as in others; e.g., Smith and Dugmore 2006) the features and deposits produced by a volcanogenic flood were not particularly noteworthy in terms of scale, particle sizes, or the volume of material. Erosion forms are poorly developed, and the size of flood-transported material has been limited by the types of sediments available rather than the capacity of the flood to move it. Total volumes of sediment are likewise limited and thus give little indication of the peak discharge or duration of the event. Tephrochronology was well suited to tackling this problem and providing a means to correlate scattered landscape evidence despite the lack of tephra production from the flank eruptions themselves.

On Eyjafjallajökull the eruption of the Skerin fissure around AD 920 (northwestern part of the glacier) coincided with a much larger eruption in the neighboring volcano Katla—an association that also occurred in AD 1821–1823 and probably in both AD 1612 and late presettlement times, leading to anxious monitoring of both volcanoes when activity began in Eyjafjallajökull in March 2010. An eruption of Katla has been expected for some time; based on the very detailed records that have existed since AD 1500 Katla's mean

**3.5.** *Gígjökull in June 2010. Tephra from the 2010 eruption of Eyjafjallajökull blankets the entire landscape; in the foreground it is about 3 cm deep. Floods from melting ice in the summit crater have deepened the channel to the right of the glacier and created the channel to the far right. The pro-glacial lake has been completely filled in. Photo by Andrew Dugmore.*

eruption interval is forty-nine years (with a standard deviation of twenty-five years). It has been more than ninety years since Katla's last eruption, an unusually long period of time. The fact that it is "overdue" suggests that another eruption will occur sooner rather than later; combine that with the 2010 eruption of Eyjafjallajökull and repeated examples of near contemporaneous activity in Eyjafjallajökull and Katla, and it seems quite probable that Katla will erupt soon and create both ash clouds and major floods.

## CONCLUSION

Volcanic eruptions have created many different hazards for the people of Iceland and contributed to some of their greatest human tragedies. Despite their frequent occurrence and sometimes very large magnitudes, they have not, however, proved to be the greatest hazard to the Icelandic people. Diseases such as the fifteenth-century plagues and later smallpox outbreaks have killed more people in discrete episodes, and other factors such as climate change and sociopolitical constraints may have led to a greater cumulative total of lives lost.

**3.6.** *The floodplain of Markarfljót valley in September 2010, pictured immediately to the north of Eyjafjallajökull, looking east. Floods from the 2010 eruption have reshaped the floodplain along the track. Visibility is poor because of dust raised from the tephra blanketing the ground. Photo by Barney Bedford.*

The impacts of volcanic hazards themselves have been exacerbated by other factors, such as bad weather, earthquakes, and economic constraints. Limitations to the effects of volcanic hazards have been created by both environmental and cultural factors. With the notable exception of Vestamanneyjar, where the largely submerged volcanic system forms a fine natural harbor, there has been little to draw people to settle in the present volcanic zones, let alone on active volcanoes. Social systems developed to cope with the vagaries of life in Iceland have proved well suited to coping with volcanic hazards: mobility within the island has been possible, and volcanically induced livestock fatalities could be offset by increased emphasis on fishing and hunting.

At a global scale, it has been argued that volcanic eruptions can represent opportunities as well as threats and that, despite their undoubted destruction, they may also spur development and innovation (Grattan 2006). In Iceland, however, the impacts may well have promoted conservatism and stifled innovation (Karlsson 2000). Having said that, communities in Iceland have successfully coped with volcanic hazards through approaches to living that is more regularly tested by bad weather and outbreaks of disease. Enduring settlement in Iceland is a testament to both Icelandic social organization and the durability of the Norse farm as a settlement strategy.

*Acknowledgments.* We acknowledge support from the Leverhulme Trust (Landscapes circum Landnám) and the US National Science Foundation through the Office of Polar Programs Arctic Social Sciences Grant 0732327 as part of the International Polar Year Humans in the Polar Regions project "IPY: Long Term Human Ecodynamics in the Norse North Atlantic: Cases of Sustainability, Survival, and Collapse." This publication is a product of the North Atlantic Biocultural Organization (NABO) cooperative.

## REFERENCES

Arnalds, Olafur, Elín F. Thorarinsdottir, Sigmar Metusalemsson, Ásgeir Jonsson, Einar Gretarsson, and Arnór Arnason
2001    *Soil Erosion in Iceland.* Soil Conservation Service and Agricultural Research Institute, Reykjavik. (English translation of original Icelandic publication from 1997).

Casely, Andrew F., and Andrew J. Dugmore
2007    Good for Glaciers, Bad for People? Archaeologically Relevant Climate Models Developed from Reconstructions of Glacier Mass Balance. *Journal of Archaeological Science* 34: 1763–1773.

Church, Mike J., Andrew J. Dugmore, Kerry-Anne Mairs, Andrew R. Millard, Gordon T. Cook, Guðrún Sveinbjarnardóttir, Philippa A. Ascough, Anthony J. Newton, and Katy Roucoux
2007    Timing and Mechanisms of Deforestation of the Settlement Period in Eyjafjallsveit, Southern Iceland. *Radiocarbon* 49(2): 659–672.

Cutler, Nick A., Lisa R. Belyea, and Andrew J. Dugmore
2008    The Spatiotemporal Dynamics of a Primary Succession. *Journal of Ecology* 96: 231–246.

Dugmore, Andrew J., Mike J. Church, Kerry-Anne Mairs, Thomas H. McGovern, Anthony J. Newton, and Guðrún Sveinbjarnardóttir
2006    An Over-Optimistic Pioneer Fringe? Environmental Perspectives on Medieval Settlement Abandonment in Thórsmörk, South Iceland. In *The Dynamics of Northern Societies*, ed. Jette Arneborg and Bjarne Grønnow. Studies in Archaeology and History 10. Publications from the National Museum, Copenhagen, pp. 333–344.

Dugmore, Andrew J., Mike J. Church, Kerry-Anne Mairs, Thomas H. McGovern, Sophia Perdikaris, and Orri Vésteinsson
2007    Abandoned Farms, Volcanic Impacts and Woodland Management: Revisiting Þjórsárdalur, the "Pompeii of Iceland." *Arctic Anthropology* 44 (1): 1–11.

Dugmore, Andrew J., Anthony J. Newton, Guðrún Larsen, and Gordon T. Cook
2000    Tephrochronology, Environmental Change and the Norse Settlement of Iceland. *Environmental Archaeology* 5: 21–34.

Einarsson, Thorleifur
1963    Pollen Analytical Studies on the Vegetation and Climate History of Ice-
        land in Late and Post-Glacial Times. In *North Atlantic Biota and Their His-
        tory,* ed. Áskell Löve and Doris Löve. Pergamon, Oxford, pp. 355–365.

Falk, Oren
2007    The Vanishing Volcanoes: Fragments of Fourteenth-Century Icelandic
        Folklore. *Folklore* 118(1): 1–22.

Grattan, John P.
1998    The Distal Impact of Volcanic Gases and Aerosols in Europe: A Review
        of the 1783 Laki Fissure Eruption and Environmental Vulnerability in
        the Late 20th Century. *Geological Society London, Special Publication* 15:
        7–53.

2006    Aspects of Armageddon: An Exploration of the Role of Volcanic Erup-
        tions in Human History and Civilization. *Quaternary International* 151:
        10–18.

Grattan, John P., Michael Durand, David Gilbertson, and F. Brian Pyatt
2003    Human Sickness and Mortality Rates in Relation to the Distant Eruption
        of Volcanic Gases: Rural England and the 1783 Eruption of the Laki Fis-
        sure, Iceland. In *Geology and Health: Closing the Gap,* ed. Anthony Berger
        and H. Catherine Skinner. Oxford University Press, Oxford, pp. 19–25.

Grattan, John P., Michael Durand, and S. Taylor
2003    Illness and Elevated Human Mortality Coincident with Volcanic Erup-
        tions. In *Volcanic Degassing,* ed. Clive Oppenheimer, David M. Pyle, and
        Jenni Barclay. Special Publication 213. Geological Society of London,
        London, pp. 401–414.

Grönvold, Karl, Níels Óskarsson, Sigfús J. Johnsen, Henrik B. Clausen,
   Claus U. Hammer, Gerald Bond, and Edouard Bard
1995    Tephra Layers from Iceland in the Greenland GRIP Ice Core Correlated
        with Oceanic and Land Based Sediments. *Earth and Planetary Science
        Letters* 135: 149–155.

Gudmundsson, Magnus T., Guðrún Larsen, Ármann Höskuldsson, and
   Ágúst G. Gylfason
2008    Volcanic Hazards in Iceland. *Jökull* 58: 251–268.

Gudmundsson, Magnus T., Freysteinn Sigmundsson, and Helgi Björnsson
1997    Ice-Volcano Interaction of the 1996 Gjálp Subglacial Eruption, Vat-
        najökull, Iceland. *Nature* 389: 954–957.

Halflidason, Halflidi, Guðrún Larsen, and Gunnar Ólafsson
1992    The Recent Sedimentation History of Thingvallavatn, Iceland. *Oikos* 64:
        80–95.

Hallsdóttir, Margret
1987    Pollen Analytical Studies of Human Influence on Vegetation in Relation
        to the Landnám Tephra Layer in Southwestern Iceland. *Lundqua Thesis*
        18: 1–45.

Haraldsson, Hreinn
1981    The Markarfljót Sandur Area, Southern Iceland: Sedimentological, Petro-
logical and Stratographical Studies. *Striae* 15: 1–60.

Jóhannesson, Haukur, and Sigmundur Einarsson
1988    Krísuvíkureldar I. Aldur Ögmundarhrauns og Miðaldalagsins. *Jökull* 38:
71–85.

Karlsson, Gunnar
2000    *Iceland's 1100 Years: History of a Marginal Society.* Mál og Menning,
Reykjavik.

Larrington, Carolyne
1996    *The Poetic Edda: A New Translation by Carolyne Larrington.* Oxford University Press, Oxford.

Larsen, Gudrun
2000    Holocene Eruptions within the Katla Volcanic System, South Iceland:
Characteristics and Environmental Impact. *Jökull* 49: 1–28.

Larsen, Gudrun, Anthony J. Newton, Andrew J. Dugmore, and Elsa Vilmundardóttir
2001    Geochemistry, Dispersal, Volumes and Chronology of Holocene Silicic
Tephra Layers from the Katla Volcanic System. *Journal of Quaternary Science* 16(2): 119–132.

Larsen, Gudrun, and Sigurdur Thórarinsson
1977    H4 and Other Acidic Hekla Tephra Layers. *Jökull* 27: 28–46.

McGovern, Thomas H., Orri Vésteinsson, Adolf Fridriksson, Mike J. Church, Ian
Lawson, Ian A. Simpson, Arni Einarsson, Andrew J. Dugmore, Gordon T. Cook,
Sophia Perdikaris, Kevin Edwards, Amanda M. Thomson, W. Paul Adderley,
Anthony J. Newton, Gavin Lucas, and Oscar Aldred
2007    Landscapes of Settlement in Northern Iceland: Historical Ecology of
Human Impact and Climate Fluctuation on the Millennial Scale. *Ameri-
can Anthropologist* 109(1): 27–51.

Sæmundsson, Kristján
1991    Jarðfræði Kröflukerfisins (The Geology of the Krafla Volcanic System). In
*Náttúra Mývatns* (The Natural History of the Mývatn Area), ed. ArnÞór
Gardarsson and Arni Einarsson. Hið íslenska náttúrufræðifélag, Reykjavík, pp. 24–95 (in Icelandic).

Self, Steve, and R.S.J. Sparks, eds.
1981    *Tephra Studies.* Dordrecht, Reidel.

Shane, Phil
2000    Tephrochronology: A New Zealand Case Study. *Earth-Science Reviews*
49(1–4): 223–259.

Smith, Kate T.
2004    Holocene Jökulhlaups, Glacier Fluctuations and Palaeoenvironment, Mýr-
dalsjökull, South Iceland. PhD dissertation, Geography, School of Geosciences, University of Edinburgh, UK.

Smith, Kate T., and Andrew J. Dugmore
2006    Jökulhlaups Circa Landnám: Mid- to Late First Millennium AD Floods in South Iceland and Their Implications for Landscapes of Settlement, South Iceland. *Geografiska Annaler* 88A(2): 165–176.

Smith, Kate T., and Hreinn Haraldsson
2005    A Late Holocene Jökulhlaup, Markarfljót, Iceland: Nature and Impacts. *Jökull* 55: 75–86.

Storm, Gustav, ed.
1888    *Islandske annaler indtil 1578*. Norsk Historisk Kildeskriftfond, Christiania, Norway.

Sveinsson, Einar Ólafur
1947    Byggð á Mýrdalssandi (Settlement in Mýrdalssandur). *Skírnir* 121: 185–210 (in Icelandic).

Thórarinsson, Sigurdur
1944    Tefrokronologiska studier på Island. *Geografiska Annaler* 26: 1–217.
1958    *The Öræfajökull Eruption of 1362*. Náttúrugripasfn Íslands, Reykjavík.
1967    The Eruptions of Hekla in Historical Times. *The Eruption of Hekla 1947–1948* 1: 1–170.
1968    *Heklueldar* (The Eruptions of Hekla). Sögufélagið, Reykjavík (in Icelandic).
1979    On the Damage Caused by Volcanic Eruptions with Special Reference to Tephra and Gases. In *Volcanic Activity and Human Ecology*, ed. Payson D. Sheets and Donald K. Grayson. Academic Press, San Diego, pp. 125–159.
1981    Jarðeldasvæði á nútíma (Volcanic Areas of the Holocene). In *Náttúra Íslands*, 2nd ed. Almenna bókafélagið, Reykjavík, pp. 81–119.

Thórarinsson, Sigurdur, and Kristján Sæmundsson
1979    Volcanic Activity in Historical Time. *Jökull* 29: 29–32.

Thordarson, Thorvaldur, and Guðrún Larsen
2007    Volcanism in Iceland in Historical Time: Volcano Types, Eruption Styles and Eruptive History. *Journal of Geodynamics* 43: 118–152.

Thordarson, Thorvaldur, and Steve Self
2003    Atmospheric and Environmental Effects of the 1783–1784 Laki Eruption: A Review and Reassessment. *Journal of Geophysical Research* 108(D1): 4011.

Tómasson, Haukur
1996    The Jökulhlaup from Katla in 1918. *Annals of Glaciology* 22: 249–254.

Vasey, Daniel E.
1996    Population Regulation, Ecology, and Political Economy in Preindustrial Iceland. *American Ethnologist* 23(2): 366–392.

Vésteinsson, Orri, Thomas H. McGovern, and Christian Keller
2002    Enduring Impacts: Social and Environmental Aspects of Viking Age Settlement in Iceland and Greenland. *Archaeologia Islandica* 2: 98–136.

Witham, Claire S., and Clive Oppenheimer
2004    Mortality in England during the 1783–4 Laki Craters Eruption. *Bulletin of Volcanology* 67: 15–26.

## UNDERSTANDING HAZARDS, MITIGATING IMPACTS, AVOIDING DISASTERS

### Statement for Policy Makers and the Disaster Management Community

A long-term view of volcanic hazards in Iceland contains an important message for policy makers: *context is vital*. Although combinations of major eruptions and unlucky circumstances have contributed to nationwide calamities, depression, and famine, we stress that it was not the size or type of volcanic eruption alone that decided this result but rather the time of year the eruption took place and the coincidence of other factors that in combination could produce catastrophic shocks to the economic system. It is notable that despite over 200 volcanic events in Iceland that could have led to a disaster, few have killed people either directly or indirectly; when bad synergies occur, however, death tolls can be great. Historical case studies suggest that human suffering on a massive scale is not necessarily a measure of system resilience (or failure): societies can absorb enormous and inhuman amounts of pain and suffering without failing.

Potential impacts of volcanic eruptions are variable depending on environmental and social contexts and are best viewed alongside other natural hazards, from disease to extreme weather. Long recurrence times and their varied nature have meant that prior to the twentieth century AD there was little specific planning to cope with volcanic impacts. However, communal resilience in Iceland that developed to face other environmental challenges, such as extreme or unpredictable weather, has been the basis of an effective response to volcanic hazards and the mitigation of their impacts. Self-reliance was key and was based on flexible strategies of farming and wildlife exploitation. Arguably, this flexibility came at the cost of economic development, which at best was sluggish until the end of the nineteenth century. Modifying or abandoning this ability to deal with setbacks in favor of economic development did not seem like an acceptable strategy until modern times. Serendipitously, the volcanic events that create hazards in Iceland have also created environmental records that are a highly effective means of assessing those hazards. Through a detailed, multidisciplinary study of the past, we can both acquire an appreciation of the likely physical effects of future events and assess how specific circumstances have led to economic cost and human suffering—or not. The key to effective anticipation of an unknowable future is to understand the importance of synergistic effects and how they might occur depending upon context.

# FOUR

# Fail to Prepare, Then Prepare to Fail: Rethinking Threat, Vulnerability, and Mitigation in the Precolumbian Caribbean

*Jago Cooper*

## INTRODUCTION AND KEY CHALLENGES

The islands of the Caribbean are a particularly interesting geographical region to examine the dynamic relationship between past human communities and sudden environmental change. This chapter examines how past peoples, living on the islands in the Caribbean Sea, were vulnerable to a number of environmental threats. The focus of this chapter is the impact of floods, droughts, and wind shear created by relative sea level rise, precipitation change, and hurricane activity. These hazards were identified as particularly relevant to current debates, given the predicted increase in the risk of such hazards in the near future (Caribbean Community Climate Change Centre 2009; Intergovernmental Panel on Climate Change 2007). The potential Precolumbian mitigation of these hazards through the development of household architecture, settlement location, food procurement strategies, and networks of community interaction is explored in this chapter; and the relative success in mitigating impact and avoiding disaster is considered. This chapter reviews different scales of analysis, from the global, regional, national, and local, to extract key themes for comparative discussion. These research themes are then examined in more detail using a case study area in north-central Cuba where the author has conducted interdisciplinary collaborative research with Cuban and international colleagues since 2002.

The absence of other causes of sudden environmental change in this chapter—namely earthquakes, volcanoes, and the impacts of El Niño/La Niña—should not be taken as an indication of their relative lack of importance. Rather, these major causes of sudden environmental change would not be given justice in this short chapter; they require, and receive, their own standalone discussion elsewhere (Handoh et al. 2006; Scheffers et al. 2009). However, the key discussions in this chapter that focus on mitigation and resilience to floods, droughts, and wind shear by Precolumbian populations have a direct relevance to all discussions of human engagement with sudden environmental change in the region. In fact, different causes behind sudden environmental change were less important for past human communities than was the similarity in their impacts on the local environment.

Therefore examples of past human engagement with the consequences of sudden environmental change often have relevance beyond their specific source of origin and geographical context. This is not because universal rules can be identified in human mitigation and transferred between different geographical regions and time periods; rather, each case study examined in isolation provides one way in which the variables of climate, environment, and human experience have played out in the past. By increasing the number of "case studies" or "experiments" (Nelson et al. this volume) and looking at the relationship between cause and effect, decisions and decision making, planning and chance, we can improve our understanding of these relationships within a global ecodynamics framework that helps us to better understand hazards, mitigate impacts, and avoid disasters. These wider lessons suggest that this Precolumbian "case study" is relevant for modern-day populations of the Caribbean, and the combination of case studies presented in this book has important lessons for the wider populations of the world that currently face sudden environmental change (Alley et al. 2003: 2005; Lenton et al. 2008).

The terms *vulnerability, hazard, impact,* and *resilience* are increasingly finding their way into academic and policy literature, although their meanings can often be appropriated differently by different disciplines. The term *vulnerability* is used in this chapter to describe exposure to hazards when the *hazard* is a potential threat to a past community that has not yet been manifested. *Impacts* are the consequences of a hazard; they can be both direct and indirect in nature and are relative as a result of potential mitigation strategies that can reduce their impact through intentional or unintentional preparation. *Resilience* is a more complex term to use given the extensive discussion of its role in ecological and social theory; however, in this chapter it is used in its broadest sense to refer to the relative ability and mechanisms with which past communities lived through the impacts of sudden environmental change while maintaining their core lifeways (Redman and Kinzig 2003).

## ENVIRONMENTAL AND CLIMATIC CONTEXT

The islands of the Caribbean are an interesting mixture of geologically diverse landforms dotted throughout the Caribbean Sea, bounded by the continental landmasses of North and South America. General trends of smaller coral limestone and volcanic islands in the southern Lesser Antilles and larger, geologically older islands in the northern Greater Antilles are often made, but in reality each island has a very different personality created by its local environment. There is evidence for a diverse range of flora and fauna in the Caribbean islands prior to human colonization, with pre-human residents, such as the giant sloth, living in caves surrounded by temperate forests during the terminal Pleistocene (Steadman et al. 2005). The environments of the different Caribbean islands were changed following the arrival of humans, whose activities and introduction of new species would have a well-discussed and profound impact on the environment (Goudie 2006; Newsom and Wing 2004; Siegel et al. 2005).

The islands of the Caribbean are particularly vulnerable to the dangers of sudden environmental change because of their location within the earth's climate system. Caribbean climate is controlled to a large, though still debated, extent by ocean currents driven by thermohaline systems in the North Atlantic (Lowe and Walker 1997: 362). The Caribbean is a key driver in this system, and consideration of sudden environmental change in the region needs to be contextualized within a global oceanic context. The Caribbean Sea generates movement in ocean currents, as well as climate patterns in the Northern Hemisphere, through the creation of warm salty water in the tropical shallow sea that drives warm energy northward up into the North Atlantic. This movement creates an extremely dynamic flow of ocean currents in and around the Caribbean that is an integral part of the wider Atlantic climatic system, which means the islands themselves are particularly vulnerable to changes and variability within this system (Clarke et al. 2003: 923; Overpeck et al. 1989: 556).

The well-established threat of hurricanes to the Caribbean islands exemplifies the importance of the oceanic context of the Caribbean as climatic fronts from the Atlantic and West Africa combine to generate deep low-pressure systems that are pushed westward toward the Caribbean (Donnelly and Woodruff 2007; Hetzinger et al. 2008; Saunders and Lea 2008). Current paleo-tempestological research examines the ways changes in past climate systems affected the frequency and intensity of prehistoric hurricanes in the Caribbean (McCloskey and Keller 2009). These same Atlantic climate systems also control precipitation on the Caribbean islands, with the movement of the intertropical convergence zone regularly changing the amount of water that falls on the Caribbean (Haug et al. 2001). So when we look at the impacts of sudden environmental change on the Caribbean, we need to consider intra-hemispheric causality and the relative vulnerability of these islands at an important interface in the global climate system. Therefore it is often necessary and informative to look to non-local data sets to provide paleoclimatic data and proxy evidence for sudden environmental change in the Caribbean (Black et al. 2007; Cronin et al. 2003; Gischler et al. 2008). More regionally specific research on climatic change in the Caribbean can facilitate an improved understanding of the relationship between global and regional climate change and local environmental hazards. Fortunately, climate change in the Atlantic is the focus of urgent and exhaustive research that can be used to explore the scale and timing of impacts in the Caribbean.

## ARCHAEOLOGICAL CONTEXT

The Caribbean is an intriguing archaeological region, not least because many of the fundamental questions of Precolumbian colonization and societal development remain embroiled in lively debate. However, painting a broad picture, the islands were colonized at some point after 7,000 BP, with early sites first appearing in Cuba and Hispaniola. These earliest "lithic" societies developed hunter-forager lifestyles in the Greater Antilles until around 4000 BP, when more complex lithic and shell artifacts and the more extensive colonization of other islands led to the "archaic" phase of hunters, fishers, and foragers being defined. Ceramics were first found in the Caribbean in about 2500 BP; during this time period incipient agriculture was developed before larger-scale communities reliant on agriculture emerged sometime around AD 600. Interestingly, "archaic" peoples with these mobile and flexible hunter-forager traditions may have continued up to contact and lived often in close proximity to agriculturalist societies with hierarchical social systems. From around AD 900 to contact, we see the development of more hierarchical societies and extensive networks of inter-island interaction that thrived up until the contact period, during which a population of up to 1 million indigenous people was estimated to have been living in the Caribbean (Curet 2005).

This broad overview of the diverse islands in the Caribbean is useful to provide a general framework, but it highlights the major challenge of divergent resolutions at which climatic, environmental, and archaeological data operate in this region. It is clear that the regional perspective is not an effective scale at which to examine archaeological evidence for the human experience of sudden environmental change. It is essential to use site-specific examples that combine local environmental and archaeological data that are informed from a regional perspective but grounded with high-resolution comparative data. Therefore this chapter will attempt to correlate different spatial and temporal scales of cause and effect linking global climatic instability to regional environmental context to local sudden environmental change before considering the relative impact on past human communities at individual Precolumbian settlement sites.

Another important challenge to this research is the definition and identification of *change*. This brief introduction has highlighted that the Caribbean is perpetually in climatic, environmental, and social flux; therefore "change" is relative to the scale at which the parameters of an assumed equilibrium are defined. However, the time depth of archaeology provides an excellent framework with which to look at the ways cyclical events operating on inter-annual, inter-decadal, inter-centennial, and inter-millennial timescales can be examined using the human lifetime as the fundamental building block with which to construct a multi-temporal, as well as multi-spatial, structural framework to better understand change (Adam 1994; Ingold 1993). With this framework in mind, the Caribbean provides an interesting backdrop to examine how past human communities lived for thousands of years in a region subjected to the multi-temporal impacts of sudden environmental change.

## KEY HAZARDS AND PAST IMPACTS

The three main creators of hazards and subsequent sudden environmental change in the Precolumbian Caribbean focused on in this chapter are relative sea level rise, precipitation change, and hurricane activity. These climate-dependent conditions create key hazards that include floods, droughts, and wind shear; but the hazard to past communities needs to be considered in a wider context in which the potential threat of the hazard is relative and dependent on issues of cyclicity, variability, and predictability. This wider consideration of the hazard requires that the human perspective be taken into account, where hazards are culturally contingent on ecological knowledge (Crate 2008). In many ways, to contextualize the hazard within a culturally, socially, and phenomenologically specific setting is in itself a means of better understanding the reality of vulnerability, impact, and resilience.

### Relative Sea Level Rise

Relative sea level rise can create profound vulnerabilities for island communities. The Caribbean has witnessed dramatic sea level change and is one of the few areas in the world that has experienced regionally increasing relative sea levels throughout the period of human occupation. This is the case because early Holocene eustatic sea level rises were replaced by Middle to Late Holocene iso-static relative sea level rise (Milne, Long, and Bassett 2004: 1183; Toscano and Macintyre 2003). Inevitably, local tectonic activity, coastal sedimentation, and erosion processes affect this picture and highlight the importance of micro-scale case studies to complement the macro-scale regional picture (Cooper and Peros 2010; Peros, Reinhardt, and Davis 2007; Ramcharan 2004).

Since the established colonization of the Caribbean, there has been at least a 5-m rise in regional relative sea levels, which has radically changed the islandscape of the Caribbean (Milne, Long, and Bassett 2004; Toscano and Macintyre 2003). The impacts of relative sea level rise on Precolumbian populations have been raised previously as an important issue for discussion (Keegan 1995; Tabio 1995). However, it is important to consider how the impacts of relative sea level rise actually manifest themselves for coastal communities. Modelers often describe long-term regional figures of relative sea level rise as 1 mm per year over an extended period. However, this is based on mean figures often averaged over thousands of years, and the reality of relative sea level rise for people living in the region is very different. In fact, the impact of relative sea level rise is a punctuated equilibrium in which abrupt coastal flooding events are instigated by catalysts such as hurricane storm surge.

These periodic flooding events are caused by long-term processes of relative sea level rise, but they create very sudden impacts for coastal communities, as paleocoastlines are breached and new coastlines formed (Cooper and Boothroyd 2011). In Cuba, 27 percent of the island was flooded by rising relative sea levels between initial colonization around 6000 BP and the arrival of Columbus in AD 1492 (figure 4.1). Detailed bathymetric models of different areas of the coastline, combined with local relative sea level change data modeled using geomorphological and archaeobotanical data, indicate tipping points at which paleocoastlines are breached and inland areas flooded. These tipping points represent episodes of sudden environmental change in which both the flooding event and subsequent impacts on coastal ecology would have been profound. The dating of such events enables the correlation with archaeological context. In the case study area in northern Cuba we see some interesting patterns of changing settlement location and food procurement strategy during this period of relative sea level rise impacts that can provide indications of Precolumbian mitigation strategies discussed further later in this chapter. Therefore the vulnerabilities created by relative sea level rise in the Caribbean exposed Precolumbian populations to important hazards. Coastal flooding and radical changes in marine and coastal ecology were important for Precolumbian populations, who often lived in coastal settlements with a marine-focused diet. The impact of long-term relative sea level rise needs to be considered in the context of short-term flooding events that occurred on perhaps inter-centennial and inter-millennial timescales. Flooding events created by increasing relative sea levels had a key impact on regional islandscapes and local coastlines through the reaching of tipping points that caused coastal flooding and sudden local environmental change.

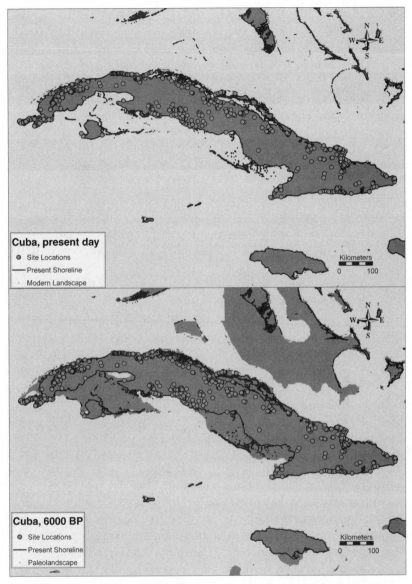

**4.1.** *Comparative map of Cuba showing 27 percent loss of landmass as a result of the 5-m rise in relative sea levels from 6000 BP to present. Map by Jago Cooper.*

## Precipitation

Precipitation change has been argued to be an important factor in creating sudden environmental change, and there are many worldwide discussions of the impacts on past human populations (Gill et al. 2007). Unfortunately, the Caribbean lacks the detailed precipitation records found in other regions, but understanding its climatic context enables the exposure and discussion of human vulnerability to precipitation variation. Much work still needs to be done to reconstruct and understand precipitation change effectively (Broecker 2009), but it is clear that changes in the Atlantic climate system affect precipitation rates in the Caribbean. Fine-grained reconstructions of precipitation change in the Caribbean require additional research; but existing data indicate fluctuating regional precipitation rates over time, with a drier period beginning 10,500 BP, a wetter period beginning 7000 BP, and an intense dryer period beginning 3200 BP (Higuera-Gundy et al. 1999: 159; Hodell et al. 1991; Nyberg et al. 2001).

These broad chronologies for precipitation variation based on lake cores and archaeobotanical evidence are too limited to provide a comprehensive regional picture, but the evidence does suggest the potential importance of such changes to the local environments of the islands of the Caribbean (Siegel et al. 2001). However, an understanding of Caribbean communities' vulnerability to precipitation variability requires a more nuanced understanding of the different spatial and temporal scales at which hazards can have an impact. Paleoprecipitation variation in the Caribbean includes low-frequency regional impacts on an inter-millennial scale that would have substantially changed the terrestrial ecology of the region, but at the same time there would have been cycles of high-frequency, inter-annual impacts on local environments that would have had a more direct and noticeable impact for human communities (Nyberg et al. 2001). Floods and droughts are often assumed to be the main hazards generated by precipitation change, but perhaps we should also consider the hazard of instability or unpredictability as a key threat for Precolumbian communities. The high variability of the frequency, seasonality, and reliability of precipitation created by the exposure to unstable Atlantic weather systems created dramatic regional and local climatic instability and variable precipitation rates (Haug et al. 2001). This hazard of instability has been well established in previous discussions, particularly in respect to the origins of agriculture (Bettinger, Richerson, and Boyd 2009; Rosen in press), and this hazard appears to have been important for the peoples of the Caribbean. While broad regional trends in precipitation variation from lake cores indicate periods of drier and wetter conditions, it is important to consider the micro-scale of shorter-term and more locally specific variation. These smaller-scale impacts therefore have to be examined locally using relevant paleoclimatic data on a case-by-case basis.

## Hurricanes

Hurricanes represent some of the most dramatic and well-publicized hazards Caribbean populations face. The production of intense low pressures in

**4.2.** *Photographs showing damage caused by Hurricane Ike in 2008. Clockwise from bottom left: two different modern house designs destroyed by the hurricane, unusable broken house tiles collected for disposal following the hurricane, and one Precolumbian house from the "Taíno" heritage village of El Chorro de Maíta being rebuilt six days after the hurricane. Photos by (clockwise from bottom left) Roberto Valcárcel Rojas, Roberto Valcárel Rojas, Jago Cooper, and Jago Cooper.*

the mid-Atlantic creates these seasonal tropical cyclones that move westward into the Caribbean. The hurricane represents one of the most frequent high-impact hazards in the Caribbean with annual regional return rates. It is difficult to appreciate the impact of such wind speeds without having witnessed the effects, but the hurricane creates some of the most profound sudden environmental changes in the Caribbean (figure 4.2). The spatial nature of hurricane impacts can often be fairly local, with wind shear damage limited to perhaps a swath 5–10 km in width. The temporality of the hurricane impacts—namely wind shear, coastal storm surges, and pluvial flooding—has both an immediate and a mid- to long-term impact on the local environment. This variation in the temporal scale of impact is important when considering mitigation of these effects by human communities. In many ways the nature of the hurricane impact is defined by the speed and cost at which human communities can "recover."

The first written record of extreme weather events appears in Columbus's diary of his first voyage (Dunn and Kelley 1989), the start of a long historical record of hurricane landfalls in the Caribbean. Evidence for prehistoric hurricane activity in the Caribbean is available from geomorphological studies of sediment cores and also the use of proxy evidence, such as coral isotope data, for changing North Atlantic sea surface temperatures that are argued to affect the frequency and intensity of hurricane activity (Beck et al. 1997: 705; Donnelly and Woodruff 2007; Elsner 2007; McCloskey and Keller 2009; Nyberg et al. 2007). These proxy data for hurricane activity are an interesting avenue for future research, but existing data show the presence and impacts of hurricanes in the Precolumbian Caribbean (Hetzinger et al. 2008). This discussion highlights that the high-frequency local impact of hurricanes should not only focus on the "event" itself but should also consider the medium- to long-term "impacts" in which reconstruction is part of the impact and essential to the development of any mitigation strategy.

## HUMAN MITIGATION AND RESILIENCE

Ethno-historical records from the contact period Caribbean suggest that Precolumbian populations had complex belief systems in which weather and the process of environmental change were well established (Oviedo 1959 [1526]). Different deities associated with different aspects of precipitation and the stages of hurricanes—Boinayel, Coatrisque, and Guabancex—show an understanding and communication of meteorological knowledge through an active symbology alive within the human community (Drewett 2003; Pané 1999 [1498]). It is intriguing to consider the role such oral histories might have played in enabling intergenerational knowledge transfer for hazards that might have had inter-decadal and inter-centennial timescales, such as different coastal flooding events on different islands. However, from an archaeological perspective this nuance of ecological understanding and knowledge transfer is more challenging to identify. This raises the important point that it is not the aim of this chapter to identify cause and effect between sudden environmental change and socio-behavioral change. Rather, this chapter has a wider aim: to examine through archaeology how Precolumbian populations lived through periods of sudden environmental change and whether their now extinct lifeways have useful lessons for mitigating similar impacts faced by populations living in the Caribbean today.

Therefore, while the causality of human behavioral change is interesting, this overview of human mitigation in the face of sudden environmental change focuses instead on whether household architecture, settlement location, food procurement strategies, and interaction networks—as understood through archaeological analysis—provided resilience to the established dangers of sudden environmental change.

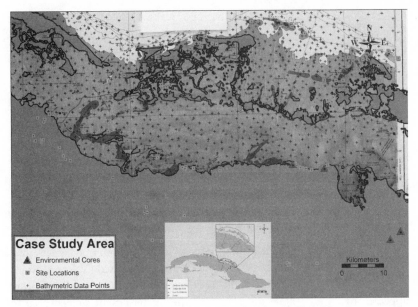

**4.3.** *Map of the case study area in north-central Cuba where fieldwork has been carried out since 2003. Map by Jago Cooper.*

### Household Architecture

Archaeological excavations of Precolumbian house structures in the Caribbean reveal the consistent use of wooden poled structures, predominantly circular or oval and ranging between 6 and 9 m in diameter (Curet 1992; Samson 2010; Schinkel 1992). Historically, the wood's poor preservation has limited the degree to which the design of these structures can be examined and fully understood. However, the recent discovery and excavation of well-preserved house structures in waterlogged conditions at the site of Los Buchillones (Valcárcel Rojas et al. 2006) has enabled a better understanding of Precolumbian household architecture and the potential resilience of these forms to known hazards.

Los Buchillones is a late Precolumbian settlement site dating AD 1250 to contact. The site is located within the case study area in north-central Cuba (figure 4.3). The house structures at Los Buchillones use two concentric rings of substantive mahogany (*Swietenia mahagoni*) posts, with diameters up to 33 cm, to form the structural framework for the house. These posts are deeply embedded up to 1.7 m into the ground. This hardwood permanent structural framework was then dressed with a lighter-weight superstructure including a slender rafter, stringer, and thatched roof. It has been hypothesized that these structures used suspended woven matted floors over lightweight timber struts, but at this stage the floors have not been excavated. However, local paleoenvironmental cores at the site indicate that these structures were located in waterlogged conditions during their occupation (Peros, Graham, and Davis 2006), so it seems likely that the floors were suspended between the structural posts.

Modern-day residents in the two neighboring coastal villages of Punta Alegre and Maximo Gomez, 2 km west and 4 km east of Los Buchillones, respectively, predominantly live in concrete structures and initially considered these Precolumbian structures to be *debil* (weak) against the hazards of wind shear, coastal storm surge, and pluvial flooding (Nelson Torna, personal communication). However, this categorization of weakness or vulnerability requires careful consideration in light of the earlier discussion of past impacts. Radiocarbon dating of different elements of the house structures and the artifact assemblages contained within them shows that the structural posts have remained in situ and in use for hundreds of years (Cooper 2010a; Cooper and Thomas in press). Excavations showed that these posts had been cut for immediate use and had not been removed from their original location or reused (Valcárcel Rojas et al. 2006). However, radiocarbon dates suggest that these structural posts appeared to have been "re-dressed" with the lighter-weight superstructures over time as roofs were replaced. This finding raises the interesting question of how weakness or vulnerability is judged in the face of specific hazards. Initially, the lightweight wooden and thatch superstructure would have been a more vulnerable place to be than a concrete structure during the high wind speeds of a hurricane, but this focus on the short-term "event" of the hazard ignores the medium- to longer-term impacts of post-hazard reconstruction that are often more destructive for Caribbean communities. Therefore, if we take the ethnohistorical sources at face value and argue that Precolumbian communities had management strategies in place to identify oncoming hurricanes, alert the community, and retreat to nearby caves for shelter during a hurricane's short-term impact, then their Precolumbian house structures were extremely resilient to the mid- to long-term "impacts" because they could be rebuilt within days of a hurricane using locally available and easily sourced materials (see figure 4.2). Therefore the potential resilience of these house structures needs to be considered in light of the different timescales at which the impacts of hazards occurred.

## Settlement Location

The majority of modern-day settlements in the Caribbean were located and founded by post-contact communities, predominantly using European settlement planning traditions. Modeling the vulnerability of different settlement locations to wind shear and flooding at a regional scale is problematic because the parameters of local topography and environment are crucial fac-

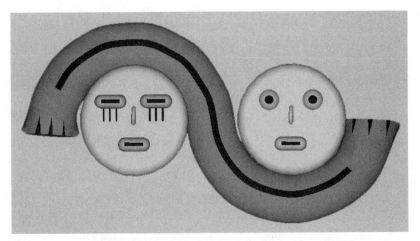

**4.4.** *Logo for the Save the Children–sponsored resettlement initiative in Holguin inspired by the iconographic representation of Guabancex, the Precolumbian deity associated with the hurricane's destructive force. Photo by Roberto Valcárel Rojas.*

tors that can be overlooked at this macro-scale. Therefore models that show that most Precolumbian settlements in Cuba are located in close proximity to caves that could be used as hurricane shelters or that topographic modeling suggests a preference for leeward settlement locations in upland areas is a somewhat statistical argument that requires a case-by-case analysis (Cooper 2010a). This caveat is particularly important when considering the changing nature of the Cuban archipelago over time and the impacts of relative sea level rise and changing climatic and environmental conditions. However, before we focus on a case study site, it is interesting to note observations by modern-day inhabitants of Cuba who consider Precolumbian settlements to be located in more flood-protected areas of the landscape.

An example of this observation put into action comes from a recent Save the Children–sponsored urban planning initiative in Holguin in eastern Cuba, which uses as its logo the Precolumbian deity Guabancex, the symbolic representation of the destructive force of the hurricane (figure 4.4). This project has identified a pattern in Precolumbian settlement locations and argues that their use of leeward hillside brows for settlements, in contrast to the more common post-contact use of river valleys, provides better protection from the common tropical storm and hurricane pluvial flooding in the region (Valcárcel Rojas 2002). Inevitably, such regional generalizations are susceptible to oversimplification, as without doubt many Precolumbian settlements do appear to be located in positions more traditionally considered "vulnerable." Therefore, general observations surrounding the relative vulnerability of Precolumbian settlement locations need to be evaluated within their individual topographic and paleoenvironmental settings if useful interpretations are to be made regarding their relative resilience.

Los Buchillones is an interesting site at which to explore these issues of settlement vulnerability in more detail. Paleoenvironmental evidence shows that the site was a Precolumbian residential settlement that straddled the coastline using stilted wooden structures over waterlogged environments. This coastal location, similar to the neighboring modern-day villages of Punta Alegre and Maximo Gomez, exposes the settlement to the impacts of the hazards discussed earlier. Therefore each of these potential hazards can be evaluated using this site-specific example. Located 1 km south of Los Buchillones is a range of hills called the Lomas de Punta Alegre, which contain a number of large limestone caves that could have been used as hurricane shelters. Precolumbian artifacts in these caves indicate their use, or at least knowledge of their location, by Precolumbian populations. Therefore these caves offered potential shelter for the occupants of Los Buchillones during the wind shear "event" of past hurricanes.

A topographic and hydrographic model of the coastal region around Los Buchillones enables the modeling of the impacts of coastal storm surges on this Precolumbian settlement (Cooper and Boothroyd 2011). Bathymetric models show that the flow of water through the offshore island archipelago is greatly restricted by a prominent reef located 30 km north of Los Buchillones, by the shallow depth of the intervening Bahia de Buena Vista, and by a series of narrow channels that limit the flow of water through a network of low-lying mangrove islands. This suggests that the location of the site behind the Jardines del Rey archipelago would have mitigated the impact of hurricane coastal storm surges.

The potential for pluvial flooding at Los Buchillones is high, as the Lomas de Punta Alegre behind the site is a water catchment area that channels rainwater down the hillsides to the coast. However, the location of the house structures in a waterlogged environment with potentially suspended floors mitigates against the impact of pluvial flooding because the water ran off the hills into the wetlands—unlike today, when the houses of Punta Alegre are regularly flooded.

Los Buchillones is just one site in the densely populated Precolumbian islandscape of the Cuban archipelago; therefore it is not possible to take these "lessons" of potential resilient settlement location and apply them elsewhere. However, this case study does show how the study of settlement location within an established paleoenvironmental setting, combined with an improved understanding of household architecture used at the site, can provide a better understanding of the vulnerabilities and potential resilience of Precolumbian communities. This study shows the importance of evaluating vulnerability contingent on the local environmental context, and, while not transferable to other sites in different environmental contexts, some of the findings are certainly relevant to the modern-day populations of Punta Alegre and Maximo Gomez.

## Food Procurement Strategies and Interaction Networks

Changing patterns in Precolumbian resource and subsistence strategies are subject to a large number of influences over time, from changing settlement locations to demographic fluctuations, seasonality, overexploitation, and new technologies. Therefore, linking the impact of sudden environmental change with changes in past food procurement strategies identified in faunal assemblage analyses is often too simplistic and deterministic to be meaningful. However, it is interesting to consider how reconstructed food procurement strategies during particular points in time would have helped mitigate against the impacts of known hazards in a particular case study area.

In the case study area around Los Buchillones, faunal assemblages from a number of sites have been studied, and they reveal some general patterns in the diversification of environmental niches exploited over time (Cooper, Valcárcel Rojas, and Calvera Rosés 2010). During the occupation of Los Buchillones, we can reconstruct a diverse and wide-reaching food procurement strategy that utilized resources from pelagic, reef, mangrove, littoral, lowland agricultural, and upland forested environments with a large catchment area drawn around each site. Evidence shows direct access by inhabitants of Los Buchillones to all of the marine environments, but the links with the upland regions in Cuba's interior raise the probability of trade and exchange networks (Cooper 2008). The use of food resources from a diverse range of environments highlights a strategy that provides resilience against sudden disruptions to local environments.

It is clear from this discussion that sudden environmental change can occur in the Caribbean at different spatial scales, but the diversification of resource sources facilitates the mitigations of these impacts. The local impacts of relative sea level rise and hurricanes indicate that to successfully live through these impacts, communities require access to resources and support beyond the affected areas. In the case study area at Los Buchillones, interaction models have been constructed using the movement of sourced materials through the islandscape (Cooper 2010b). These networks of interaction show that established relationships based on exchange and reciprocity between different coastal sites and the interior upland areas exist up to 50 km inland. References to social relationships in the late Precolumbian Caribbean indicate that these networks would have been firmly established, with strong intermarriage and social reticulation. Therefore this network of interaction provides an important framework for management following localized impacts of hazards such as hurricanes (Cooper and Peros 2010).

## SUMMARY AND FUTURE RESEARCH

The intentionality behind human decision-making processes is challenging to identify through archaeological data alone. Consequently, it is very difficult to differentiate between deliberately planned disaster management strategies that have been intentionally adopted and cultural practices that have the benefit of mitigating potential hazards. Therefore this chapter is not arguing for a mono-causal link among Precolumbian household architecture, settlement location, food procurement strategies, interaction networks, and the dangers of sudden environmental change. Rather, it uses paleoclimatic and paleoenvironmental data at different spatial and temporal scales to identify the hazards experienced by Precolumbian populations in the Caribbean. It then uses detailed archaeological investigation at different spatial and temporal scales to assess the potential resilience of their lifeways to these impacts, occasionally using modern-day comparisons for contrast (Peterson and Broad 2009). This study suggests that hazards need to be considered as culturally contingent and based on the ecological knowledge with which societies understand the nature and threat of potential hazards. In the Caribbean, Precolumbian lifeways appear to have offered some important advantages in mitigating the impacts of known hazards in the region. These advantages helped mitigate the impacts of hazards and reduced the vulnerability of Precolumbian communities to sudden environmental change.

The scaled temporality of hazard return rates in the Caribbean raises the interesting topic of intergenerational knowledge transfer and the cultural transmission of ecological knowledge over time. Archaeology, through case studies such as this one from the Caribbean, provides a deep time perspective of human engagement with environmental change that challenges the use of concepts such as stability and equilibrium. The constantly changing dynamics of human-climate-environment relations need to be understood in terms of flux rather than equilibrium; therefore hazards can only be properly understood within their individual geographic, temporal, and cultural contexts. In the Caribbean, archaeology provides one of the few tools available to access this important knowledge following the loss of an entire way of life after European contact. Therefore archaeologists can make an important contribution to ongoing debates over disaster management in the Caribbean where concepts of threat, vulnerability, and resilience can be better understood using the time depth of human experience. In this way, archaeologists should be involved in future disaster management strategies to enable a better understanding of hazards, provide critical discussion of potential mitigation strategies, and contribute to a wider interdisciplinary debate that enables modern-day communities to avoid the impending dangers of sudden environmental change in the region.

Future research needs to concentrate on providing more interdisciplinary case studies in which paleoclimatic, paleoenvironmental, and archaeological data can be brought together in an informative way. The discussion in this chapter raises some interesting observations that merit more extensive comparative discussion. More fine-grained proxy data for local paleoclimates and paleoenvironments are required to bring the impacts of sudden environmental change to the archaeological scale of human occupation at individual settlements. However, perhaps most important, an improved dialogue needs to be opened among archaeologists, climatologists, and disaster management experts, as there is no doubt that archaeology has innovative perspectives and important lessons to contribute to a much wider debate (Anderson et al. 2007; Giddens 2009; Jansen et al. 2007).

*Acknowledgments.* This research was made possible through funding from the Arts and Humanities Research Council (AH/1002596/1), Leverhulme Trust (6/SRF/2008/0267), University of Leicester School of Archaeology and Ancient History, and Natural Environment Research Council (P17233-60). This chapter was inspired by the Global Long Term Human Ecodynamics Conference organized by Andrew Dugmore, Tom McGovern, Astrid Ogilvie, and Sophia Perdikaris at Eagles Hill in 2009. I also thank Roberto Valcárcel Rojas, for his longstanding co-direction of this project, and colleagues in Cuba who have collaborated and contributed to this research, including Celso Paso Alberti, Jorge Calvera Rosés, Gabino la Rosa Corzo, Raúl Gómez Fernández, Vicente O. Rodríguez, Elena Guarch, Odalys Brito Martínez, Pedro Cruz Ramírez, Juan Carlos Mayo Rodríguez, Yanelis Buchillón López, Idania Buchillón Jorge, Iosvany Martinez, Lazaro Calvo Iglesias, Indira Mayea, Dayessy Rojas, Daima Morel, Marcos Labrada Achoa, José Calvera, Nelson Torna, and Adrián García Lebroc.

## REFERENCES

Adam, Barbara
 1994 Perceptions of Time. In *Humanity, Culture, and Social Life: Companion Encyclopaedia of Anthropology,* ed. Tim Ingold. Routledge, London, pp. 503–526.

Alley, Richard B., J. Marotzke, W. D. Nordhaus, J. T. Overpeck, D. M. Peteet, R. A. Pielke Jr., R. T. Pierrehumbert, P. B. Rhines, T. F. Stocker, and L. D. Talley
 2003 Abrupt Climate Change. *Science* 299: 2005–2010.

Anderson, David G., Kirk A. Maasch, Daniel H. Sandweiss, and Paul A. Mayewski
 2007 Climate and Culture Change: Exploring Holocene Transitions. In *Climate Change and Cultural Dynamics: A Global Perspective on Mid-Holocene Transitions,* ed. David G. Anderson, Kirk A. Maasch, and Daniel H. Sandweiss. Academic Press, London, pp. 1–24.

Beck, Warren J., Jacques Récy, Fred Taylor, Lawrence R. Edwards, and Guy Cabloch
  1997    Abrupt Changes in Early Holocene Tropical Sea Surface Temperature
          Derived from Coral Records. *Nature* 385: 705–707.

Bettinger, Robert, Peter Richerson, and Robert Boyd
  2009    Constraints on the Development of Agriculture. *Current Anthropology*
          50(5): 627–631.

Black, David E., Matthew A. Abahazi, Robert C. Thunell, Alexey Kaplan, Eric J. Tappa,
and Larry C. Petersen
  2007    An 8-Century Tropical Atlantic SST Record from the Cariaco Basin: Base-
          line Variability, Twentieth-Century Warming, and Atlantic Hurricane Fre-
          quency. *Paleoceanography* 22(PA2024): 1–10.

Broecker, Wallace S.
  2009    *The Impact of Global Warming on Precipitation Patterns. Climate Change:
          Global Risks, Challenges and Decisions.* IOP Conference Series: Earth and
          Environmental Science 6, Copenhagen.

Caribbean Community Climate Change Centre (CCCCC)
  2009    *Climate Change and the Caribbean: A Regional Framework for Achieving
          Development Resilient to Climate Change (2009–2015).* CCCCC Report
          for CARICOM Heads of State. First Congress for the Environmental
          Charter and Climatic Change, October 11–13, 2007, Caracas.

Clarke, Garry, David Leverington, James Teller, and Arthur Dyke
  2003    Superlakes, Megafloods, and Abrupt Climate Change. *Science* 301: 922–
          923.

Cooper, Jago
  2008    Creating Connections between Caribbean Islands: An Archaeological
          Perspective from Northern Cuba. In *Comparative Island Archaeologies:
          British Archaeological Reports 1829,* ed. James Conolloy and Matthew
          Campbell. Archaeopress, Oxford, pp. 179–190.
  2010a   Precolumbian Archaeology of Cuba: A Study of National Site Distribu-
          tion Patterns and Radiocarbon Chronologies. In *Island Shores, Distant
          Pasts: Archaeological and Biological Approaches to the Precolumbian Settle-
          ment of the Caribbean,* ed. S. M. Fitzpatrick and Ann H. Ross. University
          of Florida Press, Gainesville, pp. 81–107.
  2010b   Modelling Mobility and Exchange in Precolumbian Cuba: GIS Led
          Approaches to Identifying Pathways and Reconstructing Journeys from the
          Archaeological Record. In *Journal of Caribbean Archaeology,* special edi-
          tion of the journal edited by C. Hofman and A. J. Bright, pp. 122–137.

Cooper, Jago, and Richard Boothroyd
  2011    Living Islands of the Caribbean: A View of Relative Sea Level Change
          from the Water's Edge. In *Communities in Contact: Essays in Archaeology,
          Ethnohistory and Ethnography of the Amerindian Circum-Caribbean,* ed.
          C. L. Hofman and A. van Duijvenbode. Sidestone, Leiden, pp. 393–406.

Cooper, Jago, and Matthew C. Peros
  2010    The Archaeology of Climate Change in the Caribbean. *Journal of Archaeo-
          logical Science* 37(6): 1226–1232.

Cooper, Jago, and Kenneth Thomas
  In press  Constructing Caribbean Chronologies: Comparative Radiocarbon Dating of Shell and Wood Artefacts from Precolumbian Sites in Cuba. *Archaeometry*.

Cooper, Jago, Roberto Valcárcel Rojas, and Jorge Calvera Rosés
  2010  Recent Archaeological Fieldwork from the Region around Los Buchillones. In *Beyond the Blockade: New Currents in Cuban Archaeology*, ed. S. Kepecs, A. Curet, and G. De La Rosa. University of Alabama Press, Tuscaloosa, pp. 89–105.

Crate, Susan
  2008  Gone the Bull of Winter? Grappling with the Cultural Implications of and Anthropology's Role(s) in Global Climate Change. *Current Anthropology* 49(4): 569–595.

Cronin, Thomas M., G. S. Dwyer, T. Kamiya, S. Schwede, and D. A. Wilard
  2003  Medieval Warm Period, Little Ice Age and 20th Century Temperature Variability from Chesapeake Bay. *Global and Planetary Change* 36: 17–29.

Curet, Antonio L.
  1992  House Structure and Cultural Change in the Caribbean: Three Case Studies from Puerto Rico. *Latin American Antiquity* 3(2): 160–174.
  2005  *Caribbean Paleodemography: Population, Culture History and Sociopolitical Processes in Ancient Puerto Rico*. University of Alabama Press, Tuscaloosa.

Donnelly, Jeffrey P., and Jonathan D. Woodruff
  2007  Intense Hurricane Activity over the Past 5000 Years Controlled by El Niño and the West African Monsoon. *Nature* 447: 465–468.

Drewett, Peter
  2003  Feasting at the Ball Game: The Belmont Project, Tortola, British Virgin Islands. *Archaeology International* 6: 56–59.

Dunn, Oliver, and James E. Kelley Jr.
  1989  *The Diario of Christopher Columbus's First Voyage to America 1492–1493 (Abstracted by Fray Bartolomé de Las Casas)*. University of Oklahoma Press, Norman.

Elsner, James B.
  2007  Tempests in Time. *Nature* 447: 647–649.

Giddens, Anthony
  2009  *The Politics of Climate Change*. Polity, Cambridge.

Gill, Richardson B., Paul A. Mayewski, Johan Nyberg, Gerald H. Haug, and Larry C. Peterson
  2007  Drought and the Maya Collapse. *Ancient Mesoamerica* 18: 283–302.

Gischler, Eberhard, Eugene A. Shinn, Wolfgang Oschmann, Jens Fiebig, and Noreen A. Buster
  2008  A 1500-Year Holocene Caribbean Climate Archive from the Blue Hole, Lighthouse Reef, Belize. *Journal of Coastal Research* 24(6): 1495–1505.

Goudie, Andrew
   2006   *The Human Impact on the Natural Environment.* Blackwell, Oxford.
Handoh, Itsuki C., Adrian J. Matthews, Grant R. Bigg, and David P. Stevens
   2006   Interannual Variability of the Tropical Atlantic Independent of and Associated with ENSO. Part 1: The North Tropical Atlantic. *International Journal of Climatology* 26: 1937–1956.
Haug, Gerald H., Konrad A. Hughen, L. C. Peterson, D. M. Sigman, and U. Rohl
   2001   Southward Migration of the Intertropical Convergence Zone through the Holocene. *Science* 293: 1304–1308.
Hetzinger, Steffen, Miriam Pfeiffer, Wolf-Christian Dullo, Noel Keenlyside, Mojib Latif, and Jens Zinke
   2008   Caribbean Coral Tracks Atlantic Multidecadal Oscillation and Past Hurricane Activity. *Geology* 36(1): 11–14.
Higuera-Gundy, Antonia, Mark Brenner, David A. Hodell, Jason H. Curtis, Barbara W. Leyden, and Michael W. Binford
   1999   A 10,300 14C Yr Record of Climate and Vegetation Change from Haiti. *Quarternary Research* 52: 159–170.
Hodell, David A., Jason H. Curtis, Glenn A. Jones, Antonia Higuera-Gundy, Mark Brenner, Michael W. Binford, and Kathleen T. Dorsey
   1991   Reconstruction of Caribbean Climate Change over the Past 10,500 Years. *Nature* 352: 790–793.
Ingold, Tim
   1993   The Temporality of the Landscape. *World Archeology* 25(2): 152–174.
Intergovernmental Panel on Climate Change
   2007   *Climate Change 2007. The Physical Science Basis: Contribution of Working Group I to the Fourth Assessment Report of the Intergovernmental Panel on Climate Change,* ed. S. Solomon, D. Qin, M. Manning, Z. Chen, M. Marquis, K. B. Averyt, M. Tignor, and H. L. Miller. Cambridge University Press, Cambridge.
Jansen, Eystein, J. Overpeck, K. R. Briffa, J.-C. Duplessy, F. Joos, V. Masson-Delmotte, D. Olago, B. Otto-Bliesner, W. R. Peltier, S. Rahmstorf, R. Ramesch, D. Raynaud, D. Rind, O. Solomina, R. Villalba, and D. Zhang
   2007   Paleoclimate. In *Climate Change 2007: The Physical Science Basis. Contribution of Working Group I to the Fourth Assessment Report of the Intergovernmental Panel on Climate Change,* ed. S. Solomon, D. Qin, M. Manning, Z. Chan, M. Marquis, K. B. Averyt, M. Tignor, and H. L. Miller. Cambridge University Press, Cambridge, pp. 433–497.
Keegan, William F.
   1995   Recent Climatic and Sea Level Fluctuations in Relation to West Indian Prehistory. *Proceedings of the 16th International Congress for Caribbean Archaeology* 16: 95–104.
Lenton, Timothy M., Hermann Held, Elmar Kriegler, Jim W. Hall, Wolfgang Luch, Stefan Rahmstorf, and Hans J. Schellnhuber
   2008   Tipping Elements in the Earth's Climate System. *Proceedings of the National Academy of Sciences* (USA) 105(6): 1786–1793.

Lowe, John J., and Mike J.C. Walker
    1997    *Reconstructing Quaternary Environments*. Longman, London.

McCloskey, Terrence A., and Gerta Keller
    2009    5000 Year Sedimentary Record of Hurricane Strikes on the Central Coast of Belize. *Quaternary International* 195(1–2): 53–68.

Milne, Glenn A., Antony J. Long, and Sophie E. Bassett
    2004    Modelling Holocene Relative Sea-Level Observations from the Caribbean and South America. *Quaternary Science Review* 24: 1183–1202.

Newsom, Lee A., and Elizabeth S. Wing
    2004    *On Land and Sea: Native American Uses of Biological Resources in the West Indies*. University of Alabama Press, Tuscaloosa.

Nyberg, Johan, Antoon Kuijpers, Bjorn A. Malmgren, and H. Kunzendorf
    2001    Late Holocene Changes in Precipitation and Hydrography Recorded in Marine Sediments from the Northeastern Caribbean Sea. *Quarternary Research* 56: 87–102.

Nyberg, Johan, Bjorn A. Malmgren, Amos Winter, Mark R. Jury, K. Halimeda Kilbourne, and Terrence M. Quinn
    2007    Low Atlantic Hurricane Activity in the 1970s and 1980s Compared to the Past 270 Years. *Nature* 447: 698–701.

Overpeck, Jonathan T., Larry C. Petersen, Nilva Kipp, John Imbrie, and David Rind
    1989    Climate Change in the Circum–North Atlantic Region during the Last Deglaciation. *Nature* 338: 553–557.

Oviedo, Gonzalo Fernández
    1959    *Natural History of the West Indies*. University of North Carolina Press,
    [1526]   Chapel Hill.

Pané, Fray Ramon
    1999    [1498] *An Account of the Antiquities of the Indians*. Duke University Press, Durham, NC.

Peros, Matthew C., Elizabeth Graham, and Anthony M. Davis
    2006    Stratigraphic Investigations at Los Buchillones, a Taìno Site on the North Coast of Central Cuba: Evidence from Geochemistry, Mineralogy, Paleontology, and Sedimentology. *Geoarchaeology* 21(5): 403–428.

Peros, Matthew C., Eduard G. Reinhardt, and Anthony M. Davis
    2007    A 6000 Cal Yr Record of Ecological and Hydrological Changes from Laguna de la Leche, North Coastal Cuba. *Quarternary Research* 67: 69–82.

Peterson, Nicole, and Kenneth Broad
    2009    Climate and Weather Discourse in Anthropology: From Determinism to Uncertain Futures. In *Anthropology and Climate Change: From Encounters to Actions*, ed. S. Crate and M. Nuttall. Left Coast Press, Walnut Creek, CA, pp. 70–86.

Ramcharan, Eugene K.
    2004    Mid-to-Late Holocene Sea Level Influence on Coastal Wetland Development in Trinidad. *Quaternary International* 120: 145–151.

Redman, Charles L., and Ann P. Kinzig
2003    Resilience of Past Landscapes: Resilience Theory, Society, and the Longue Durée. *Conservation Ecology* 7(1): 1–14.

Rosen, Arlene
In press    Change and Stability in an Uncertain Environment: Foraging Strategies in the Levant from the Early Natufians through the End of the Pre-Pottery Neolithic A. In *Environmental Risk and Resilience as Long Term Factors of Culture Change*, ed. N. F. Miller and K. Moore. University of Pennsylvania Press, Philadelphia.

Samson, Alice V.M.
2010    *Renewing the House: Trajectories of Social Life in the Yucayeque (Community) of El Cabo, Higüey, Dominican Republic, AD 800 to 1504.* Sidestone, Leiden.

Saunders, Mark A., and Adam S. Lea
2008    Large Contribution of Sea Surface Warming to Recent Increase in Atlantic Hurricane Activity. *Nature* 451: 557–560.

Scheffers, Sander R., Jay Haviser, Tony Browne, and Anja Scheffers
2009    Tsunamis, Hurricanes, the Demise of Coral Reefs and Shifts in Prehistoric Human Populations in the Caribbean. *Quaternary International* 194(1–2): 69–87.

Schinkel, Kees
1992    The Golden Rock Features. In *The Archaeology of St. Eustatius the Golden Rock Site,* ed. A. Versteeg and K. Schinkel. Publication of the St. Eustatius Historical Foundation 2. St. Eustatius Historical Foundation, St. Eustatius, Virgin Islands, pp. 143–212.

Siegel, Peter E., John G. Jones, Deborah M. Pearsall, and Daniel P. Wagner
2001    Culture and Environment in Prehistoric Puerto Rico. *Proceedings of the 18th International Congress for Caribbean Archaeology* 18: 281–290.
2005    Environmental and Cultural Correlates in the West Indies: A View from Puerto Rico. In *Ancient Borinquen: Archaeology and Ethnohistory of Native Puerto Rico,* ed. P. E. Siegel. University of Alabama Press, Tuscaloosa, pp. 88–121.

Steadman, David W., Paul S. Martin, Ross D.E. MacPhee, A.J.T. Jull, Gregory McDonald, Charles A. Woods, Manuel Iturralde-Vinent, and Gregory W.L. Hodgins
2005    Asynchronous Extinction of Late Quaternary Sloths on Continents and Islands. In *Proceedings of the National Academy of Sciences of the United States of America,* ed. W. R. Dickinson; originally published on-line on August 5, 2005, doi:10.1073/pnas.0502777102, pp. 11763–11768.

Tabio, Ernesto E.
1995    *Introducción a la Arqueología de las Antillas.* Editorial de Ciencias Sociales, La Habana.

Toscano, Marguerite A., and Ian G. Macintyre
2003    Corrected Western Atlantic Sea-Level Curve for the Last 11,000 Years Based on Calibrated 14C Dates from *Acropora palmata* Framework and Intertidal Mangrove Peat. *Coral Reefs* 22: 257–270.

Valcárcel Rojas, Roberto

2002    *Inundaciones y Sociedad Aborigen en el Territorio de los Municipios Mayari y Sagua de Tanamo*. Departamento Centro, Oriental de Arqueologia, Holguin, Cuba.

Valcárcel Rojas, Roberto, Jago Cooper, Jorge Calvera Rosés, Odalys Brito, and Marcos Labrada

2006    Postes en el Mar: Excavación de una estructura constructiva aborigen en Los Buchillones. *El Caribe Arqueológico* 9: 76–88.

## UNDERSTANDING HAZARDS, MITIGATING IMPACTS, AVOIDING DISASTERS

### Statement for Policy Makers and the Disaster Management Community

Five thousand years of human experience in the Caribbean can provide important lessons for modern-day policy makers and practitioners working with the impacts of climate change in the region. Case studies in this chapter show that regional climate change creates unavoidable threats to everyone living in the islands of the Caribbean. However, different communities' relative experience of these threats is entirely dependent on very local conditions and the lifestyle choices of different societies. The importance of the way local conditions affect the experience of environmental hazards highlights the fact that centralized planning strategies at national or international scales currently fail to prepare people for what they will experience and how they should best prepare themselves.

The reliance of Precolumbian mitigation strategies on local preparation for local threats greatly helped reduce vulnerability in the past. This chapter reveals that the Precolumbian selection of secure settlement locations, the creation of diverse food distribution networks, and the use of readily rebuilt household architecture maximized the potential for mitigation based on local environmental conditions. These Precolumbian lifeways contrast strongly with modern-day lifestyles in the Caribbean that have been strongly influenced by non-local European and North American traditions. Examples such as the colonial legacy of European selection of river valley settlement locations or more recent developments, such as the centralized distribution of non-local food staples and the development of architectural designs reliant on imported materials, highlight changes in the Caribbean that have increased vulnerability to known hazards in the region.

A clear argument arises from this research that the current focus on short-term "impact" mitigation in the Caribbean is emphasized at the expense of more robust preparation and reconstruction strategies that take into account the complexity of decision-making in human societies and the need for long-term strategies to change human behavior. Such a lesson shows the importance of local education strategies that try to foster improved traditional ecological knowledge within communities that helps people understand the nature of the threats they face and feel empowered to plan for themselves. Both in the past and in the present, the real "cost" of an environmental disaster is often not from the "event" itself but from the weeks, months, and years of devastation that ensue. The devastating impacts of sea level rise, rainfall change, and hurricane activity are inevitable for modern-day communities in the Caribbean. Therefore this research suggests adopting the perspective of how quickly human communities can return to "life as before" rather than focusing on how robustly they can "withstand" the inevitable hazards that loom on the horizon. Practitioners' work should emphasize local education, decentralized planning empowerment, and post-impact reconstruction. The current reliance on centralized power structures for dealing with the impacts of climate change in the Caribbean fosters a dangerous sense of absolved responsibility and highlights why the lessons from the past, contained in this chapter, are important for the challenges of the future.

# FIVE

# Collation, Correlation, and Causation in the Prehistory of Coastal Peru

*Daniel H. Sandweiss and Jeffrey Quilter*

To the casual visitor and even many archaeologists, the mountains and deserts of Peru (figure 5.1) appear timeless and unchanging. Indeed, mountains are frequently metaphors for long-term stability and slow change: "how many years can a mountain exist, before it is washed to the sea?" asked Bob Dylan. So, too, the coastal strip shared by much of Chile and Peru hosts one of the driest deserts in the world (figure 5.2), which imbues the visitor with a sense of constancy. Regional archaeology features a great variety of unearthed artifacts made of perishable materials—wood, bone, shell, cloth—that would have disintegrated long ago in other environments. Subspecialties in scholarship have developed from the products of the dry, coastal environment: textile experts who study brightly colored, intricately woven textiles of coastal Peru, and biological anthropologists who can investigate ancient diseases and pathologies thanks to well-preserved human remains. But the apparent stability of the landscape of western South America belies a highly dynamic geological and biophysical terrain.

To address issues of prehistoric human ecodynamics in this extraordinary place, we begin by describing the region. We then consider in general terms the methodological and epistemological challenges to understanding collation, correlation, and causation in the archaeological record, with particular reference to human-environment interaction. We conclude with a detailed case

**5.1.** *Map of Peru. Map by Daniel H. Sandweiss.*

study from coastal Peru (a medium-term perspective) and a longer-term perspective on millennial-scale trends in risk, population, and complexity in this extreme environment.

## THE CENTRAL ANDEAN COAST

The central Andean coast (figure 5.1) is subject to significant natural disasters that tend to recur frequently but without a predictable periodicity. The Andes are located on a subducting plate margin (the oceanic Nazca Plate is sliding

**5.2.** *Typical dunes on the Peruvian coast. Photo by Daniel H. Sandweiss.*

under the continental South American Plate), so the region experiences frequent seismic activity and volcanism. Earthquakes, volcanic eruptions, and the tsunamis sometimes associated with seismic activity have a devastating impact not only on the people but also on the towns, cities, and economic infrastructure, such as irrigation works systems (e.g., Giesecke and Silgado 1981). However, because of the unusual shallow-angle subduction under northern and central Peru, active volcanism does not occur here as it does in Ecuador and in southern Peru, Bolivia, northern Chile, and Argentina (Barazangi and Isacks 1976). Consequently, this sector of the central Andes lacks catastrophic volcanic eruptions.

El Niño Southern Oscillation (ENSO) dominates present-day climatic variability on inter-annual timescales in the tropics and involves both the atmosphere and the ocean in the tropical Pacific (e.g., Maasch 2008). On the central Andean coast, El Niño warms near-shore waters, bringing torrential rainfall to the land and depressed biotic productivity to the adjacent ocean. Frequency, intensity, and duration of El Niño events generally follow a latitudinal gradient, decreasing toward the south. However, each event is different, and rainfall can skip valleys or occur in different sectors of valleys, with variable consequences. In this largely unvegetated region, the rains often lead to destructive flooding as well as plagues of insects and diseases. Earthquakes produce abundant debris on the landscape; El Niño flooding mobilizes this unconsolidated sediment, often resulting in coastal progradation (seaward expansion of the shoreline) and inland dune incursions (see Sandweiss et al. 2009 and discussion later in this chapter).

## CHALLENGES

To understand how short-, medium-, and long-term geological, climatological, and environmental processes are interrelated with one another and with human activities, we must take into account epistemological foundations and fundamental principles of scientific methodology. The epistemological issues concern the dimensions by which we measure phenomena under scrutiny, while the methodological concerns focus on relating phenomena and events to one another.

In attempting to insert rigor into archaeological investigations, many years ago Albert C. Spaulding (1960) underscored the importance of distinguishing among three different analytical dimensions: space, time, and form. By definition, a dimension is a phenomenon that requires its own measuring device, and such is the case for these three. The distance from, say, Cambridge, Massachusetts, to Orono, Maine, is a constant (so long as it is "as the crow flies" or along the same route) and is measured in kilometers, miles, or some other standardized units. The time it takes to get from one city to the other, however, varies depending on mode of travel and many other factors and is measured by time units that may be expressed as minutes, hours, days, or even weeks (depending on the traffic). One measurement system cannot be converted into the other, and neither the distance between the cities nor the time it takes to travel to them can be converted into "form." Time itself is a form of measurement. It marks change and duration. As in the cases of space and time, form has its own intelligibility. It comprises not only the shape of things but also their qualities, such as color and texture (see Wagensberg 2008).

Investigators, whether archaeologists, Shakespearean scholars, or crime detectives, commonly use secure information in one dimension to infer information in one or more others. "Secure information" is often derived from generalized principles or laws. For example, the geological law of superposition (that, without later modification, lower strata are older than upper strata) is used to infer that differences between the fossils or artifacts distinctive to particular strata or ranges of strata represent change through time. Form— the distinctive fossils or artifacts—and (the products of) time—the inferred change—are thus accounted for in such exercises.

Fairly commonly, secure information in two dimensions aids in learning something in the third dimension. For example, the consistent identification of artifacts with distinctive attributes, such as decoration or mode of manufacture (formal dimension), within a restricted geographical region (spatial dimension) may help to identify or at least narrow the range of possibilities for the time period of their use or popularity in a new region of investigation when the time of use is known elsewhere. These simple rules for relating data from different dimensions have wide use and are essential for many different kinds of studies.

As we are concerned with changing human-environmental relations over time, issues of relations between the formal and temporal dimensions are particularly relevant to our interests. We chronicle forms that endure or change through time, and we are interested in the relationships of different forms to one another through time, such as different settlement types in relation to environmental changes.

This leads us to issues of collation, correlation, and causation (Sandweiss and Quilter 2008), which are steps in a chain of increasingly significant activities leading to plausible explanations for past events. They are mutually and sequentially dependent on one another so that without collation, the other two steps cannot be carried out and without correlation, causation cannot be reasonably posited.

Collation is the demonstration that events occurred simultaneously. We collate manuscript papers by placing them together in the same pile or group, and we collate events by showing that they occurred at the same time. This first and apparently simple step is extremely difficult to achieve in archaeology, however, especially for short-term events. As with most things in archaeology, when the temporal scales of events are of long duration, we can be fairly confident in collating them. For example, we can collate a gradual decrease in rainfall with changing environments and settlement patterns by showing that these events occurred at the same time. So long as anthropological archaeology saw change as slow, within evolutionary or neo-evolutionary theoretical frameworks, the focus was on looking at the "big picture" and concomitant big events. With an awareness of the potential for short-term events to have long-term consequences, such as in punctuated equilibrium, we are faced with the difficulty of trying to collate events when chronological measuring devices in archaeology are generally coarse, with resolutions at a century or half-century scale at best. Except in rare and special cases, for now and perhaps the foreseeable future there is no solution to this problem except to wait for more precise temporal measuring tools that will allow for tighter collations of events of interest to be made.

There are cases in which we can make tighter collations, however. For instance, if we excavate a shell heap and find a mollusk shell that incorporates growth or geochemical anomalies known to be caused by El Niño, we can infer that the associated stratum was deposited very close in time to the event (although various exceptions can be raised). More broadly, we can look at environmental history encoded in a shell across its lifespan and know something about conditions and changes in conditions for that span and thus for associated archaeological events. Over time, the development of collations of these kinds can lead to fairly robust data sets that can be inferred to have value in developing correlations.

Correlation, in formal terms, refers to demonstrating that events of interest covary in a statistically significant way. Correlation therefore requires even more rigor than does collation in linking events occurring through time. To continue with the case previously mentioned, the observation that, for a particular region, there was a change in rainfall in the past and that at the same time there was a changing environment and that, further, human settlement patterns appear to have changed while these other events were taking place must be more strongly associated to proceed further, to causation. In archaeology it is often difficult if not impossible to show covariance in a statistically significant way. This is again a result of the high values for standard deviations in our attempts to gain confidence that events are occurring at the same time and because it is hard to know what to quantify, how to quantify it, and how to establish an acceptable degree of uncertainty in what we might consider significant covariance.

A significant challenge in archaeology is the fact that our sample size is commonly very small and the population from which it is drawn is usually, at best, highly uncertain while the universe from which it was taken is invariably unknown. There is commonly high variability in the distribution of archaeological materials throughout a site, even if the site itself is fairly well delimited. The quantity and distribution of shells or human burials in middens may vary considerably from one place to another within the entire distribution of middens. Although archaeologists commonly employ stratified and other forms of random sampling of deposits, we cannot always rely on these methods to provide information about the overall quantity and nature of the materials that could be sampled.

As might be expected, causation is the most difficult level of all of these linked investigative procedures. Events as rapid, obvious, and well reported as the eruption of Vesuvius can clearly document, following our example, that a settlement pattern changed as a result of environmental factors. "Quality" here is important: a well-known case of a volcanic eruption that sent waves of ashes (whether at Pompeii or Ceren [Sheets 2006]) leaves little doubt as to the cause of what we might banally refer to as a "change in settlement."

In the case noted earlier—the changing rainfall-environment-settlement pattern chain that could be collated and might be correlated—it becomes much more difficult to move to the next level of causation, simply because human beings are complex and their reasons for doing things may or may not be a result of other events that are seen to collate or correlate. What appear to be clear-cut cases of intense causal agents, such as volcanoes, do not always provide sufficient evidence for causality. Volcanic eruptions have the advantage (for archaeologists at least) that most societies lack the capacity to clean up after them, but both hurricanes and earthquakes are short-term, strong causal agents that may leave few archaeological traces after sufficient time has passed and recovery has occurred (see, for instance, Wilkerson 2008). The degree to which societies are vulnerable even to volcanoes, however, is highly variable, as is the rate of recovery (Sheets 2008). The same must therefore hold true for other disasters, with the precise nature of the catastrophe, the rate at which it occurs, and the various components of the society experiencing the catastrophic process all playing important roles in how events play out in human terms.

## SCALES

Consideration of intense causal agents leads us to ponder the scales of impacts, societies, and responses. Scales cannot be seen as isolates, however, because size alone is insufficient to understand processes occurring through time. Just as a single drop of water on a boulder will have little effect but many drops of water over a long time will bore a hole through granite, so, too, small events over long periods of time can have grand consequences. Again, when archaeology is encumbered by coarse resolution in its view of phenomena in the three dimensions of space, time, and form, it is forced to look mostly at large-scale impacts occurring on grand societal levels and to see responses on similar scales.

The chronologies archaeologists commonly create are cultural-historical periods. They consequently represent major ruptures in human societies and, frequently, drastic environmental change as well. This creates its own problems in that many different events are seen as collated and correlated, but causation, especially simple, straightforward, mono-causal varieties, becomes elusive. Whether it be the Roman Empire or the Classic Maya, the breakdown of what appear to have been relatively stable (though, in reality, constantly changing) systems seems to occur in many different sectors of the natural and cultural worlds simultaneously. Even if causation could theoretically be narrowed to a few key components of the system, doing so becomes extremely difficult for archaeologists, who should take some comfort in the fact that it seems equally elusive for historians who often claim superior data sets for understanding the past.

The relation of the complexity of a system to its ability to withstand changes in its environment is, fittingly, a complex issue. *Complexity* is a loaded term, especially when applied to human cultures or social systems, and, as noted earlier, simplistic notions of sociocultural evolution no longer seem valid as approaches to understanding the long-term human story. The classic case of the Western Desert Aborigines can be cited. Their technology might be termed "stone age" by a previous generation of anthropologists, but it is actually highly efficient and technologically sophisticated—as in the case of compound tools that, in Swiss Army knife fashion, provide multiple working edges and surfaces in a single, light, portable instrument (Gould 1970). Furthermore, while Aboriginal technology *might* be considered simple, Western Desert kinship systems are among the world's most complex. Because it was important to them, Western Desert Aborigines easily kept track of marriage rules and clan affiliations that can boggle the mind of an outsider. Finally, both the technology and the social system of the Western Desert Aborigines were potentially the products of the same number of centuries as Western European or East Asian systems, so they cannot be assumed to be some kind of relicts from the past.

At the same time we can recognize that ethnographically known, apparently simple societies are not so simple and that they are not fossils of a distant past, we are faced with the demonstrated fact that, in broad view, human life on the planet has gone through dramatic changes since the Lower Paleolithic, as Timothy Kohler states so elegantly in his chapter in this volume. Long ago, V. Gordon Childe (1925) emphasized the Neolithic, Urban, and Industrial Revolutions; since then, other scholars have noted additional dramatic changes, such as the Broad Spectrum Revolution (Flannery 1969), among others. However many revolutions one wishes to cite, the underlying fact of the matter is that 30,000 or 40,000 years ago, all humans were hunter-gatherers. Through time, the number of hunter-gatherers has diminished while the number of agriculturalists has grown, and, increasingly, more people are living in urban centers and are not directly involved with food production. These changes have been accompanied by a great number of others, such as increased dependence on fossil fuels and the machinery that runs on them and, more recently, on computer technology. All of these changes and more have occurred on an increasingly global scale, so even people who do not have many machines or computers are affected by them.

These global changes can be referred to as increasing "complexity" in the sense that Emile Durkheim (1984 [1893]) proposed that societies consist of increasingly specialized subunits that interrelate in complex ways. Recently, Ian Hodder (2006) has referred to the increasing "entanglements" people have with material culture, including such things as infrastructure, on which people become dependent and which consequently traps them in systems of dependency. For Peru, this trend is clear in the change from early gathering-fishing-hunting communities that had low investments in complex infrastructure and so could adapt to changing circumstances, such as the dramatic changes in resource availability and locations during El Niño events and the increasing complexity and entanglements that occurred with the growth in dependence on irrigation agriculture, urban settlements, and the associated socio-political and economic systems that were tied to them.

**5.3.** *The Ascope Canal in the Chicama Valley is reputed to have been built by the Chimu (ca. AD 1100–1450), though irrigation systems are notoriously difficult to date. Photo by Jeffrey Quilter.*

The advantages of mobility and flexibility in the face of changing circumstances that existed in Peru and everywhere else during early prehistory also had negative aspects. One price of irrigation agriculture was a reduction in the number of buffering mechanisms that could overcome short-term shortages and other recurring negative events that could not be solved by moving to a different place or exploiting a different resource. Through time, the challenges of the "known unknowns" of preparing for the next famine were met by narrowing the range of subsistence strategies to grains and other foods that could be stored for relatively long terms and by building infrastructure—irrigation canals (figure 5.3) and storage facilities—that would both maximize the amount of resources ("quantity is its own kind of quality") and provide buffering systems, through storage, to get through the bad times.

Once Peruvian coastal economies became dependent on irrigation agriculture as the primary means of subsistence, issues of resilience, vulnerability, and hazards arose similar to those of the Hohokam, as discussed by Margaret Nelson and her colleagues in this volume. A future comparison of the two situations might be enlightening, especially because while many of the advantages and disadvantages of irrigation agriculture were similar in both societies, there was also a fundamental difference. In the case of coastal Peru, the huge protein larder of the Humboldt fisheries provided a distinct advantage in surviving times when agriculture failed. A further complication is that maritime resources primarily provided protein while agriculture mostly offered carbohydrates in the form of maize and tubers, though the importance of beans, fruits, and other foods is not to be taken lightly.

Whether foragers, fisherfolk, or agriculturalists, it is the "unknown unknowns" that create the most problems when those unknowns provide challenges to prosperity or survival that cannot be met successfully or, sometimes, at all. Commonly, short- or medium-term successful adaptations have within them the seeds of their own downfall. Common examples include directly overexploiting a resource or creating a situation that indirectly results in the unsustainability of what was thought to be a stable adaptive system. The latter includes such activities as short- or medium-term behaviors that have long-term consequences.

While many generalizations can be made regarding general patterns of human-environmental relations, as well as the theories and methodologies by which we may try to understand past events, much depends on the particular circumstances of a given region and the people who inhabit it. Science depends as much on induction as on deduction, and thus we will turn to the specific conditions of coastal Peru to explore many of the issues presented earlier from both a particularist and a general perspective.

## CONTRIBUTIONS

### Key Hazards

We do our research in an extreme environment—the central and north coast of Peru. Because the area is lapped by the Pacific Ocean and lies well within the tropics (between about 3°30' and 18°20' S latitude), those unfamiliar with the region might imagine balmy waters and waving palms. The truth is far different, however. The coastline shared by northern Chile and Peru (see figure 5.1) is one of the world's driest deserts (no palm trees without irrigation) thanks to the rain shadow effect of the Andes Mountains rising abruptly to the east and the cool Humboldt or Peru Current that sweeps up the western side of South America from the Antarctic (no balmy waters) (Lettau and Lettau 1978).

Despite the general lack of precipitation, however, humans have inhabited the Peruvian and Chilean coast for at least 13,000 years (Sandweiss 2008; Sandweiss et al. 1998). Over time, populations grew, socio-political complexity emerged, and eventually large-scale empires arose. The economic basis for these developments rested on two key environmental factors: the high productivity of the marine environment resulting from intense nutrient upwelling in the Peru Current, and the potential for irrigation agriculture using water from streams arising in the adjacent Andes and flowing west to the coast (Moseley 1992, 2001).

Extreme aridity is not the only disaster that plagues the South American coast. The Andes Mountains exist for a reason: the oceanic Nazca Plate is subducting under the South American continental plate along the western margin of Peru and Chile, pushing up the Andes and causing frequent earthquakes (see Lamb 2006). On August 15, 2007, for instance, a magnitude 8.0 earthquake struck near Ica on the coast south of Peru, killing hundreds of people and destroying tens of thousands of buildings (Quakes 2007). Many sectors of the Andes also suffer volcanic eruptions, although the north-central part of Peru on which we focus does not experience this disaster; here, the Nazca Plate is subducting at a shallower angle than elsewhere, so it does not go deep enough to melt and produce magma (Barazangi and Isacks 1976).

"Normal" conditions, consisting of a cool ocean and arid land, are interrupted at irregular intervals by El Niño, the eastern Pacific expression of the inter-annual climatic perturbation known as El Niño Southern Oscillation (NOAA n.d.). El Niño warms the coastal waters from Ecuador south into Chile. This has consequences on land and sea. In the ocean, deepening of the thermocline (the boundary between warmer, mixed surface water and deep, cooler water) suppresses nutrient upwelling. From plankton up the food chain to small and large fish, birds, and sea mammals, major El Niño events result in tremendous loss of biomass through mortality and out-migration (e.g., Barber and Chávez 1983). Some northern, warm-adapted species migrate south along the coast and replace the local biota that has died or headed even further south, but total available biomass is significantly reduced.

On land, the warmer sea surface temperatures lead to convective storms. Rain in a desert disrupts the "normal" system when people have adapted to aridity. With a tectonically destabilized hydrological system, abundant earthquake-produced debris, and little vegetation to hold surface sediment in place, El Niño rains cause destructive erosion. In today's regime, floods blow out roads, bridges, and buildings (see, for instance, photos from the 1982–1983 El Niño in Canby [1984]). People drown. Standing water creates breeding grounds for insects that carry diseases such as malaria and dengue fever, and plagues of locusts and rodents consume crops not destroyed by the floods. The early colonial inhabitants of the northern coastal region faced these same hazards, as dramatically described by local witnesses following the first major El Niño event of the Colonial period, in 1578 (Copson and Sandweiss 1999; Huertas 2001; Quilter 2011). One, a Spanish priest in the Lambayeque Valley, described the attempts at farming after the rains:

> After the canals were fixed, the Indians hurried to plant and there came the
> plagues ... such that any seed that grew a hand's width above the ground

was eaten by crickets and locusts and some green worms and yellow ones and other black ones that were bred from the putrefaction of the earth because of the said rains . . . [After several plantings], when the fruit was ready to harvest there was such a multitude of mice that this witness didn't believe the Indians and went to some fields and saw mounds of mice like piles of sand . . . the mice were the size of medium rabbits . . . This witness counted a mound of them and there were 500 more or less. (Francisco de Alcocer 2001 [1580]: 42 [f. 220v./221r.]; authors' translation)

The hazards associated with El Niño are bad enough, but the risks to humans on the Peruvian coast are even worse because of synergistic interactions, what Michael Moseley has called convergent catastrophes (e.g., Moseley 1999; Satterlee et al. 2001). Following earlier work on coastal processes and prehistory (Moseley and Richardson 1992; Moseley, Wagner, and Richardson 1992; Sandweiss 1986), Moseley and his colleagues have identified a devastating suite of sequential disasters for the Peruvian coast (Sandweiss et al. 2009).

Earthquakes destabilize the drainage system and produce loose debris on the largely barren desert surface. El Niño–driven floods then erode the surface, moving the debris into the rivers and out to the shoreline. In addition to destruction by flooding of planting surfaces and infrastructure such as houses and canals, El Niño brings diseases and crop plagues while depressing productivity in the marine environment.

The sediment that reaches the coast forms large, temporary deltas at river mouths and then gets strung out along the shore to the north as beach ridges. This reduces the extent and productivity of intertidal zones. Sand from the beach ridges blows inland on the constant onshore breezes (see figure 5.2), eventually covering field systems and reducing agricultural productivity.

### Past Impacts

Working with Peruvian archaeologist Ruth Shady—who has been excavating large Late Preceramic sites such as Caral (figure 5.4) in the Supe Valley (e.g., Shady Solis 2005; Shady Solis, Haas, and Creamer 2001), 200 km north of Lima—Moseley, Sandweiss, and colleagues were able to track the coastal disaster sequence beginning about 3,800 years ago (Sandweiss et al. 2009). Several sites had clear evidence of earthquake damage followed by reconstruction. A massive beach ridge formed along the shore and eventually blanketed about 100 km of coastline. Bays filled with sediment, and sand began blowing inland. In several sites, sand deposits were covered by a final construction level, less well made than earlier structures, and then the sites were abandoned.

In the Supe case, collation is clear, frozen in time by human construction. Given the tight chronology, there is almost certainly correlation between the disasters and the human activities culminating in abandonment. Whether the

**5.4.** *Two of the six major mounds at the Late Preceramic site of Caral in the Supe Valley, Peru, the largest Late Preceramic site on the Peruvian coast. Photo by Daniel H. Sandweiss.*

disasters were causative remains an intractable question, though it is tempting to assign them some role in the regional cultural changes at the end of the Late Preceramic Period. It may help to look at this case from a broader spatial and temporal perspective. First, "abandonment" refers strictly to the monumental sites; we do not know what happened to the population of the Supe and adjacent valleys after the large sites fell out of use. This is an urgent topic for future research. Second, monumental, preceramic, or aceramic sites continued for several hundred years on the peripheries of the Supe Culture area, to the north at Salinas de Chao (Alva 1986) and to the south at El Paraíso (Quilter 1985), beyond the reach of the massive beach ridge that fed the invading sand sheets. Were these sites homes to different societies with different cultural dynamics? Were they successful for longer simply because they were safe from the sand and other disasters? Did they receive migrants fleeing the Supe area who enhanced their labor pools and contributed to their longer survival as monumental sites?

Regardless of whether synergistic disasters caused the cessation of monument building by the Supe Culture, earthquakes, El Niño, and related coastal processes continue to operate in the region today. Because these processes interact at an intermediate timescale, over the course of decades, modern planners are unlikely to take them into account. These are the kinds of lessons for today that archaeology can draw from the past because of its privileged view of human-environment interaction at intermediate (decadal) to long (centennial to millennial) timescales.

Turning to a longer timescale, we see an intriguing pattern in the relation among demography, complexity, and risk from disasters on the Peruvian coast. Through time, population grew, though it is notoriously difficult to quantify prehistoric population levels. To substantiate our assertion of the direction and approximate rates of growth, we spliced and smoothed John Rick's (1987) radiocarbon date–based curve for the Preceramic Period (ca. 13,000–3600 calendar years before present) with David Wilson's (1988) site survey–based curve for the coastal Santa Valley (~9°S) for the Initial Period through the Middle Horizon (ca. 3,600 to 1,000 years ago, or 1600 BC to AD 1000).

For the final two prehistoric periods, the Late Intermediate Period time of the north coast Chimu Empire and the Late Horizon or Inca Empire (ca. AD 1000–1532), Wilson's curve shows a population decline in the Santa Valley; however, he recognizes that continuity in the local ceramic tradition may mask the continued occupation of sites under Chimu and Inca domination. Considering ethno-historic records relating to population at the time of the Spanish Conquest in AD 1532 (e.g., Cook 1981) and broader archaeological patterns (e.g., Moseley 2001), our figures (5.5–5.8) show continued population growth through these final two prehistoric periods. The early historical record is very clear on the demographic disaster that followed the Spanish Conquest, with depopulation ratios of as much as 100:1 in less than a century for some coastal valleys (Cook 1981).

The archaeological record shows a general increase in social complexity through time along the coast (e.g., Moseley 2001; Richardson 1994). The earliest settlers were mobile or semi-sedentary hunter-fisher-gatherers (Sandweiss in press) who became sedentary shortly before 5,000 years ago, when they began to build large monuments. Despite fluctuation in monument building, such as the Supe case outlined earlier, the volume of construction and the nature of social and economic organization evidenced in the archaeological record and (for the latest period) in the ethno-historic record show a general trend toward larger volumes and more complex arrangements.

The frequency of volcanism and tectonically driven earthquake and tsunami activity should not have fluctuated through the time of human occupation; these events do not have a regular recurrence interval but do recur at average rates through time that are independent of climate on a human timescale. In contrast, El Niño frequency did change throughout the period of human occupation of Peru (Keefer et al. 1998; Rein et al. 2005; Sandweiss et al. 2007), and we therefore use El Niño as our proxy for risk (figures 5.5–5.8).

- From ca. 13,000 to 8,000 years ago, El Niño occurred at an unknown frequency; we assess risk as high, but complexity and population were low (figure 5.5).

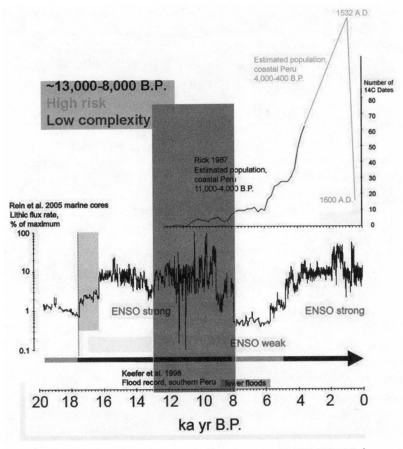

**5.5.** *Population, risk, and complexity on the Peruvian coast, 13,000–8000 BP (years before present/AD 1950). Population curve drawn from Cook (1981), Moseley (2001), Rick (1987), and Wilson (1988) (see text). Risk is based on frequency/ intensity of El Niño, from Rein et al. (2005) and Sandweiss et al. (2007). Complexity is based on the authors' experience and the general literature (e.g., Moseley 2001; Richardson 1994). Figure drafted by Kurt Rademaker.*

- From ca. 8000 to 6000 cal BP, few or no El Niño events took place, coastal waters were seasonally warmer than present in northern Peru, and there was probably seasonal rainfall north of 10°S. At this time, population began to grow but remained low overall. Complexity increased as the first sedentary villages were founded. Risk was minimal (figure 5.6).

- From ca. 6,000 to 3,000 years ago, El Niño events were strong but infrequent; coastal waters were cool along all of Peru. Complexity increased with the onset of large-scale monument building, evidence of different

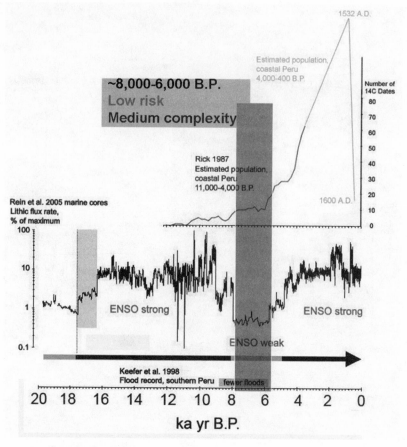

**5.6.** *Population, risk, and complexity on the Peruvian coast, 8000–6000 BP. See figure 5.5 caption for sources. Figure drafted by Kurt Rademaker.*

social classes at monumental centers, and a diversifying economy. The rate of population growth increased notably (figure 5.7).

- From ca. 3000 cal BP to present, El Niño variability fluctuated within the range of modern variability. Population grew rapidly until the Spanish Conquest in the early 1530s and then plunged precipitously. Complexity also increased, from state-level societies to large (ultimately pan-Andean) empires (figure 5.8).

Though very broadly painted, this record shows that through the prehistoric era on the coast of Peru, increasing population and growing complexity were accompanied by ever greater risk from natural hazards. In stark contrast, the demographic collapse after the 1530s was *not* caused by natural disasters but instead resulted from human-induced disasters—warfare, economic and

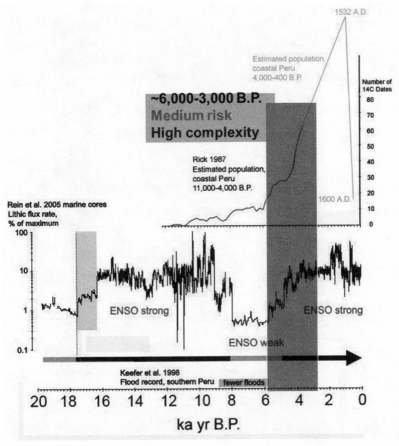

**5.7.** *Population, risk, and complexity on the Peruvian coast, 6000–3000 BP. See figure 5.5 caption for sources. Figure drafted by Kurt Rademaker.*

social disruption, and disease (Cook 1981; cf. Kiracofe and Marr 2009). This pattern seems counterintuitive at first glance but may hold important lessons.

## CONCLUSION

As noted earlier, the coarse resolution of archaeological views of the past results in many issues remaining unclear. The turbulent times of change between recognizable cultural periods are difficult to interpret. Even if fine-grained resolution were available, some issues would be elusive. For example, demographic collapse as a result of diseases that leave no easily recognizable signatures on human remains (especially in regions where only bones remain) would be hard

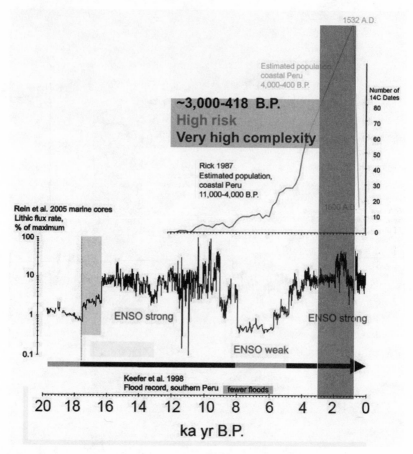

**5.8.** *Population, risk, and complexity on the Peruvian coast, 3000 BP–present. See figure 5.5 caption for sources. Figure drafted by Kurt Rademaker.*

to determine directly. Population drops marked by reduced village sizes may be difficult to recognize when archaeologists cannot be sure if particular houses were abandoned or, if abandonment is noted, of the reasons for a smaller population when many reasons are possible. These negative aspects of archaeological research must be balanced, however, with the discipline's great potential to examine long-term changes.

The clear pattern of increasing population sizes on the Peruvian coast, apparently throughout prehistory and certainly in its later phases, is a testament to humanity's success as a species in adapting to a challenging and changing environment. Embedded in this grand narrative are interesting questions about the shorter-term patterns of the rise and fall of what are generally termed "complex" societies. From a shorter-term perspective, complexity is never totally lost, but the geographic extent of complex systems and the proportion of the overall population incorporated at any given moment in a single system oscillated through time. Complexity, however conceived, came early to Peru, but there was a clear pattern of development followed by disintegration of complex systems over periods that appear to have lasted for more than a few generations. While these are among the most difficult archaeological periods to examine, they offer the potential of telling the most interesting stories, both in and of themselves and as means by which to understand how societies respond to stresses and reorganize themselves in their wake.

As a final note, if the growth in population in Peru is marked as a general success story, it seems clear that this is part of a general trend throughout the world. We are all too cognizant of the fact, however, that the general upward trend in growth of human populations is also tied to the increasing interconnectivity of events in one place in the globe with those in another. Indeed, the demographic collapse brought by the Spanish invasion was correlated with the introduction of new plant and animal species in both the Old World and the New. This process was the creation of the Modern World. As human populations are growing, they are not only becoming more interrelated but are also affecting the natural environment more radically. It remains to be seen whether the global natural-cultural system can be sustained for the long-term health of human inhabitants without undergoing drastic alterations that will be viewed as catastrophes by those who experience the sharpest changes.

## REFERENCES

Alcocer, F. de
  2001      Probanzas de indios y españoles referentes a las catastróficas lluvias de
  [1580]    1578, en los corregimientos de Trujillo y Saña. In *Diluvios andinos a través de las fuentes documentales*, comp. L. Huertas. Fondo Editorial Pontificia Universidad Católica del Perú, Lima, pp. 78–279.

Alva, W.
  1986      Las Salinas de Chao. *Materialien zur Allgemeinen und Vergleichenden Archäologie*, Band 34. Verlag, Munchen, Germany.

Barazangi, M., and B. L. Isacks
  1976      Spatial Distribution of Earthquakes and Subduction of the Nazca Plate beneath South America. *Geology* 4: 686–692.

Barber, R. T., and F. P. Chávez
  1983      Biological Consequences of El Niño. *Science* 222: 1203–1210.

Canby, T. Y.
  1984      El Niño's Ill Wind. *National Geographic* 165 (February): 144–183.

Childe, V. G.
  1925      *The Dawn of European Civilization.* Knopf, New York.

Cook, N. D.
1981　　*Demographic Collapse, Indian Peru, 1520–1620.* Cambridge University Press, New York.

Copson, W., and D. H. Sandweiss
1999　　Native and Spanish Perspectives on the 1578 El Niño. In *The Entangled Past: Integrating History and Archaeology,* ed. M. Boyd, J. C. Erwin, and M. Hendrickson. Proceedings of the 1997 Chacmool Conference. University of Calgary, Calgary, Alberta, pp. 208–220.

Durkheim, E.
1984　　*The Division of Labour in Society.* Translated by W. D. Hall. Macmillan,
[1893]　Basingstoke.

Flannery, K.
1969　　Origins and Ecological Effects of Early Domestication in Iran and the Near East. In *The Domestication and Exploitation of Plants and Animals,* ed. P. J. Ucko and G. W. Dimbleby. Aldine, Chicago, pp. 73–100.

Giesecke, A., and E. Silgado
1981　　*Terremotos en el Perú.* Ediciones Rikchay, Lima.

Gould, R. A.
1970　　Spears and Spear-Throwers of the Western Desert Aborigines of Australia. *American Museum Novitates* 2403: 1–42.

Hodder, I.
2006　　*The Leopard's Tale: Revealing the Mysteries of Catalhoyuk.* Thames and Hudson, London.

Huertas, L.
2001　　*Diluvios andinos a través de las fuentes documentales.* Fondo Editorial Pontificia Universidad Católica del Perú, Lima.

Keefer, D. K., S. D. deFrance, M. E. Moseley, J. B. Richardson III, D. R. Satterlee, and A. Day-Lewis
1998　　Early Maritime Economy and El Niño Events at Quebrada Tacahuay, Peru. *Science* 281: 1833–1835.

Kiracofe, J. B., and J. S. Marr
2009　　Marching to Disaster: The Catastrophic Convergence of Inca Imperial Policy, Sand Flies, and El Niño in the 1524 Andean Epidemic. In *El Niño, Catastrophism, and Culture Change in Ancient America,* ed. D. H. Sandweiss and J. Quilter. Dumbarton Oaks Research Library and Collection, Washington, DC, pp. 145–164.

Lamb, S.
2006　　*Devil in the Mountain: A Search for the Origin of the Andes.* Princeton University Press, Princeton, NJ.

Lettau, H. H., and K. Lettau
1978　　*Exploring the World's Driest Climate.* Center for Climatic Research, Institute for Environmental Studies, University of Wisconsin, Madison.

Maasch, K. A.
2008    El Niño and Interannual Variability of Climate in the Western Hemisphere. In *El Niño, Catastrophism, and Culture Change in Ancient America*, ed. D. H. Sandweiss and J. Quilter. Dumbarton Oaks Research Library and Collection, Washington, DC, pp. 33–55.

Moseley, M. E.
1992    Maritime Foundations and Multilinear Evolution: Retrospect and Prospect. *Andean Past* 3: 5–42.
1999    Convergent Catastrophe: Past Patterns and Future Implications of Collateral Natural Disasters in the Andes. In *The Angry Earth*, ed. A. Oliver-Smith and S. M. Hoffman. Routledge, New York, pp. 59–71.
2001    *The Inca and Their Ancestors*, rev. ed. Thames and Hudson, London.

Moseley, M. E., and J. B. Richardson III
1992    Doomed by Natural Disaster. *Archaeology* 45(6): 44–45.

Moseley, M. E., D. Wagner, and J. B. Richardson III
1992    Space Shuttle Imagery of Recent Catastrophic Change along the Arid Andean Coast. In *Paleoshorelines and Prehistory: An Investigation of Method*, ed. L. L. Johnson and M. Stright. CRC Press, Boca Raton, FL, pp. 215–235.

NOAA (National Oceanographic and Atmospheric Administration)
n.d.    El Niño Theme Page, http://www.pmel.noaa.gov/tao/elnino/el-nino-story.html.

Quakes
2007    http://earthquake.usgs.gov/earthquakes/recenteqsww/Quakes/us2007gbcv.php.

Quilter, J.
1985    Architecture and Chronology at El Paraíso, Peru. *Journal of Field Archaeology* 12: 279–297.
2011    Cultural Encounters at Magdalena de Cao, Viejo in the Early Colonial Period. In *Enduring Conquests: Rethinking the Archaeology of Resistance to Spanish Colonialism in the Americas*, ed. M. Liebmann and M. Murphy. School of American Research, Santa Fe, NM, pp. 103–125.

Rein, B., A. Lückge, L. Reinhardt, F. Sirocko, A. Wolf, and W.-C. Dullo
2005    El Niño Variability off Peru during the Last 20,000 Years. *Paleoceanography* 20: PA4003, doi:10.1029/2004PA001099.

Richardson, J. B., III
1994    *People of the Andes*. Smithsonian Institution Press, Washington, DC.

Rick, J.
1987    Dates as Data: An Examination of the Peruvian Preceramic Radiocarbon Record. *American Antiquity* 52: 55–73.

Sandweiss, D. H.
1986    The Beach Ridges at Santa, Peru: El Niño, Uplift, and Prehistory. *Geoarchaeology* 1: 17–28.

2008      Early Fishing Societies in Western South America. In *Handbook of South American Archaeology*, ed. H. Silverman and W. H. Isbell. Springer, New York, pp. 145–156.

In press    The Early Prehistory of the Central Andean Coast. In *The Cambridge Prehistory*, ed. C. Renfrew and P. Bahn. Cambridge University Press, Cambridge.

Sandweiss, D. H., K. A. Maasch, C.F.T. Andrus, E. J. Reitz, M. Riedinger-Whitmore, J. B. Richardson III, and H. B. Rollins
2007      Mid-Holocene Climate and Culture Change in Coastal Peru. In *Climatic Change and Cultural Dynamics: A Global Perspective on Mid-Holocene Transitions*, ed. D. G. Anderson, K. A. Maasch, and D. H. Sandweiss. Academic Press, San Diego, pp. 25–50.

Sandweiss, D. H., H. McInnis, R. L. Burger, A. Cano, B. Ojeda, R. Paredes, M. C. Sandweiss, and M. D. Glascock
1998      Quebrada Jaguay: Early Maritime Adaptations in South America. *Science* 281: 1830–1832.

Sandweiss, D. H., and J. Quilter
2008      Climate, Catastrophe, and Culture in the Ancient Americas. In *El Niño, Catastrophism, and Culture Change in Ancient America*, ed. D. H. Sandweiss and J. Quilter. Dumbarton Oaks Research Library and Collection, Washington, DC, pp. 1–11.

Sandweiss, D. H., R. Shady Solís, M. E. Moseley, D. K. Keefer, and C. R. Ortloff
2009      Environmental Change and Economic Development in Coastal Peru between 5,800 and 3,600 Years Ago. *Proceedings of the National Academy of Sciences* 106: 1359–1363.

Satterlee, D. R., M. E. Moseley, D. K. Keefer, and J. Tapia A.
2001      The Miraflores El Niño Disaster: Convergent Catastrophes and Prehistoric Agrarian Change in Southern Peru. *Andean Past* 6: 95–116.

Shady Solís, R.
2005      *La Civilización de Caral-Supe: 5000 Años de Identidad Cultural en el Perú.* Instituto Nacional de Cultura, Proyecto Especial Arqueológico Caral-Supe, Lima.

Shady Solís, R., J. Haas, and W. Creamer
2001      Dating Caral, a Preceramic Site in the Supe Valley on the Central Coast of Peru. *Science* 292: 723–726.

Sheets, P.
2006      *The Ceren Site: An Ancient Village Buried by Volcanic Ash in Central America*, 2nd ed. Case Studies in Archaeology. Thomson Wadsworth, Belmont, CA.

2008      Armageddon to the Garden of Eden: Explosive Volcanic Eruptions and Societal Resilience in Ancient Middle America. In *El Niño, Catastrophism, and Culture Change in Ancient America*, ed. D. H. Sandweiss and J. Quilter. Dumbarton Oaks Research Library and Collection, Washington, DC, pp. 167–186.

Spaulding, A. C.
  1960    The Dimensions of Archaeology. In *Essays in the Science of Culture in Honor of Leslie A. White*, ed. G. E. Dole and R. L. Carneiro. Thomas Y. Crowell, New York, pp. 437–456.

Wagensberg, J.
  2008    Understanding Form. *Biological Theory* 3: 325–335.

Wilkerson, S.J.K.
  2008    And the Waters Took Them: Catastrophic Flooding and Civilization on the Mexican Gulf Coast. In *El Niño, Catastrophism, and Culture Change in Ancient America*, ed. D. H. Sandweiss and J. Quilter. Dumbarton Oaks Research Library and Collection, Washington, DC, pp. 243–271.

Wilson, D. J.
  1988    *Prehispanic Settlement Patterns in the Lower Santa Valley, Peru: A Regional Perspective on the Origins and Development of Complex North Coast Society*. Smithsonian Institution Press, Washington, DC.

## UNDERSTANDING HAZARDS, MITIGATING IMPACTS, AVOIDING DISASTERS

### Statement for Policy Makers and the Disaster Management Community

Peru is famous for the soaring, seemingly ageless Andes Mountains and a coastal desert that preserves archaeological remains as if they had been abandoned decades instead of centuries ago. These impressions of long-term stability are illusions, however. Instead, the Andes and the coastal desert are the results of highly dynamic processes.

The jagged Andes are young mountains still in the process of forming as the Nazca Plate, under the ocean, pushes below the continent and shoves the mountains upward. The desert is a product of the cold, offshore Humboldt Current that prevents rain from falling on the coast. The pressure of the Nazca Plate results in a steady uplifting of the desert coast, while the pressures of the geological plates create volcanoes, earthquakes, and tsunamis. The slow uplift of the coast disrupts irrigation systems and other infrastructure in time periods that are best noted over the span of centuries and are thus imperceptible in a single human lifetime. Changes in the Humboldt Current and the release of pressure on the tectonic plates, however, occur suddenly and unexpectedly.

The overriding of the cold waters of the Humboldt by warm waters from the north is referred to as El Niño Southern Oscillation events, or "El Niño" events in the popular press. Once barely known, El Niños are now understood as related to distinct weather patterns throughout a huge area of the globe. Nevertheless, scientific understanding of how El Niños are patterned is still under investigation. The only way to fully investigate this issue and related events is through archaeology and allied sciences because they provide views of (pre)history in remote times.

There are challenges to archaeological investigations of past human-environment interaction, but they do not hinder them. In our chapter we present a long-term view of hazards and the human response for the desert coast of Peru and then focus on a specific example of synergistic hazards. At the broader scale, we collate El Niño events and major cultural and population changes from 13,000 BP to the present. Through time, increasing population sizes and growing complexity correlate with greater risks from natural hazards, with implications for human resilience—as life became riskier, populations increased and so did social complexity until a human hazard, the Spanish Conquest, brought local societies to their knees and decimated their populations.

Looking specifically at the end of the first period of monumental society, we see synergistic hazards operating in ways that must still occur today. The chain of events starts with earthquakes producing debris. El Niño rains wash this debris to the coast, coastal processes expose the sand portion of the debris to the wind, and the sand turns agricultural fields into deserts. These processes are ongoing but at a timescale too great to be easily recognized except by extensive study.

Current research is starting to examine the details of human ecodynamics in these periods to see how specific societies responded to changing events and how we can learn of them for our own future.

# SIX

# Silent Hazards, Invisible Risks: Prehispanic Erosion in the Teotihuacan Valley, Central Mexico

*Emily McClung de Tapia*

The prehispanic urban center of Teotihuacan (ca. AD 1–650) dominated the landscape of a watershed situated in the northeast sector of the Basin of Mexico (figure 6.1), a closed hydrological basin characterized in prehispanic times by a lake system that has since been largely drained and otherwise modified in historical and modern times. It is the site of the first major city in the Americas, the capital of a complex state society that grew to dominate the basin and adjacent valleys of central Mexico, with contacts in southern Mesoamerica (Millon 1988). While the region undoubtedly offered an attractive habitat for early Holocene hunter-gatherer-fishers between volcanic events (González et al. 2006), the earliest agricultural settlements date much later, to approximately 1150 BC (Sanders, Parsons, and Santley 1979). The results of detailed settlement studies in the region provide a framework for understanding the evolution of human communities, their spatial distribution, and potential resource use (ibid.).

Paleoenvironmental studies in the Basin of Mexico have focused mainly on the Late Glacial Maximum and the Pleistocene-Holocene transition. Unfortunately, the period of human occupation is poorly represented as a result of inconsistent sedimentation, volcanic ash deposits, surface deflation, and the effects of tectonics; the last three to five millennia are usually grouped together as a single period marked by human impact, understood as agricultural activities and related deforestation.

**6.1.** *Prehispanic urban zone of Teotihuacan, Mexico. Photo by Horacio Tapia-McClung.*

## THE TEOTIHUACAN REGION

The study area is characterized today as semiarid, with a marked seasonal rainfall regime alternating between a rainy season from April-May to September-October and a dry season that dominates the remainder of the year. Average annual precipitation is approximately 500 mm, with some variation at different elevations, and average annual temperature is 15° C. Five main vegetation types are predominant: grassland, xerophytic scrub, oak scrub, oak forest, and aquatic vegetation. Elevation ranges and key plant taxa associated with these communities are summarized in table 6.1 (Castilla-Hernández and Tejero-Diez 1987; Rzedowski et al. 1964). Archaeological plant remains indicate that these communities, together with pine and mixed pine-oak forest, were present during prehispanic times (Adriano-Morán 2000; Adriano-Morán and McClung de Tapia 2008).

Although the Basin of Mexico bore witness to a long sequence of devastating volcanic eruptions, the Teotihuacan region itself (figure 6.2) seems to have been largely spared—at least since the Middle Holocene—perhaps because of its location north of a low range of hills that forms an eastern extension of the higher mountain chain known as the Sierra Nevada. The exception to this situation is evident in the southwestern portion of the alluvial plain, which drains into the former Lake Texcoco. Here, lacustrine sediments are mixed with volcanic ash from several tephras (Lamb et al. 2009). However, several millennia of natural events and human activities have modified the entire region, thus

**Table 6.1.** Present-day vegetation types in the Teotihuacan Valley, Mexico. Pine (*Pinus* spp.) or mixed pine-oak forest was present during the prehispanic period.

| Vegetation Type/Elevation Range | Key Species |
| --- | --- |
| Oak forest (3,000–3,050 masl) | *Quercus crassipes, Q. greggii, Q. mexicana* |
| Oak scrub (2,800–3,000 masl) | *Quercus frutex, Baccharis conferta, Eupatorium glabratum* |
| Xerophytic scrub (2,300–2,750 masl) | *Opuntia streptacantha, Zaluzania augusta, Mimosa aculeaticarpa* var. *biuncifera* |
| Grassland (2,400–3,050 masl) | *Buchloe dactyloides, Hilaria cenchroides, Bouteloua gracilis* |
| Aquatic vegetation (2,240–2,260 masl) | *Cyperus* spp., *Eleocharis* sp., *Hydrocotyl ranunculoides, Polygonum* spp., *Scoenoplectus tabernaemontani, S. pungens, Typha latifolia, Nymphaea* sp., *Potomogeton* sp. |
| Riparian Gallery (2,240–2,300 masl) | *Salix bonplandiana, Alnus glabrata, Populus arizonica, Taxodium micronatum, Fraxinus uhdei* |

Note: masl = meters above sea level.
*Sources:* Vegetation types: Castilla-Hernández and Tejero-Diez 1987; Rzedowski et al. 1964. Forest data: Adriano-Morán and McClung de Tapia 2008.

complicating the reconstruction of past landscapes and understanding of the challenges faced by human populations.

The enormous growth of Teotihuacan around approximately AD 200 has recently been attributed to the mass influx of migrants from the central and, especially, the southern sectors of the Basin of Mexico as a consequence of a catastrophic eruption of Popocatepetl, dated to around 100 BC–AD 70 (Plunket and Uruñuela 2006, 2008; cf. Siebe et al. 1996). Earlier investigators had noted the immense growth of the city around this time (Millon 1970, 1973), coincident with significant decline elsewhere in the basin (Sanders, Parsons, and Santley 1979). In the early years of the Basin of Mexico surveys, however, little was known about the sequence of volcanism and its impact on human communities in central Mexico, and almost no systematic geoarchaeological investigation was undertaken in the region until the late twentieth century (Cordova 1997; Córdova and Parsons 1997; Frederick 1997; Frederick, Winsborough, and Popper 2005; Hodge, Cordova, and Frederick 1996). Consequently, the apparent depopulation of a large part of the Basin of Mexico at the time of Teotihuacan expansion was hypothesized to be a result of the immense attraction offered by the growing city to the north—as a pilgrimage center and multiethnic enclave, a commercial hub, and similar attributes (Millon 1973). Obsidian mining and production were firmly controlled by the state, initially dependent on a source of black obsidian available within the valley close to Otumba and eventually expanding to dominate the source of green obsidian at Cerro de las Navajas north of Pachuca (ibid.;

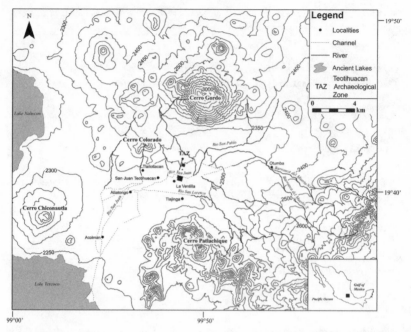

**6.2.** *Location of the Teotihuacan region in the Basin of Mexico, central Mexico. Map by Rodrigo Tapia-McClung.*

Sanders, Parsons, and Santley 1979). Diverse products were obtained from distant regions—ceramics, jade, and other types of greenstone; mineral and organic substances for the elaboration of paints; and animal species (live as well as skins), to name a few.

The Teotihuacan state collapsed around AD 600–650. While the direct causes are still open to discussion, growing evidence supports the idea that internal social conflicts were a potential factor and that the elite sector of the society gradually distanced itself from such mundane realities as meeting the subsistence needs of the highly controlled population (Gazzola 2009). Some authors have proposed that degradation of the landscape resulting from deforestation and exhaustion of the soils in the region may have provoked an ecological collapse at the end of the Classic period (Sanders 1965; Sanders, Parsons, and Santley 1979), while others have suggested that climate change affected the region (Manzanilla 1997). Although many references in the literature emphasize the city's destruction and subsequent abandonment, this appears to have been associated mainly with ceremonial areas in the central sector and high-status residential areas; overall population decline seems to have taken place over a period of about two centuries (Charlton and Nichols 1997; Cowgill 1974; Millon 1988). There is considerable evidence for the influx of new groups with different cultural traditions at the time of Teotihuacan's collapse (Manzanilla 2005; Rattray, Litvak, and Diaz 1981). A process of continual, albeit gradual, resettlement was apparent beginning around AD 900, culminating in a Late Postclassic (ca. AD 1350–1520) regional population estimated at around 150,000 inhabitants. Although this figure parallels the population at the height of the Classic Teotihuacan period, during the Aztec occupation several important administrative centers were dependent on the kingdom of Texcoco, but no single major urban center dominated the political scene (Evans 2001).

The jury is still out on these issues. Research in the Teotihuacan Valley has focused on developing a methodological approach to the study of landscape evolution in this highly modified setting and facilitating a better understanding of the relative dangers of sudden environmental change in the region (Lounejeva-Baturina et al. 2006, 2007; McClung de Tapia 2009; McClung de Tapia et al. 2003, 2004, 2005, 2008; Rivera-Uria et al. 2007; Sedov et al. 2010; Solleiro-Rebolledo et al. 2006).

## ADAPTIVE CYCLES AND HUMAN ECODYNAMICS AT TEOTIHUACAN

In an attempt to go beyond the description of the more evident components of the complex system of the Teotihuacan state and to focus on its interaction with the landscape within which the city was situated, the history of the region was explored within the framework of a socio-ecological system in which change was viewed in terms of resilience, adaptability, and transformability (Walker et al. 2004). If *resilience* is conceived as the capacity of a system to absorb perturbation and reorganize as a consequence of change, *adaptability* indicates the capacity of actors within the system to influence or manage resilience, and *transformability* refers to the ability to create a fundamentally new system when ecological, economic, or social structures render the present system unviable. The interaction among these variables determines either the direction of change in a socio-ecological system when stress surpasses latitude or the maximum degree of change the system can support before it can no longer recover.

On a superficial level, it appeared that the collapse of the Teotihuacan state and its effects on urban life represented the crossing of a threshold, as did the introduction of Colonial administration at the beginning of the sixteenth century. In fact, this latter event resulted in a major transformation. However, these events were considered from the perspective of the landscape's response rather than that of the political-economic systems, based on the assumption that it was necessary to develop a detailed understanding of what the environment may have been like at different moments in the past before the socio-ecological structure of prehispanic societies in the region could be analyzed. Although the importance of scale in understanding interactions was clear, no real idea existed of how the landscape operated at different temporal and spatial scales.

## CHALLENGES

One of the major challenges of this research has been to sort through modern and historical impacts on the landscape in an attempt to recognize evidence for processes and events dating to the Classic and Late Postclassic periods. Another challenge is presented by the generally poor preservation of organic remains in both archaeological contexts and soil profiles. Although a considerable amount of paleoethnobotanical investigation has been undertaken in the region, only after decades of research has it been possible to assemble a broad collection of macro- and micro-plant remains representative of the vegetation types that were present in the prehistoric past. In soils studied to date in the region, charcoal has rarely been recovered from stratigraphic contexts, and in many cases ceramics were absent as well (McClung de Tapia et al. 2005). Pollen is generally poorly preserved; however, although it has not been possible to quantify pollen data, it has been feasible to determine the key taxa consistently present in the samples from different time periods. On the other hand, phytoliths (silica particles formed in tissues of certain plants) are fairly well preserved, and types associated with grasses (subfamilies Pooideae, Panicoideae, Chloridoideae, and Aristoideae) are predominant (McClung de Tapia et al. 2008).

The instability of the landscape over time, together with a long history of perturbations, limited the kinds of soil analyses that could be successfully employed in large parts of the region. Soil properties that are not affected by diagenesis (physical and chemical changes occurring through time) and that are deemed indicators of "soil memory" have been studied in numerous profiles (vertical cross-sections) throughout the area (Rivera-Uria et al. 2007; Solleiro-Rebolledo et al. 2006). In addition, radiocarbon dating as well as the determination of stable carbon isotope ratios ($\delta^{13}C$) have been carried out for selected soil horizons (specific layers or strata of soil or subsoil in vertical cross-sections) (Lounejeva-Baturina et al. 2006, 2007; McClung de Tapia et al. 2005; Rivera-Uria et al. 2007).

## HAZARDS

Among the key hazards prehispanic populations in the region faced were tectonic movements, volcanic events, and agricultural risks such as early or late frosts, as well as drought, torrential rainfall events, hailstorms, floods, and erosion. Needless to say, these factors are often interrelated.

To date, the effects of earthquakes in the region have not been detected in the archaeological record. While there is little doubt about their occurrence and presumed frequency based on historical and modern events, the ravages of time and related post-depositional processes have obscured the evidence. Some of the rebuilding of structures at Teotihuacan may have been motivated on occasion by earthquake damage, but no clear evidence has been reported either in the city of Teotihuacan or in rural habitation areas outside the dense urban zone. Periodic rebuilding at the site seems to have been related to aggrandizement of the elite and to have been deeply couched in ritual practices (Sugiyama and López-Luján 2007).

As mentioned, documented volcanic events do not seem to have directly affected the region since the Late to Middle Holocene (Barba 1995; McClung de Tapia et al. 2005), although the bedrock (*tepetate*) is derived from consolidated volcanic ash, and volcanic materials comprise a major component of the soils in the region. What are referred to here as *agricultural risks* are mainly seasonal events related to the intensity of storms and runoff during the summer months, when approximately 80–90 percent of the annual precipitation occurs. However, these kinds of events do not only affect agriculture but may have had much more drastic effects on human groups comprising the different sectors of Teotihuacan society. Because historical records are not available for this time period, many parallels have been drawn with Aztec society for which a number of historical and ethno-historical documents exist. It is important to remember, though, that a period of 700–1,000 years separates these two societies.

## EVIDENCE FOR DEFORESTATION, EROSION, AND FLOODS

The analysis of charcoal specimens recovered from controlled contexts in several archaeological excavations representing the period from the Late Formative (ca. 400–100 BC) through the Late Postclassic (ca. AD 1350–1520) did not reveal clear evidence for deforestation (Adriano-Moran and McClung de Tapia 2008). A particularly notable aspect of this research was the consistent presence of essentially the same arboreal taxa characteristic of the region today, with the exception of pine (*Pinus* spp.), which has disappeared from the local flora. Pollen of these same taxa is consistently recorded in archaeological samples and soils as well; unfortunately, the low representation of pollen overall precludes a more detailed comparison.

In spite of the lack of conclusive evidence for deforestation, it undoubtedly occurred, given the large quantities of wood required as construction material and fuel for ceramic production as well as household consumption (Barba 1995). Deforestation is also indicated indirectly by evidence for erosion (McClung de Tapia et al. 2005). On the other hand, soil studies conducted in the region, together with the distribution of elevation zones and the biotic requirements of key forest taxa identified from the archaeological plant remains, suggest that the Teotihuacan Valley, at the time of the city's development, was not characterized by broad extensions of dense forest. GIS modeling of these factors revealed that a maximum of approximately 13 percent of the valley surface was likely covered by forest (McClung de Tapia and Tapia-Recillas 1996).

Erosion in the study region constitutes a long-term process composed of numerous episodes, often of differing intensities. The short-term impacts vary from barely noticeable dust storms (surface deflation by eolic erosion), to sediment carried in runoff from torrential storms of relatively limited duration, to severe landslides. The long-term effect is a highly modified, unstable landscape. All of these processes were active in the Teotihuacan Valley as well as elsewhere in the Basin of Mexico during the prehispanic occupation of the region. Deforestation of the surrounding slopes, particularly following the Spanish Conquest, greatly contributed to vegetation change and landscape instability. The cumulative effect of erosion, as evidenced from stratigraphy in the Teotihuacan region, has been the burial of past soils that were productive in prehispanic times as well as significant changes in the hydrology of the valley.

In general terms, the evidence from soils studied in the region indicates mainly polycyclic profiles (associated with two or more partially completed cycles of soil formation), poorly developed for the most part and often truncated, where part of the profile has been lost by erosion. Moderate to well-developed soil horizons are rare, indicating relatively young or degraded soils, and considerable evidence is present for pedosediments (in the process of development) overlying buried soils (McClung de Tapia et al. 2005).

Two examples in the alluvial plain are interesting because ceramics recovered from buried A horizons can be associated with prehispanic occupations and thus dating in relative terms of the overlying erosion sequence. In particular, in the Tlajinga area, ceramics from predominantly Miccaotli and Tlamimilolpa phase (AD 200–400) in a 2A (buried surface) horizon were covered by a C horizon with mainly Xolalpan phase materials (AD 400–550), over which redeposited sherds from earlier Teotihuacan occupations were situated. At Otumba, Mazapan phase ceramics (AD 900–1100) were predominant in the 2A horizon, which in turn was covered by a C horizon without ceramic materials and overlain by Aztec II–III sherds (AD 1300–1500) in approximately 100 cm of additional sediments (Pérez-Pérez 2003). Both areas have detailed histories of prehispanic irrigation detected through excavation (Charlton 1990; Nichols 1987), but the important aspect for this discussion is the evidence for erosion. Both irrigation systems are buried under later redeposited sediments. Particularly at Otumba, the sediments contain high proportions of sand (60–80 percent).

The presence of Aztec II–III ceramics in the uppermost layers of the Tlajinga sequence indicates that eroded sediments covered the earlier irrigation system prior to the Late Postclassic period. The presence at Otumba of Aztec II–III ceramics in the redeposited sediments overlying Mazapan phase ceramics indicates a still later erosion event, represented by post-Aztec sediments on the surface.

Both Tlajinga and Otumba were situated in close proximity to rivers that have suffered severe incision, probably related to intensive deforestation of upper slopes, apparently dating from the Colonial period (figure 6.3). The presence of sand lenses attests to the deposition of sand on the cultivated surface as the water from these rivers was diverted to provide humidity for irrigation. Once incision lowered the available flow of water with respect to the field surface, irrigation was no longer feasible. The evidence for Aztec agricultural activities at both sites indicates that this process took place at a later time.

The evidence for major hydraulic works in and around the city of Teotihuacan implies that seasonal flooding was a significant problem, for the urban center as well as surrounding agricultural areas. The city's ceremonial center, the so-called Street of the Dead, stretches over 2 km north-south, with a difference in elevation of approximately 30 m from one extreme to the other—suggesting that runoff from the *barrancas* (gorges) and streams that discharged into the Rio San Juan had been channeled to divert excess water from the ceremonial center. It is hard to believe that channeling of the river was undertaken simply to conform to the urban grid, although it undoubtedly served to divert excess rainwater and waste from structures along the Street of the Dead. George L. Cowgill (2000, 2007) suggests that the Rio San Lorenzo may also have been channeled, based on its unusually straight course slightly south of the limits of urban Teotihuacan.

The presence of waterlogged features and sediments was detected by Florencia Müller in archaeological tunnels excavated in the interior of the Sun Pyramid, associated with an earlier structure built prior to the monumental edifice (Gómez-Chávez 2008); similar conditions were encountered in recent excavations (Sarabia and Sugiyama 2010). Although a definitive explanation for this phenomenon is elusive, inundation water from the Rio San Juan may have permeated parts of the structure.

## URBAN EXPANSION AND VULNERABILITIES
## IN AGRICULTURAL PRODUCTION

Many aspects of architectural and other material remains of Teotihuacan society evoke in the observer impressions of hierarchy, rigid social control, and even arrogance, with their overwhelming emphasis on detailed planning, control of access to spaces and resources, together with frequent expansion and periodic urban renewal—in a word, aggrandizement. Although investigators earlier suggested that Teotihuacan's residents were primarily agriculturalists who

**6.3.** *Erosion and stream incision near Otumba in the eastern sector of the Teotihuacan Valley. Photo by Julia Pérez-Pérez.*

cultivated the surrounding fields (Millon 1976) and that food resources were unlikely to have been imported (Sanders 1976), emerging evidence for a highly structured elite dominating a large dependent class challenges this view.

Although prehispanic populations here developed canal systems for irrigation and terraces for water control as well as increased soil depth in the piedmont, the population of Teotihuacan surpassed the potential carrying capacity of maize-based agricultural production early in the city's developmental history and ultimately reached approximately 100,000–150,000 inhabitants (Millon 1973). Cowgill (1974) estimated that the city's population reached 50,000–60,000 inhabitants during the Tzacualli phase (AD 1–100), whereas other investigators calculated a regional carrying capacity of between 40,000 and 50,000 (Charlton 1970; Lorenzo 1968; Sanders 1976). Evidently, to support a significant proportion of the population, it was necessary to obtain subsistence products from adjacent valleys in central Mexico: the remainder of the Basin of Mexico, the Toluca Valley to the west, and the Puebla-Tlaxcala region to the east (McClung de Tapia 1987). Carrying capacity may in fact have been much lower than previous estimates, given recent evidence suggesting that the drained fields in the area of springs southwest of San Juan Teotihuacan were of Colonial rather than prehispanic origin (Gazzola 2009; González-Quintero and Sánchez-Sánchez 1991). Thus economic control of adjacent regions was fundamental to the urban support system. Certainly, the inherent risks to agricultural production were unpredictable except in the very short term—as they are in modern rural agricultural zones in central Mexico—and it would have required a highly efficient institutional organization to obtain resources from different areas from year to year as harvests were lost by the effects of weather variability. If population estimates for this phase approximate reality, then Teotihuacan established and maintained this mode of subsistence organization for roughly five to six centuries.

Under these circumstances, removing water-control systems from operation and from the lands they irrigated would appear counterproductive. However, the expansion of the urban zone over time took place at the expense of agricultural production, as demonstrated by discoveries in recent years of buried irrigation canals underlying Teotihuacan structures at Tlailotlacan (Nichols, Spence, and Borland 1991), Tlajinga (Nichols 1987), and La Ventilla (Gazzola 2009).

In addition to building over earlier irrigation systems, as the city grew, potentially productive agricultural zones were affected in other ways. The analyses of macro- and micro-botanical remains recovered from sediments that constitute the fills for a sequence of seven superimposed structures comprising the Moon Pyramid at the northern extreme of the Street of the Dead indicate that these materials were obtained from agricultural fields. Similarly, macro-botanical remains identified from the Sun Pyramid (McClung de Tapia 1987) and the Feathered Serpent Temple (McClung de Tapia and Rodríguez-Bejarano 1995) are consistent with this hypothesis. Luis Barba (1995) postulated that an immense amount of soil had to have been removed from the surface to provide construction fill for the major buildings along the Street of the Dead. The detriment to potentially productive agricultural lands is evident.

## CLIMATE CHANGE

No clear evidence has been recovered to date indicating the effect of significant climate change toward the end of the Classic period in the Teotihuacan Valley or elsewhere in the Basin of Mexico. Societies in this region developed under semiarid conditions, particularly in the northeast sector of the basin, and created agro-ecological and social mechanisms to cope with occasional droughts. Although it would be expected that cold events resulting from equatorial shifts of the Intercontinental Convergence Zone could produce droughts in central Mexico (Hassan 2009: 59), this evidence is not straightforward in the archaeological record. The fact that such events occurred, however, is clearly attested in sixteenth-century documents (García-Acosta, Pérez-Zevallos, and Molina del Villar 2003; Kovar 1970).

Results from geoarchaeological research undertaken by Carlos Cordova (1997) in the Texcoco region south of Teotihuacan suggest that the period immediately following the collapse of the Teotihuacan state, known as the Epiclassic period (AD 650/700–900), was characterized by episodes of torrential precipitation together with erosion and catastrophic floods. Comparable evidence has yet to be detected in the Teotihuacan Valley, but it is hoped that ongoing research will permit researchers to determine if similar processes can be identified in the alluvial record. However, drought may be indicated toward the end of the Early Postclassic period (AD 1100–1300), associated in cultural terms with the fall of Tula further north in the Basin of Mexico. The analysis of phytoliths recovered from soils in the Teotihuacan region reports a significant increase in grasses associated with semiarid conditions with respect to those associated with cool-humid conditions corresponding to this time period (McClung de Tapia et al. 2008). Unfortunately, none of the paleoenvironmental studies carried out to date in the lake sediments of the Basin of Mexico provides information for this period.

## MITIGATION

Mitigation involved several aspects. Clearly, water was a vital element at Teotihuacan, as expressed in iconography and ideology, and elaborate rituals associated with water are symbolized in mural representations and burial offerings (Sugiyama and López-Luján 2007). The need to propitiate rains and appease the deities was a fundamental aspect of agricultural practice.

Hydraulic works modified the landscape significantly. Rivers were channeled to avoid flooding, and irrigation systems helped control seasonal water flow in addition to increasing agricultural productivity. Terraces were constructed to control erosion and increase soil buildup as well as humidity (Sanders, Parsons, and Santley 1979).

The acquisition of a significant proportion of subsistence products from elsewhere provided a solution to the subsistence demands of the growing population, faced with the unpredictability of agricultural risks as well as an apparent decrease in suitable agricultural lands locally. An added benefit, from a political and economic perspective, would have been the establishment and maintenance of control over adjacent regions.

Seasonal flooding undoubtedly increased following the collapse of the Teotihuacan state, reaching a peak during the Colonial period. The remains of Aztec structures in the area of springs southwest of the Classic period city of Teotihuacan are found at depths of 3.5–4.0 m below the modern surface, with some Teotihuacan remains at still greater depths (Cabrera-Castro 2005). The analysis of sediments in the area of Atlatongo, slightly further to the south, revealed approximately 3 m of redeposited sediments (Rivera-Uria et al. 2007).

Overall, it looks as though the landscape of the Teotihuacan Valley was sufficiently resilient to withstand the effects of human impact during the Classic period, during which Teotihuacan developed and prospered. While it is beyond the scope of this chapter to provide a detailed discussion of events at the end of the Late Postclassic period and the initial Colonial period, it is evident that the fragile limit between sustainable productivity and catastrophe represented a threshold that was overshot as a result of numerous interrelated factors. Changes in land use resulting from the introduction of Spanish agricultural techniques, significant indigenous population reduction as a result of numerous epidemics, *congregación* (relocation and concentration of remnant communities partially devastated by disease or situated in rural areas particularly far from Spanish administration centers), and the construction of dams to minimize flooding that affected the colonial capital built on top of the ruins of Aztec Tenochtitlan all contributed to the abandonment of agricultural systems in the piedmont zone and to land degradation in general, as well as to erosion and devastating floods.

The region's ecosystems were severely damaged following the Spanish Conquest. Hydraulic works—based first on frequent repairs of the prehispanic system built to control flooding of Tenochtitlan to avoid contamination by saline waters from Texcoco of the freshwater sector in the south by means of a system of dikes and raised causeways and, later, on the drainage of Lake Texcoco (initiated in 1637)—constantly failed. A document dated to 1555 shows that the Spaniards were conscious of the need to relocate the vulnerable colonial city while at the same time recognizing the impossibility of such an endeavor in the face of exorbitant costs and the opposition of the indigenous population (McClung de Tapia 1990). The hydrological system of the Teotihuacan region drained into Lake Texcoco and therefore contributed substantially to the problem of colonial flooding. The fluvial network of the lower Teotihuacan Valley was possibly channeled in the mid-fifteenth century, at the time of Nezahualcoyotl, ruler of Texcoco (Cordova 1997). In 1604 a dam was constructed approximately 3 km south of Acolman in the southern sector of the alluvial plain of the Teotihuacan Valley to control the Rio San Juan and flooding in Mexico City. The effect was to create a large artificial lake; historical documents report continual inundations in this area culminating in the disappearance of several towns, most notably Acolman itself, which was ultimately relocated to its present site in 1781. In 1772 the Augustinian convent of Acolman was submerged in several meters of sediments, and the church of Atlatongo was similarly inundated (ibid.; Gamio 1922). Meanwhile, the floods continued, and despite constant repairs to the dam, the attempt to control the seasonal flow of water to Lake Texcoco was fruitless.

## FUTURE RESEARCH

Attempts to differentiate the landscape impacts of Aztec occupation of the Teotihuacan Valley from the earlier Classic period have been limited by the difficulty of separating Colonial impacts from prehispanic events and processes. Following more than a decade of detailed soil studies and paleoethnobotanical analyses in the region with the objective of reconstructing the Classic period landscape—what was the valley like when the Teotihuacanos occupied it?—it has become clear that the initial Colonial period was a time of major demographic upheaval and associated landscape change. Although some authors have suggested that perhaps the central part of the Teotihuacan Valley was not as intensively exploited as other sectors of the Basin of Mexico (Gibson 1964), this information needs to be gathered, in historical archives as well as from paleoenvironmental and geoarchaeological studies. A research effort has recently been undertaken that seeks to look at historical records to trace vegetation change through land-use practices. It is clear that a better understanding of Colonial period processes and events, including the impact of new technologies, socioeconomic organization, and worldview during this period, is necessary to better understand the Late Postclassic and, finally, prior periods such as the Classic.

The social component of the complex society described here is largely unknown, although it can be assumed that adaptability was operational (the city and state endured for approximately five centuries following an earlier century of less complex development). Yet because little is known of the perceptions and expectations of the multiple levels of human groups that occupied the city, beyond speculating about elite control over the rest of the society, there appears to be no suitable measure of adaptability. Possibly, a potential measure of landscape adaptability following the collapse of Teotihuacan could be the rate at which different vegetation communities were reestablished in relation to the gradual resettlement of the region. It is hoped that ongoing research will contribute to this question.

## CONCLUSION

Many parallels can be drawn with the plight of the modern metropolitan area in the Basin of Mexico. The perpetual effort to control erosion and seasonal flooding continues to this day. The inability of local authorities to impede settlement by marginal populations in high-risk areas in the Federal District and the adjacent State of Mexico, such as steep slopes and *barranca* edges, fosters severe damage from saturated soils and consequent landslides or stream avulsion, causing flash floods. A recent disaster, resulting from atypical torrential rains together with continual showers that lasted for several days in February 2010—traditionally the dry season in this region—affected domestic and commercial properties, mainly in lower-elevation, high-density population centers. Breaches in a drainage canal for wastewater inundated one of the major highways and caused considerable economic losses related to transportation of products between Mexico City and the Gulf Coast (figure 6.4).

Although Intergovernmental Panel on Climate Change projections for the region (Christensen et al. 2007) predict an overall decrease in mean annual precipitation for Central America in general, considerable local variability is expected, especially in mountainous areas such as central Mexico and particularly the Basin of Mexico. Atypical precipitation events, in addition to sporadic torrential showers in summer and seasonal hurricanes, may well continue to affect the region. While it is not difficult to imagine the trauma of prehispanic communities faced with severe flood damage, including erosion, the resilience of those settlements and the landscape in general was far greater than that of modern industrial and service-based urban communities in the Basin of Mexico.

*Acknowledgments.* The research reported in this chapter was supported by the Consejo Nacional de Ciencia y Tecnología, Mexico (101988), as well as the Instituto de Investigaciones Antropológicas, Instituto de Geología, and Dirección General de Asuntos del Personal Académico, Universidad Nacional Autónoma de México (UNAM). The author thanks Diana Martínez-Yrizar, Emilio Ibarra-Morales, and Cristina Adriano-Morán of the Laboratorio de Paleoetnobotánica y Paleoambiente and Jorge Gama-Castro, Elizabeth Solleiro-Rebolledo, and Sergey Sedov of the Instituto de Geología, UNAM.

**6.4.** *Flooding of the major highway between the Gulf Coast and Mexico City and adjacent communities in February 2010. Courtesy,* La Jornada.

## REFERENCES

Adriano-Moran, C. C.

2000    Estudio del Carbón Arqueológico como Indicador de los Cambios en la Vegetación, en el Valle de Teotihuacan, Estado de México. MS thesis, Biology, Facultad de Ciencias, Universidad Nacional Autónoma de México, México, DF.

Adriano-Moran, C. C., and E. McClung de Tapia

2008    Trees and Shrubs: The Use of Firewood in Prehispanic Teotihuacan. *Journal of Archaeological Science* 35: 2927–2936.

Barba, L. A.

1995    El Impacto en la paleogeografía de Teotihuacan. Unpublished PhD dissertation, Facultad de Filosofía y Letras, Universidad Nacional de México, México, DF.

Cabrera-Castro, R.

2005    Nuevas evidencias arqueológicas del manejo del agua en Teotihuacan. El campo y la ciudad. In *Arquitectura and urbanismo: pasado y presente de los espacios en Teotihuacan*, ed. M. E. Ruiz Gallut and J. Torres Peralta. Memoria de la Tercera Mesa Redonda de Teotihuacan, Instituto Nacional de Antropología e Historia, México, DF, pp. 121–161.

Castilla-Hernández, M. E., and J. D. Tejero-Diez

1987    Flora y vegetación del Cerro Gordo (San Juan Teotihuacan) y regiones aledañas, Valle de México, México. *Biotica* 12(4): 231–255.

Charlton, T. H.

1970    Contemporary Agriculture of the Valley. In *The Natural Environment, Contemporary Occupation and 16th Century Population of the Valley*, ed. W. T. Sanders, A. Kovar, T. H. Charlton, and R. A. Diehl. The Teotihuacan Valley Project: Final Report, vol. 1. Occasional Papers in Anthropology 3. Department of Anthropology, Pennsylvania State University, University Park, pp. 253–384.

1990    Operation 12, Field 20, Irrigation System Excavations. In *Preliminary Report on Recent Research in the Otumba City-State*, ed. T. H. Charlton and D. L. Nichols. Research Report 3, vol. 1. Mesoamerican Research Colloquium, Department of Anthropology, University of Iowa, Iowa City, pp. 201–212.

Charlton, T. H., and D. L. Nichols

1997    Diachronic Studies of City-States: Central Mexico from 1700 B.C. to A.D. 1600. In *The Archaeology of City-States,* ed. D. L. Nichols and T. H. Charlton. Smithsonian Institution Press, Washington, DC, pp. 169–207.

Christensen, J. H., B. Hewitson, A. Busuloc, A. Chen, X. Gao, I. Held, R. Jones, R. K. Kolli, W.-T. Kwon, R. Laprise, V. Magaña Rueda, L. Mearns, C. G. Menéndez, J. Räisänen, A. Rinke, A. Sarr, and P. Whetton

2007    Regional Climate Projections. In *Climate Change 2007: The Physical Science Basis. Contribution of Working Group 1 to the Fourth Assessment Report of the Intergovernmental Panel on Climate Change*, ed. S. Solomon,

D. Qin, M. Manning, Z. Chen, M. Marquis, K. B. Averyt, M. Tignor, and H. L. Miller. Cambridge University Press, Cambridge, pp. 847–940.

Cordova, C. E.
1997    Landscape Transformation in Aztec and Spanish Colonial Texcoco, Mexico. Unpublished PhD dissertation, Department of Geography, University of Texas, Austin.

Córdova, C. E., and J. R. Parsons
1997    Geoarchaeology of an Aztec Dispersed Village on the Texcoco Piedmont of Central Mexico. *Geoarchaeology* 12(3): 177–210.

Cowgill, G. L.
1974    Quantitative Studies of Urbanization at Teotihuacan. In *Mesoamerican Archaeology: New Approaches*, ed. N. Hammond. University of Texas Press, Austin, pp. 363–396.
2000    Intentionality and Meaning in the Layout of Teotihuacan, Mexico. *Cambridge Archaeological Journal* 10(2): 358–365.
2007    The Urban Organization of Teotihuacan, Mexico. In *Settlement and Society: Essays Dedicated to Robert McCormick Adams,* ed. E. C. Stone. Cotsen Institute of Archaeology, University of California, Los Angeles, and the Oriental Institute of the University of Chicago, Chicago, pp. 261–295.

Evans, S. T.
2001    Aztec-Period Political Organization in the Teotihuacan Valley. *Ancient Mesoamerica* 12: 89–100.

Frederick, C. D.
1997    *Landscape Change and Human Settlement in the Southeastern Basin of Mexico.* Department of Archaeology and Prehistory, University of Sheffield, Sheffield, UK.

Frederick, C. D., B. Winsborough, and V. S. Popper
2005    Geoarchaeological Investigations in the Northern Basin of Mexico. In *Production and Power at Postclassic Xaltocan,* ed. E. M. Brumfiel. University of Pittsburgh, Pittsburgh, and INAH, México, DF, pp. 71–115.

Gamio, M.
1922    *La Población del Valle de Teotihuacan.* Tomo 1(2). Secretaria de Agricultura y Fomento, Dirección de Antropología, México, DF.

García-Acosta, V., J. M. Pérez-Zevallos, and A. Molina del Villar
2003    *Desastres Agrícolas en México. Catálogo Histórico. Épocas prehispánica y colonial (958–1822).* Fondo de Cultura Económica, Centro de Investigaciones y Estudios Superiores en Antropología Social, México, DF.

Gazzola, J.
2009    *Una propuesta sobre el proceso, factores y condiciones del colapso de Teotihuacan, Revista Dimensión Antropológica, Instituto Nacional de Antropología e Historia,* available at http://www.dimensionantropologica.inah.gob.mx/?p=794; accessed March 30, 2010.

Gibson, C.
1964    *The Aztecs under Spanish Rule.* Stanford University Press, Stanford, CA.

Gómez-Chávez, S.
2008    Florencia Emilia Jacobs Müller. Contribuciones a la Arqueología y cono-
cimiento de Teotihuacan. *Arqueología* 38: 206–219.

González, S., J. C. Jiménez-López, R. Hedges, J. A. Pompa y Padilla, and D. Huddart
2006    Early Humans in Mexico: New Chronological Data. In *El Hombre
Temprano en América y sus implicaciones en el poblamiento de la Cuenca
de México. Primer Simposio Internacional,* ed. J. C. Jiménez-López, S.
González, J. A. Pompa y Padilla, and F. Ortiz-Pedraza. Instituto Nacional
de Antropología e Historia, México, DF, pp. 67–76.

González-Quintero, L., and J. E. Sánchez-Sánchez
1991    Sobre la existencia de chinampas y el manejo del recurso agrícola-
hidraúlico. In *Teotihuacan 1980–1982. Nuevas Interpretaciones,* ed. R.
Cabrera-Castro, I. Rodríguez-García, and N. Morelos-García. Instituto
Nacional de Antropología e Historia, México, DF, pp. 345–375.

Hassan, F. A.
2009    Human Agency, Climate Change, and Culture: An Archaeological Perspective. In *Anthropology and Climate Change: From Encounters to Action,* ed. S.
A. Crate and M. Nuttall. Left Coast Press, Walnut Creek, CA, pp. 39–69.

Hodge, M. G., C. E. Córdova, and C. D. Frederick
1996    Los asentamientos prehispánicos y el medio cambiante del sureste de la
Cuenca de México. In *Tierra, agua y bosque,* ed. A. Tortolero Villaseñor.
Historia y medio ambiente en el México central, Centre Français d'Études
Mexicaines et Centraméricaines, Instituto de Investigaciones Dr. José
María Luis Mora, Potrerillos Editores, Universidad de Guadalajara, pp.
49–68.

Kovar, A.
1970    The Physical and Biological Environment of the Basin of Mexico. In *The
Natural Environment, Contemporary Occupation and 16th Century Popu-
lation of the Valley,* ed. W. T. Sanders, A. Kovar, T. Charlton, and R. A.
Diehl. The Teotihuacan Valley Project: Final Report, vol. 1. Occasional
Papers in Anthropology 3. Department of Anthropology, Pennsylvania
State University, University Park, pp. 13–67.

Lamb, A. L., S. González, D. Huddart, S. E. Metcalfe, C. H. Vane, and A.W.G. Pike
2009    Tepexpan Palaeoindian Site, Basin of Mexico: Multi-Proxy Evidence for
Environmental Change during the Late Pleistocene–Late Holocene. *Quaternary Science Reviews* 28: 2000–2016.

Lorenzo, J. L.
1968    Clima y agricultura en Teotihuacan. In *Materiales para la arqueología de
Teotihuacan,* ed. J. L. Lorenzo. Instituto Nacional de Antropología e Historia, México, DF, pp. 53–72.

Lounejeva-Baturina, E., P. Morales-Puente, H. V. Cabadas-Báez, E. Cienfuegos-
Alvarado, S. Sedov, E. Vallejo-Gómez, and E. Solleiro-Rebolledo
2006    Late Pleistocene to Holocene Environmental Changes from $\delta^{13}C$ Deter-
minations in Soils at Teotihuacan, Mexico. *Geofísica Internacional* 45(2):
85–98.

Lounejeva-Baturina, E., P. Morales-Puente, E. Cienfuegos-Alvarado, S. Sedov, and E. Solleiro-Rebolledo
2007    Late Quaternary Environment in the Teotihuacan Valley, Mexico, Inferred from $\delta^{13}$C in Soils. *SAS Bulletin* 30(1): 6–11.

Manzanilla, L.
1997    The Impact of Past Climate Change on Past Civilizations: A Revisionist Agenda for Future Research. *Quaternary International* 43–44: 153–159.

Manzanilla, L., ed.
2005    *Reacomodos demográficos. Del Clásico al Posclásico en el Centro de Mexico.* Instituto de Investigaciones Antropológicas, Universidad Nacional Autónoma de México, México, DF.

McClung de Tapia, E.
1987    Agriculture and the Formation of the Teotihuacan State. In *Studies in the Neolithic and Urban Revolutions: The V. Gordon Childe Colloquium, Mexico, 1986,* ed. L. Manzanilla. BAR International Series 349, Oxford, England, pp. 353–364.
1990    Ecología, agricultura y ganadería durante la Colonia, Medicina novohispana. In *Historia General de la Medicina en México,* tomo 2. Siglo 16, ed. G. Aguirre Beltrán and R. Moreno de los Arcos. Academia Nacional de Medicina, Universidad Nacional Autónoma de México, México, DF, pp. 60–77.
2009    *Los ecosistemas del Valle de Teotihuacan a lo largo de su Historia, Teotihuacan: Ciudad de los Dioses.* Instituto Nacional de Antropología e Historia, México, DF.

McClung de Tapia, E., H. Cabadas Baez, E. Solleiro, J. Gama-Castro, and E. Vallejo
2008    Phytoliths of Soils and Paleosols of the Teotihuacan Valley, Mexico. In *Interdisciplinary Nuances in Phytolith and Other Microfossil Studies,* ed. M. P. Babot and A. Korstanje. BAR International Series, Oxford, England, pp. 67–76.

McClung de Tapia, E., I. Domínguez-Rubio, J. Gama-Castro, E. Solleiro-Rebolledo, and S. Sedov
2005    Radiocarbon Dates from Soil Profiles in the Teotihuacan Valley, Mexico: Indicators of Geomorphological Processes. *Radiocarbon* 47(1): 159–175.

McClung de Tapia, E., and R. Rodríguez-Bejarano
1995    *Botanical Remains from the Temple of Quetzalcoatl.* Informe Técnico 2. Laboratorio de Paleoetnobotánica y Paleoambiente, Instituto de Investigaciones Antropológicas, Universidad Nacional Autónoma de México, México, DF.

McClung de Tapia, E., E. Solleiro-Rebolledo, J. Gama-Castro, J. L. Villalpando, and S. Sedov
2003    Paleosols in the Teotihuacan Valley, Mexico: Evidence for Paleoenvironment and Human Impact. *Revista Mexicana de Ciencias Geológicas* 20(30): 270–282.

McClung de Tapia, E., and H. Tapia-Recillas
1996    Statistical Analysis Using GIS: Application to the Study of Prehispanic Settlement Location in the Teotihuacan Region, Mexico. Archaeological Applications of GIS. Proceedings of Colloquium II, ed. I. Johnson and N. North. UISPP 13th Congress, Forlí, Italy. Sydney University Archaeological Methods Series 5, Sydney, Australia.

McClung de Tapia, E., J. L. Villalpando, E. Solleiro, and J. E. Gama
2004    Prácticas agrícolas prehispánicas en el valle de Teotihuacan, Estado de México: evidencias químicas y morfológicas. In Homenaje a Jaime Litvak, ed. A. Benavides, L. Manzanilla, and L. Mirambell. Instituto Nacional de Antropología e Historia, Instituto de Investigaciones Antropológicas, Universidad Nacional Autónoma de México, México, DF, pp. 63–80.

Millon, R.
1970    Teotihuacan: Completion of Map of Giant Ancient City in the Valley of Mexico. Science 170(3962): 1077–1082.
1973    Urbanization at Teotihuacan, Mexico, vol. 1: The Teotihuacan Map. University of Texas Press, Austin.
1976    Social Relations in Ancient Teotihuacan. In The Valley of Mexico: Studies in Pre-Hispanic Ecology and Society, ed. E. R. Wolf. School of American Research, University of New Mexico Press, Albuquerque, pp. 205–248.
1988    The Last Years of Teotihuacan Dominance. In The Collapse of Ancient States and Civilizations, ed. N. Yoffee and G. L. Cowgill. University of Arizona Press, Tucson, pp. 102–164.

Nichols, D. L.
1987    Prehispanic Irrigation at Teotihuacan, New Evidence: The Tlajinga Canals. In Teotihuacan. Nuevos Datos, Nuevas Síntesis, Nuevos Problemas, ed. E. McClung de Tapia and E. C. Rattray. Instituto de Investigaciones Antropológicas, Universidad Nacional Autónoma de México, México, DF, pp. 133–160.

Nichols, D. L., M. Spence, and M. Borland
1991    Watering the Fields of Teotihuacan: Early Irrigation at the Ancient City. Ancient Mesoamerica 2: 119–129.

Pérez-Pérez, J.
2003    La agricultura en Teotihuacan. Una forma de modificación al paisaje. Unpublished master's thesis, Anthropology, Facultad de Filosofía y Letras, Universidad Nacional Autónoma de México, México, DF.

Plunket, P., and G. Uruñuela
2006    Social and Cultural Consequences of a Late Holocene Eruption of Popocatépetl in Central Mexico. Quaternary International 151: 19–28.
2008    Mountain of Sustenance, Mountain of Destruction: The Prehispanic Experience with Popocatépetl Volcano. Journal of Volcanology and Geothermal Research 170(1–2): 111–120.

Rattray, E., J. Litvak, and C. Diaz, eds.
1981    Interaccion cultural en Mexico central. Instituto de Investigaciones Antropológicas, Universidad Nacional Autónoma de México, México, DF.

Rivera-Uria, M. Y., S. Sedov, E. Solleiro-Rebolledo, J. Pérez-Pérez, E. McClung, A. González, and J. Gama-Castro
2007    Degradación ambiental en el valle Teotihuacan: evidencias geológicas y paleopedológicas. *Boletín de la Sociedad Geológica Mexicana* 59(2): 203–217.

Rzedowski, J., G. Guzmán, A. Hernández, and C. Muñiz
1964    Cartografía de la vegetación de la parte norte del valle de México. *Anales de la Escuela Nacional de Ciencias Biológicas* 13: 31–57.

Sanders, W. T.
1965    *The Cultural Ecology of the Teotihuacan Valley.* Department of Sociology and Anthropology, Pennsylvania State University, University Park.
1976    The Agricultural History of the Basin of Mexico. In *The Valley of Mexico: Studies in Pre-Hispanic Ecology and Society*, ed. E. R. Wolf. School of American Research, University of New Mexico Press, Albuquerque, pp. 101–159.

Sanders, W. T., J. R. Parsons, and R. S. Santley
1979    *The Basin of Mexico: Ecological Processes in the Evolution of a Civilization.* Academic Press, New York.

Sarabia, A., and S. Sugiyama
2010    *Informe de los trabajos realizados durante la temporada 2008–2009. Programa de Conservación e Investigación en el Complejo Arquitectónico de la Pirámide del Sol, Teotihuacan.* Instituto Nacional de Antropología e Historia, Coordinación Nacional de Arqueología, Dirección de la Zona Arqueológica de Teotihuacan, México, DF.

Sedov, S., S. Lozano-Garcia, E. Solleiro-Rebolledo, E. McClung de Tapia, B. Ortega-Guerrero, and S. Sosa-Najera
2010    Tepexpan Revisited: A Multiple Proxy of Local Environmental Changes in Relation to Human Occupation from a Paleolakeshore Section in Central Mexico. *Geomorphology*, doi:10.1016/j.geomorph.2009.09.003; accessed November 26, 2009.

Siebe, C., M. Abrams, J. L. Macías, and J. Obenholzner
1996    Repeated Volcanic Disasters in Prehispanic Times at Popocatépetl, Central Mexico: Past Key to the Future? *Geology* 24(5): 399–402.

Solleiro-Rebolledo, E., S. Sedov, E. McClung de Tapia, H. Cabadas, J. Gama-Castro, and E. Vallejo-Gómez
2006    Spatial Variability of Environmental Change in the Teotihuacan Valley during the Late Quaternary: Paleopedological Inferences. *Quaternary International* 156–157: 13–31.

Sugiyama, S., and L. López-Luján
2007    Dedicatorial Burial/Offering Complexes at the Moon Pyramid, Teotihuacan. *Ancient Mesoamerica* 18: 127–146.

Walker, B., C. S. Holling, S. R. Carpenter, and A. Kinzig
2004    Resilience, Adaptability and Transformability in Social-Ecological Systems. *Ecology and Society* 9(2): 5, available at http://www.ecologyand society.org/vol9/iss2/art5; accessed July 5, 2005.

## UNDERSTANDING HAZARDS, MITIGATING IMPACTS, AVOIDING DISASTERS

### Statement for Policy Makers and the Disaster Management Community

The Basin of Mexico, where modern Mexico City and its surrounding metropolitan area are located, has been populated by relatively dense urban centers since prehispanic times, as early as 100 BC. Therefore many of the problems inherent to sustaining large populations in areas where natural and anthropogenic hazards are present can be traced back several millennia. Factors such as volcanic eruptions, tectonic events, irregular precipitation, flooding, and erosion are all interrelated and exacerbated by deforestation and intensive agricultural activities; their impact has been felt since the earliest settlements. Needless to say, increasing population density in certain areas through time, in addition to decline and abandonment in others, has also contributed to significant landscape degradation.

Prehispanic communities in the region, such as Teotihuacan, confronted these risks by developing and maintaining complex agro-ecological systems, hydraulic works, and strategically located settlements close to terraces in rural zones at higher elevations to control erosion. Many of these facilities were abandoned or significantly modified following the Spanish Conquest in the sixteenth century. The intentional drainage of the lake system during the Colonial period is perhaps the most drastic example of this landscape modification. What has ensued over the past four centuries is a complete transformation of the landscape, paralleled by population increase, resource depletion, and increased risk of natural hazards. Dense urban populations are concentrated in precarious, unstable areas where risks were always present but are now greater because of irregular urban development. Central Mexico has always been at risk, but it will undoubtedly suffer an increase in the irregularity and unpredictability of hazards, subjecting modern and future populations to more frequent disasters along with their economic and social consequences. Therefore, key lessons from this research show that the Teotihuacan landscape was sufficiently resilient during the Classic period when the ancient city developed and prospered. This resilience of prehispanic settlement strategies and their methods of landscape management should inform current urban planning strategies for modern industrial and service-based communities in the Basin of Mexico.

# SEVEN

# Domination and Resilience in Bronze Age Mesopotamia

*Tate Paulette*

Although Mesopotamia has long occupied a prominent position in the public imagination, recent events—in particular, the military occupation of Iraq and the large-scale looting of museums and archaeological sites—have drawn the Iraqi present and the Mesopotamian past vividly into the spotlight. Images of legendary ancient cities, now stranded in arid wastelands, and broken monuments to kings of vanished civilizations resonate powerfully with modern audiences, themselves increasingly uncertain about our collective future. For a world in which environmental disaster and economic collapse loom on the horizon, ancient Mesopotamia can provide both cautionary tales and success stories. Recurring hazards such as drought, flooding, and locust attacks were regularly planned for, counteracted, and endured in Mesopotamia; however, several much-debated episodes of political and economic collapse testify to the precarious nature of human-environment dynamics in the region.

This chapter provides an introduction to the range of hazards—whether strictly environmental or human-induced—that confronted the inhabitants of Bronze Age (ca. 3000–1200 BC) Mesopotamia. Particular emphasis is placed on institutional organization and institutional management as key factors in determining the impact of these hazards. The chapter begins with an introduction to Bronze Age Mesopotamia and to the most pertinent archaeological and written sources; it then focuses more narrowly on the evi-

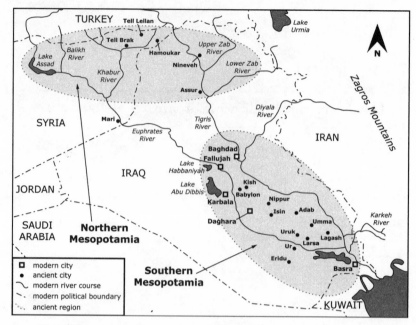

**7.1.** *Map of Mesopotamia. Base map provided by the Oriental Institute Map Series, Oriental Institute, University of Chicago.*

dence for hazards and hazard management before closing with a look toward the future.

## BRONZE AGE MESOPOTAMIA

The ancient region known as Mesopotamia encompasses much of modern Iraq and northeastern Syria (figure 7.1).[1] Traversed by two major rivers, the Tigris and the Euphrates (figure 7.2), this arid land has long supported a subsistence economy centered on cereal cultivation and the herding of sheep and goats. Rainfall is typically meager and erratic, with a high frequency of drought years, but impressive agricultural yields can be achieved across much of the region. On the alluvial plains of Southern Mesopotamia, this is possible only with the aid of irrigation, but in Northern Mesopotamia rain-fed agriculture (also known as "dry farming") is the norm. Today, as in the distant past, crops are sown in October-November and are then harvested and processed for storage in April-May (Adams 1965: 16; Postgate 1992: 167).

Throughout Mesopotamian history, settlement has been concentrated within the two agricultural zones—Southern and Northern Mesopotamia— but these zones are separated by a broad band of arid steppe better suited to exploitation by mobile pastoralists. Even within the cultivated zone, the herd-

**7.2.** *The Euphrates River in modern Syria, irrigated fields in the foreground. Photo taken at the site of Dura Europos, near Mari in the Middle Euphrates region (see figure 7.1). Photo by Tate Paulette.*

ing of sheep and goats is (and was) a major component of the economy and is carefully factored into the daily and seasonal scheduling of agricultural activities. The need for pasture requires that sheep and goats be taken out to graze on a daily basis; when the herds become too large or when local pasture is scarce, they are often taken out to more distant grazing areas for longer periods of time.

Falling immediately on the heels of the famous Urban Revolution,[2] the Bronze Age was a time of demographic flux, economic transformation, and intense political competition in Mesopotamia. During several episodes of political centralization, expansionist dynasties created regional-scale polities encompassing portions of both Northern and Southern Mesopotamia, but these efforts toward unification and integration were typically fleeting. More commonly, Mesopotamia was divided into a patchwork of relatively autonomous city-states, whose territorial boundaries and relations with neighboring polities were in constant motion. Chronologically, archaeologists distinguish among the Early Bronze Age, Middle Bronze Age, and Late Bronze Age. For each geographical region (i.e., Northern and Southern Mesopotamia), this tripartite division is then broken down further into sub-periods (figure 7.3).

Over the course of the Bronze Age, the inhabitants of Mesopotamia found themselves increasingly at the mercy of a series of powerful urban institutions. Although community organizations, corporate groups, and judicial

| Dates BC (approximate) | Mesopotamia (primary archaeological periods) | Southern Mesopotamia (region-specific periods) | Northern Mesopotamia (region-specific periods) |
|---|---|---|---|
| 1000 | Early Iron Age | Second Dynasty of Isin | Neo-Assyrian Period |
| | | | Middle Assyrian Period |
| | Late Bronze Age | Kassite Period | Mitanni Period |
| | Middle Bronze Age | Old Babylonian Period | Kingdom of Shamshi-Adad |
| | | | Old Assyrian Period |
| 2000 | | Ur III Period | |
| | | Akkadian Period | |
| | Early Bronze Age | | Early Jezireh Period |
| | | Early Dynastic Period | |
| 3000 | | Jemdet Nasr Period | |
| | Late Chalcolithic Period | Uruk Period | Late Chalcolithic Period |

**7.3.** *Chronological chart showing the primary archaeological divisions (Early, Middle, and Late Bronze Age) and the corresponding, region-specific subdivisions of the Bronze Age in Mesopotamia (3000–1200 BC); also includes the preceding Late Chalcolithic period and the succeeding Early Iron Age.*

bodies played an important role in city governance, the centralized political and religious organizations ("the palace" and "the temple") emerged as major economic powers, managing huge tracts of land and able to mobilize labor on a massive scale. Many people were dependent on these institutions for their livelihoods, and institutional demands for taxes, tribute, and labor became an ever-present fact of life (e.g., Powell 1987).

It is often unclear, however, exactly how institutional interference impacted the domestic economy of individual households. Did the imposition of institu-

**7.4.** *A typical* tell, *or mound, in the Upper Khabur region of northeastern Syria (near Tell Brak and Tell Leilan; see figure 7.1) Photo by Tate Paulette.*

tional control entail a shift in economic planning, in risk-buffering strategies, or in other forms of hazard management on the household level? Did different systems of institutional organization affect the localized impact of specific types of hazard? Did some forms of institutional control invite disaster or increase the chances of large-scale collapse, while others incorporated higher degrees of flexibility and resilience? These remain open questions.

## TYPES OF EVIDENCE

The archaeological exploration of ancient Mesopotamia began in earnest during the later part of the nineteenth century, and fieldwork has continued in Iraq and Syria up to the present day, with some notable interruptions during times of war and political unrest.[3] The typical archaeological site in Mesopotamia is the *tell*, which means "mound" in Arabic (figure 7.4). *Tell* sites are the remains of ancient towns and cities, once constructed on level ground but now rising high above the surrounding landscape thanks to the gradual buildup of debris (from successive settlements built one on top of the other) over hundreds and often thousands of years. These mounds can be as small as half of a hectare (1.2 acres) or as large as 600 hectares (1,483 acres), and they may rise only 1 m or as much as 40 m above the surrounding landscape.

Thousands of *tells* have been examined by archaeologists, through excavation and a range of noninvasive methods. Excavations regularly uncover the remains of houses, workshops, burials, temples, and palaces—all made of sun-dried mud bricks and, less commonly, stone or oven-baked bricks. Many different types of artifacts are recovered, including pottery, stone tools, metal objects, beads, figurines, seals, cuneiform tablets, human bones, animal bones, and plant remains. The most important noninvasive method is archaeological survey, which involves the systematic examination and recording of remains that are visible on the surface (e.g., artifacts, architecture, and landscape features; see, e.g., Wilkinson 2000a). Traditional survey is now supplemented by a host of remote-sensing techniques that use innovative technologies—such as magnetometry, ground-penetrating radar, and satellite imagery—to obtain new perspectives on surface remains and to probe beneath the surface in a nondestructive manner. The results in Mesopotamia have been spectacular, from the detailed mapping of buried streets and buildings to the identification of extensive ancient road systems (Meyer 2007; Ur 2003).

Natural scientists and physical scientists also play an active role in many archaeological projects. For example, recent debates over the evidence for climate change and societal collapse in Early Bronze Age Mesopotamia (discussed later in the chapter) have drawn together archaeologists, soil scientists, climatologists, botanists, and volcanologists, among others (e.g., Dalfes, Kukla, and Weiss 1997; Weiss et al. 1993). Joint projects involving specialists in digital imaging, database management, and computer modeling are also increasingly common (e.g., Wilkinson et al. 2007a, 2007b).

It is the written record, however, that really sets Mesopotamia apart as a source of information about human-environment dynamics in the ancient world. Cuneiform writing was invented in Mesopotamia near the end of the fourth millennium BC (Late Chalcolithic period). By the middle of the third millennium BC, it was being employed for a range of purposes, from administration and record keeping to royal inscriptions and literary works (e.g., Nissen, Damerow, and Englund 1993; Postgate 1992: ch. 3). It was during the Early Bronze Age, therefore, that writing truly emerged as a major data source, taking its place alongside archaeological evidence—the primary source of information about earlier, prehistoric periods.

Several caveats should be kept in mind with regard to the written evidence. First, the preservation of written material in Mesopotamia is extremely uneven, both chronologically and geographically. This situation is partially a reflection of actual trends in the production of written documents by Mesopotamian scribes, but it is also an effect of the accidents of discovery. Second, most cuneiform tablets were produced by and for the palace and temple institutions. They typically provide only a very partial perspective, biased toward the needs and desires of the institutional powers. Many segments of society remain anonymous and without a voice in the written record.

## HAZARDS AND HAZARD MANAGEMENT IN MESOPOTAMIA

Hundreds of thousands of cuneiform documents have been uncovered from archaeological sites in Mesopotamia, but the Mesopotamian scribes did not leave behind any detailed compilations of climate statistics or any manuals outlining strategies for coping with environmental stress.[4] To understand ancient hazards and their impacts, modern scholars must piece together archaeological evidence, scattered textual references, and paleoenvironmental data while also making judicious use of modern climate records and more recent ethnographic or historic accounts.

Magnus Widell, for example, has recently drawn attention to the value of a Medieval document known as the *Chronicle of Michael the Syrian* (Widell 2007). Compiled during the late twelfth century AD, this twenty-one–volume historical account provides annual references to environmental hazards and their impacts in Northern Mesopotamia over a 600-year period.[5] The most common hazards were cold winters, locust infestations, and droughts; but the full list also includes snow, storm winds, freezes, hail, floods, plagues, mildew, rain, and attacks by rats and weevils. This Medieval chronicle cannot be taken as an accurate reflection of conditions during the Bronze Age, but it provides the kind of long-term, synoptic view on environmental hazards that is lacking in the ancient data. The pages that follow introduce a number of the most common and most devastating hazards in Mesopotamia, relying on ancient sources where possible but also supplementing them with data from more recent sources.

### Drought

In arid zones, the threat of drought is a constant concern. This was especially the case in Northern Mesopotamia, where agriculture was dependent on rainfall rather than on artificial irrigation (figure 7.5). Tony Wilkinson calls this northern region the "Zone of Uncertainty," drawing attention to "the considerable risk that is inherent in cropping an area with such a wide interannual fluctuation in rainfall" (2000b: 3). Near the boundary of the zone defined as adequate for rain-fed cultivation—where rainfall averages 250 mm per year—the percentage of years with no harvest is 36 percent. Wilkinson estimates that five to ten major droughts, each lasting six years or longer, would have occurred during the thousand-year span of the Early Bronze Age alone (1997: 75).

Throughout history, water deficits have led to conditions of hunger, malnutrition, and, in the worst cases, starvation. In Mesopotamia, surprisingly

**7.5.** *A dust storm in the modern village of Hamoukar (also a large Early Bronze Age site) in northeastern Syria. The photo was taken in 2010 during a region-wide drought that had already lasted more than three years. Photo by Amanda Schupak.*

little documentary evidence directly links drought with famine, aside from a few letters dating to the Old Babylonian period and a series of documents from the very end of the Late Bronze Age (Neumann and Parpola 1987: 178; Widell 2007: 59). The archaeological identification of drought and its impacts has, however, recently emerged as a major research focus, largely in response to a series of provocative hypotheses proposed by Harvey Weiss and colleagues. Their basic argument is that, during the later part of the third millennium BC, a sudden climatic shift toward more arid conditions led to widespread collapse in Northern Mesopotamia and across a much broader zone stretching from Egypt to India (Weiss 2000; Weiss and Courty 1993; Weiss et al. 1993). There is now general agreement that this drying trend did occur (e.g., Roberts et al. 2011), but debate continues over the suddenness of the climatic shift, the causes of the aridification, and, most important, the impact on Mesopotamian societies (e.g., Kuzucuoglu and Marro 2007).

Whatever the eventual verdict in this debate, it is certain that drought posed a significant and recurring threat to the people of Bronze Age Mesopotamia. In many cases—especially when droughts were short-lived and infrequent—the negative impacts of crop failure appear to have been successfully avoided through a variety of buffering strategies (Halstead and O'Shea 1989; Wilkinson 2000b):

**7.6.** *In the fields surrounding the modern village of Hamoukar in northeastern Syria, sheep, goats, cows, horses, and donkeys are allowed to graze on piles of hay left in the fields following the cereal harvest. The manure deposited by the animals during grazing acts as a natural fertilizer for the fields. Like the related buffering strategy whereby animals are allowed to consume failing crops (e.g., during times of drought), this practice demonstrates the interdependence of agriculture and pastoralism in the region. Photo by Tate Paulette.*

1. Storage of agricultural surpluses (on the household and the institutional levels)[6]

2. Increased mobility (e.g., moving flocks to better-watered areas)

3. The transport of food to affected areas (especially in Southern Mesopotamia, where riverine transport of high-bulk staple goods is more efficient than the overland transport necessary in Northern Mesopotamia)

4. Increased local and interregional exchange (e.g., exchanging high-value items such as metals and textiles for cereals and animals)

5. Salvaging failing crops (e.g., harvesting green crops early or allowing sheep and goats to graze on them; figure 7.6).

## Severe Winters

Although the region was prone to drought and was beset by brutally hot summers, severe winter weather could also wreak havoc on crops and on human and animal populations in ancient Mesopotamia. The mountains to the north and east of the region are more prone to cold weather, but even southern Iraq occasionally experiences low nighttime temperatures and crop-killing frosts during the months of December, January, and February—right in the middle of the growing season (Adams 1981: 12; British Admiralty 1944; Willcocks 1911: 69).

There are numerous references in the cuneiform record to cold weather and its effects. Most commonly, low temperatures, snow, and ice are decried for making transportation routes difficult or impassable, thereby disrupting the flow of tribute, messengers, and troops. Harsh winter weather is also blamed for the deaths of animals and people, especially soldiers (Neumann and Parpola 1987: 181; van Driel 1992: 46; Widell 2007: 55). Although direct evidence is absent in the cuneiform sources, Widell also draws attention to olive trees. Like the ubiquitous date palms of Southern Mesopotamia, olive trees are valuable productive resources, representing a significant investment of time; their death at the hands of a harsh winter could have produced long-term economic consequences (Widell 2007: 55).

On a positive note, severe winters were regularly associated with higher levels of precipitation and, therefore, with normal or better-than-normal crop harvests in Mesopotamia. J. Neumann and Simo Parpola have argued that this correlation linking cold weather to rainfall and abundant harvests—and the opposing correlation linking warm weather to drought and famine—are visible in the Mesopotamian documentary record. Using this evidence, they argue that a major climatic shift toward warmer and drier conditions played a role in the decline of Assyria and Babylonia (i.e., Northern and Southern Mesopotamia) at the end of the Late Bronze Age (Neumann and Parpola 1987).

### Floods

Floods were a regular occurrence in Mesopotamia, and the danger of destructive flooding was very real. Unlike the Nile, whose annual flood arrived at an ideal point within the agricultural cycle, "the timing of the arrival of high water in both the Tigris and the Euphrates [was] poorly synchronized with the needs of cultivators" (Adams 1981: 3). The Tigris typically reached its highest levels in April and the Euphrates in early May. On this schedule, even minor floods, which may have occurred once every three to four years, could destroy mature crops in the fields (Verhoeven 1998: 202). More destructive high-magnitude floods may have occurred two or three times per century, with Tigris floods typically more severe than those of the Euphrates (ibid.: 203).

Floods could not be entirely prevented, but a number of flood-control measures were employed. In modern Iraq, overflow from the Tigris and the Euphrates is directed into specially constructed storage reservoirs. During the Bronze Age, it is likely that a series of natural depressions—especially the modern-day Habbaniyah and Abu Dibbis depressions near Fallujah and Karbala—served a similar purpose. The Old Babylonian (i.e., Middle Bronze Age) king Samsuiluna may even have undertaken a massive project designed to connect these two natural reservoirs to one another (Cole and Gasche 1998: 11; Verhoeven 1998: 201). When such reservoirs were not available, a method known as *controlled breaching* appears to have been employed. For example, a letter written by the Old Babylonian king Hammurabi instructs an official to open a series of canals to direct floodwaters into a marshy area (Cole and Gasche 1998: 11). The physical remains of massive dikes, constructed to protect settlements from flooding, have also been excavated at a number of sites (ibid.: 7–9).

Despite these protective measures, floods did reach fields and settlements, sometimes causing great damage. Thick layers of water-laid sediment excavated at a number of sites testify to the incursion of floodwaters, and written evidence from both Northern and Southern Mesopotamia refers to the inundation of fields, the destruction of bridges and canal works and the collapse of houses and palace walls (ibid.; Gibson 1972: 83–86).

### River Channel Shift

On the irrigated plains of Southern Mesopotamia, Bronze Age settlements were strung out along natural and artificial watercourses like beads on a necklace. Sudden river channel shifts could have catastrophic results for associated settlements, leading, for example, to the drying up of irrigation canals and the disruption of transportation and communication networks. Most channel shifts would have been triggered by a process known as *avulsion*, when a watercourse breaks through the bank of its levee and flows down the bank to create a new channel. Avulsions can be caused by natural flooding events, the weakening of levee banks through human interference (e.g., the cutting of irrigation canals), or a combination of these factors (Wilkinson 2003: 84).

There is clear evidence for a "sporadic but continuing and cumulative westward movement of the Euphrates" over time (Adams 1981: 18; cf. Gibson 1973: 454). This long-term process was the result of numerous distinct episodes of sudden channel shift. For example, the easternmost channel of the Euphrates, located to the north and east of the ancient city of Nippur (in Southern Mesopotamia), appears to have been abandoned by the river in favor of a more westerly branch during the later part of the Uruk period (Adams 1981: 61; Gibson 1973: 450).

Sudden channel shifts can lead to the abandonment of settlements, to population dispersal, and, in arid zones like Southern Mesopotamia, to desertification (Gibson 1992: 12). For example, during the nineteenth and early twentieth centuries AD, the Hilla branch of the Euphrates in Iraq lost nearly all of its water to the more westerly Hindiyah branch, leading to hunger, disease, the abandonment of settlements and farmland, and migration toward better-watered areas (Gibson 1972: 26–29). During the Old Babylonian period (Middle Bronze Age), a similar river channel shift in Southern Mesopotamia may have been responsible for the abandonment of a series of major cities (Gasche 1989; Gibson 1980: 199). Channel shifts can also, however, create new opportunities for those positioned to exploit the situation. In fact, McGuire Gibson has argued that the Uruk period channel shift just described played a crucial role in the emergence of powerful states in Mesopotamia during the same period (Gibson 1973: 461; Wilkinson 2003: 84).

### Salinization

The alluvial soils of Southern Mesopotamia are rich in salts carried down from the mountains by the Tigris and the Euphrates. These salts tend to accumulate at the water table and can be brought toward the surface either through capillary action or through a rising of the water table. Once a certain threshold of salt near the surface is reached, crop growth becomes nearly impossible, and the land must be left uncultivated—sometimes for as long as fifty or a hundred years (Adams 1981: 4; Gibson 1974: 10; Jacobsen and Adams 1958: 1251). One of the most common causes of this *salinization* process is the excessive application of irrigation water. Complex drainage systems and fallowing regimes can help to both prevent the onset of salinization and alleviate its effects, but continued agricultural success then becomes dependent on these practices (Gibson 1974).

Direct evidence for salinization in Bronze Age Mesopotamia comes largely from cuneiform documents. For example, surveyors' reports dating to the late Early Dynastic period and the Ur III period (Early Bronze Age) record the existence of large parcels of land that could not be cultivated because of high salinity. Later, during the Kassite period (Late Bronze Age), curses inscribed on field boundary stones also testify to the threat of saline soils; one curse reads, "May the god Adad, chief irrigation officer of Heaven and Earth, cause wet-salt to disturb his fields, make the barley thirst, and not allow green to come up" (Jacobsen 1982: 8). There is currently no foolproof method for measuring the frequency or ubiquity of salinization in Bronze Age Mesopotamia. Efforts to use declining agricultural productivity and changing crop preferences as proxy indicators for increasing salinization (Jacobsen 1982; Jacobsen and Adams 1958: 1252), for example, have met with significant criticism (Powell 1985).

The negative impacts of salinization can be devastating. In his ethnographic study of the town of Daghara in southern Iraq, Robert Fernea reports that, in recent times, increasingly saline soils had forced the inhabitants to abandon rice and then wheat cultivation, leaving only the more salt-tolerant barley. According to villagers, between the years 1958 and 1966, the total area of cultivable land surrounding Daghara had been reduced by one-third (Fernea 1970: 22, 38). There can be little doubt that salinization was also a persistent threat in Southern Mesopotamia during the Bronze Age. Several authors have drawn attention to the close connection between salinization and the cyclical rise and fall of centralized powers in Mesopotamia. During periods of political centralization, it is argued, the drive toward agricultural intensification led to increased irrigation, the violation of fallowing regimes, and, eventually, widespread salinization. The ultimate impact was a collapse of state power and, consequently, a return to more decentralized political structures and more resilient agricultural practices (Adams 1978; Gibson 1974).

## Soil Degradation

The effects of other types of soil degradation—for example, nutrient depletion, loss of organic carbon, and soil erosion—in Bronze Age Mesopotamia are not well understood. The issue has, however, emerged as a research focus within the broader debate over late third-millennium climate change and settlement collapse in Northern Mesopotamia. In particular, T. J. Wilkinson has argued that the interlinked processes of population growth, settlement nucleation (i.e., a focus on fewer, larger settlements), and agricultural intensification may have encouraged a process of soil degradation that left settlements vulnerable to even minor climatic variations (1997: 76–86, 2000b: 16).

The best evidence supporting this model derives not from direct indications of soil degradation but instead from a practice that was intended to combat soil degradation: the application of fertilizer. In a pioneering application of "off-site" survey techniques (i.e., focusing on the areas between settlements), Wilkinson has identified low-density artifact scatters extending out like a halo around many Early Bronze Age sites in Northern Mesopotamia. Drawing on ethnographic and historic parallels, he interprets these field scatters as the remnants of manuring, a common practice in which household refuse is spread across agricultural fields as fertilizer. The evidence suggests that manuring was widely employed in Northern Mesopotamia but only during a relatively restricted period of time—the mid- to late third millennium BC. During this period of urbanization and population growth, it appears that fertilizer was regularly applied to fields in an attempt to combat the declining fertility associated with agricultural intensification (Wilkinson 1982, 1989, 1994: 491). The eventual abandonment of many of these third-millennium settlements suggests, however, that these attempts may not have been entirely successful over the long term.

## Pests

For farmers everywhere, insects, rodents, birds, and other vermin are not only a perpetual nuisance; in many cases they represent a serious threat to agricultural success and economic viability. A whole range of such creatures confronted the farmers of Bronze Age Mesopotamia,[7] but the pest with the most potential for catastrophic damage was the locust. In modern Syria and Iraq, swarms of locusts can spread out over an area 400 km in diameter, devouring as much as 70 percent of a year's cereal crop, as well as vegetables, trees, and pastureland (British Admiralty 1944: 464; Widell 2007: 57). The periodicity and therefore the predictability of modern locust outbreaks have been a matter of some debate. In the data collected by Michael the Syrian (see earlier reference), however, Widell sees no particular pattern; a calculated average of 22.6 years between successive infestations actually conceals a much broader range of variation, with outbreaks separated by as few as 1 or as many as 74 years (2007: 58).

Cuneiform documents provide a wealth of detail about locust outbreaks in Bronze Age Mesopotamia and about methods for preventing and combating them. For example, a series of letters written to the king of Mari (Old Babylonian period, i.e., Middle Bronze Age) describes a regional governor's fight against two back-to-back years of locust infestation. The locusts were ravaging agricultural fields, and many residents were fleeing to neighboring regions. The methods employed against the locusts included hitting them, trampling them with oxen and sheep, and filling canals with water to serve as barriers (Heimpel 2003: 420). References elsewhere indicate that locusts were also collected in jars and eaten (George 1999: 291; Widell 2007: 61). Preventative measures included a set of special-purpose rituals performed in agricultural fields to protect them from Locust Tooth and from the so-called Dogs of Ninkilim, a general term for field pests. One ritual included offerings to a range of gods, a series of prayers or incantations, more offerings specifically for the god Ninkilim, and the burning of locust figurines made out of wax. It ended with this incantation: "O great dogs of Ninkilim, you have received your fodder, now go away" (George 1999: 295).

## RESILIENCE

The term *resilience* is now in such widespread use that it may be in danger of losing some of its analytical and explanatory power. The collaborators who have contributed to the current volume, however, are in general agreement that the notion of resilience still holds great potential as a tool of cross-cultural comparison and as a way of conceptualizing human-environment dynamics over the short and the long term. The following paragraphs present a brief examination of the concept of resilience—as it is typically employed by Mesopotamian specialists—to introduce a crucial caveat. Resilience is a powerful concept, but an analytical focus on resilience *at the system level* should not blind us to the importance of actions and consequences *on the human scale*.

A number of contributors to the present volume have drawn upon the conceptual repertoire of resilience theory. Originally developed to explain the nature of stasis and change in ecosystems, resilience theory places particular emphasis on the inevitability of change and transformation. The basic unit of analysis is typically the *system* (e.g., the ecosystem or the social system), and systems are understood to develop along a trajectory known as the *adaptive cycle* (see, e.g., Redman 2005; Redman, Nelson, and Kinzig 2009). In discussions of ancient Mesopotamia, the term *resilience* appears with some frequency, though typically without an explicit connection to resilience theory. A brief look at how this term is used by Mesopotamian specialists will help to draw out two critical points regarding the dangers of an exclusive analytical focus on the resilience of social systems.

The first point is that a focus on systemic resilience may downplay the role of human agency. In a now classic discussion of resilience in ancient Mesopotamia, Robert McC. Adams (1978) borrows his basic definition of resilience from the ecological literature, but he makes the important analytical move toward what he calls *strategies* of resilience and stability. For Adams, resilience and stability in social systems are not only properties or behaviors that manifest themselves at the system level; they are also tied closely to the goals pursued by the specific actors and social groups that make up the system. Even though individuals and groups may have little control over the cumulative impact of their practices and decisions, certain types of strategy are more likely to encourage either resilience or stability at the system level.

In Mesopotamia, for example, the centralized institutions were built on complex systems of redistribution that required the maintenance of steady, predictable flows of agricultural goods into and out of centralized storage facilities. The institutional powers therefore tended to favor a maximizing approach to agricultural production, with the ultimate goal of maintaining stability in the supply of staple goods over the short term. Importantly, it appears that these institutional strategies of stability and maximization led repeatedly to system-level *instability*, resulting in the well-known boom-and-bust cycle that defines the broad contours of Mesopotamian political history (Adams 1978: 334). Although they are more difficult to identify in the available sources, some other segments of society—Adams calls them "the protagonists of flexibility"—appear to have been more fluid and resilient over the long term. Adams points in particular to "the tribally organized, semi-nomadic elements" whose mobility and diversified subsistence strategies allowed them to survive throughout the turbulent ups and downs of institutional history (ibid.).

The second point regarding resilience is that an analysis focused on systemic resilience may inadvertently overlook the existence and the effects of institutionalized inequality and exploitation. Mesopotamian specialists are often ambivalent in their assessments (positive versus negative) of the role of institutional dependency in Mesopotamia, and this ambivalence is particularly noticeable in discussions of resilience. Although Adams's discussion of the concept is regularly cited, the term *resilience* is often used in a looser, less explicit sense that actually merges the notions of stability and resilience rather than contrasting them, as Adams does. Many scholars tend to assume that the Mesopotamian institutions, by virtue of their size and wealth, were intrinsically better equipped to weather environmental or economic crises than were individual households (e.g., Postgate 1992: 299; Stein 2004: 77; Stone 2007: 224; Westenholz 2002: 26). If true, this assumption (often presented without supporting evidence) would seem to contradict Adams's argument that the maximizing strategies favored by the central institutions were unsustainable and produced significant instability.

Even if it is eventually shown that the institutions actually contributed to system-level resiliency, this in itself says little about the effects of their practices on the people of Mesopotamia. In the highly stratified societies of Bronze Age Mesopotamia, the impacts of environmental hazards would not have been equally distributed across the social and economic spectrum. Resilience at the system or the institutional level might mask significant disruption and suffering for some segments of the population.

## INSTITUTIONAL POWER, RESILIENCE, AND COLLAPSE

Exactly how successful were efforts by the palaces and temples to prevent and mitigate environmental hazards in Bronze Age Mesopotamia? To what extent did institutional efforts to maximize and intensify production increase the likelihood of systemic failure or the vulnerability of specific segments of society? First, it is important to recall that the institutional landscape was neither static nor spatially homogeneous. The local balance of power between palace and temple was under continual negotiation, and regional power blocs grew and dissolved with relative frequency. At the same time, the forms and methods of institutional management were far from uniform; administrative reforms and large-scale restructurings were regularly instituted by newly ascendant regimes. Generalizations about the scope, effects, and effectiveness of institutional control in Mesopotamia are seldom possible.

The study of collapse has, however, generated a series of vigorous debates over the changing relationship between institutional power and resilience in Mesopotamia (e.g., Yoffee 1988). The paragraphs that follow provide a brief look at the three best-known episodes of collapse. The explanations offered for these episodes range across the spectrum, from environmental crisis to barbarian invasion and economic or political meltdown (Richardson in prep; Yoffee 1988).

## Late Third Millennium BC

The second half of the third millennium BC witnessed the rise and fall of two legendary political dynasties. The Akkadian and Ur III states were the first successful attempts to unite the entirety of Southern Mesopotamia within one centralized political system, but neither lasted much more than a century.[8] Explanations for the collapse of Akkadian and, later, Ur III hegemony have pointed variously to external pressures (e.g., invading Gutians and Amorites), organizational weaknesses (e.g., the bypassing of local power bases, hyper-centralization, and micro-management), and overextension (e.g., preoccupation with military expansion and disregard for internal problems).

Others have credited environmental hazards with a primary causal role. For example, Thorkild Jacobsen links the decline of the Ur III state to a long-term process of progressive salinization in Southern Mesopotamia (1982: 55; Powell 1985). The possibility of a sustained period of aridification during the later third millennium (discussed earlier) has also generated significant debate in recent years. One contentious theory suggests that a climate-induced agricultural crisis in Northern Mesopotamia may have led indirectly to the collapse of the Akkadian state in Southern Mesopotamia (Weiss et al. 1993: 1002).

The late third-millennium collapse episodes bring up two important points. First, the suggested "environmental" causes were closely intertwined with institutional management practices. Salinization is a naturally occurring process, but it would have been accelerated by institutional efforts to intensify irrigation agriculture in Southern Mesopotamia. The aridification scenario, on the other hand, assumes and hinges on a degree of interregional integration that was only achieved in Mesopotamia during a few periods of state expansion and extreme centralization. Second, a distinction should be made between political collapse and the collapse of a settlement system. The breakdown of the Akkadian and Ur III states as political entities may not have significantly impacted the routines of daily life for much of the population. Widespread agricultural failure and settlement abandonment, however, could indicate a more devastating and potentially far-reaching historical transformation.

## End of the Old Babylonian Period

During the 1760s BC, Hammurabi of Babylon undertook a series of conquests that gave him control over much of Southern Mesopotamia and established Babylon as the dominant power in the region. By early in the reign of Hammurabi's successor, Samsuiluna, however, the unified Babylonian state was already beginning to fall apart. Samsuiluna gradually lost control over cities in the southern and then the central part of the alluvial plain. The dynasty itself remained in power for another four generations, but the territory controlled by the state had shrunk to a core area around Babylon itself.

Some theories ascribe the Old Babylonian collapse, at least in part, to "natural" processes. Economic decline, for example, has been linked to a drop in agricultural productivity, which might have resulted from either soil salinization or a series of major river channel shifts (Gasche 1989; Gibson 1980: 199; Stone 1977). More commonly, though, explanations for the collapse of the Old Babylonian state have pointed to economic, administrative, and political problems, such as inflation, spiraling debt, administrative inflexibility, and pressure from external groups (Richardson in prep). This brings up an important point. The present chapter has emphasized the impact of environmental hazards, perhaps downplaying the equally disruptive effect of other (often interrelated) forces, such as social conflict, economic crisis, and political tension (Robertson 2005).

### End of the Late Bronze Age

During the period from approximately 1500 to 1200 BC (the Late Bronze Age), Mesopotamia was linked into an interregional interaction sphere of unprecedented proportions. Southern Mesopotamia was ruled over by the Kassite dynasty, while Northern Mesopotamia first played host to the Mitanni empire and then to the emerging Assyrian empire. The rulers of these powerful states exchanged letters, gifts, and marriage partners with one another and with the rest of the Great Powers—a group that included New Kingdom Egypt, Hittite Anatolia, Mycenaean Greece, and Elamite Iran. Around 1200 BC the system collapsed, ushering in a "Dark Age" characterized by widespread socio-political upheaval. The eastern Mediterranean in particular witnessed significant disruptions, including fiery destructions at many sites and the disappearance of the powerful Hittite state. In Mesopotamia the long-lived Kassite dynasty came to an end, and Assyrian power waned. In both Northern and Southern Mesopotamia, cities went into decline, and many people appear to have adopted a more mobile lifestyle (Van De Mieroop 2004: 179).

Explanations for the synchronized breakdown and collapse of states across such a broad region have been varied and numerous. External invaders, for example, have featured prominently. Most famously, a number of documents describe the movements of marauding "Sea People" around the coasts of the eastern Mediterranean. It has also been suggested that the elite-centered regional system was built on the increasingly harsh exploitation of much of the population. As debts and labor obligations mounted, many of these people managed to escape from the system (e.g., Liverani 1987) and may even have risen up in revolt.

Although environmental factors have played a relatively small part in the broader debate about Late Bronze Age collapse, the breakdown of Kassite and Assyrian power in Mesopotamia has been linked to climate change. As mentioned earlier, Neumann and Parpola argue that a shift toward warmer and drier conditions around 1200 BC coincides with textual evidence for "crop failure, famine, outbreaks of plague, and repeated nomad incursions." Ultimately, they suggest that this climate change contributed strongly to "the political, military, and economic decline of Assyria and Babylonia" (1987: 161).

## CONCLUSION: INSTITUTIONAL(IZED) RESILIENCE IN THE PAST, PRESENT, AND FUTURE

To draw the chapter to a close, it is worth reflecting briefly on the lessons that can be learned from a study of environmental hazards in Bronze Age Mesopotamia. Many of the hazards faced during the Bronze Age still confront the region's inhabitants today. They are joined by a host of new hazards, including the reduction and pollution of water supplies (as a result of extensive dam construction), the disappearance of the marshes in southern Iraq, pollution related to oil extraction and production (figure 7.7), and unsustainable levels of population increase (McGuire Gibson personal communication). It is possible that an examination of ancient forms of hazard management and mitigation could resurrect some forgotten techniques that could be directly applied in the modern world.[9] There is also, however, another less obvious but equally valuable way in which knowledge of ancient Mesopotamia can inform the present world. The study of the past is as much about learning to ask the right questions as it is about uncovering exciting new discoveries. As we learn to ask the right questions about ancient Mesopotamia, we can achieve a better understanding of the potential impact of the decisions that are made and the policies that are adopted in our own increasingly global society.

The title of this chapter draws attention to the intertwined themes of domination and resilience, both crucial to an understanding of hazards and hazard management in Bronze Age Mesopotamia. Our knowledge of human-environment dynamics in Mesopotamia is still far from complete, but we are increasingly learning to ask the right questions. These questions center on the complex intersection between resilience and the institutionalized forms of domination that emerged in Mesopotamia—for the first time in world history—during the fourth and third millennia BC. I would like to draw particular attention to two issues that bear directly on our efforts to create a more resilient, sustainable future for the present world.

**7.7.** *Cereal fields near the village of Hamoukar in northeastern Syria. The Tur Abdin Mountains of Turkey are visible in the distance, and to the right a gas flare burns off waste material from an oil well. Photo by Amanda Schupak.*

First, it is crucial that we pay careful attention to the effects and the effectiveness of different institutional forms. Over the course of the Bronze Age, Mesopotamia witnessed the rise and fall of a number of distinct systems of centralized political and economic organization. In some cases (e.g., the Ur III state), centralized control was tight and regional economic integration carefully orchestrated; in others (e.g., the Old Babylonian period), private entrepreneurs and agents played a stronger role, and the institutions managed the economy less closely. Throughout the Bronze Age the institutional powers regularly made efforts to prevent and combat environmental hazards, but in many cases their practices also contributed to the creation or exacerbation of hazards (e.g., soil salinization and channel shift).

In the modern world, when natural disasters strike, the inadequacy of institutional (i.e., state-organized) responses is often painfully obvious. One need only recall, for example, controversies over the US government's response to Hurricane Katrina in 2005 or to the oil spill in the Gulf of Mexico in 2010. There is a pressing need to fine-tune our own institutional structures, developing ways to increase their flexibility and the speed of their responses. In these efforts to improve the functioning of our institutions, the archaeological and historical records provide an invaluable, but largely untapped, resource. They offer the chance to examine countless examples of successful and unsuccessful responses to environmental crises and therefore to evaluate the effectiveness of a wide diversity of institutional forms over both the short and the long term.

The second issue is inequality—in particular, the unequal distribution of risks and benefits. We have seen that evidence for resilience at the level of the society or the system might mask the existence of deeply entrenched inequality and exploitation. Risk and the negative impacts of environmental hazards may be unequally distributed among the people and groups within a society, even when that society is, at a higher level of abstraction, resilient to repeated environmental crises.

The states of Bronze Age Mesopotamia were built on high levels of institutionalized inequality, but we still know relatively little about the distribution of risk within these societies. It is commonly asserted that the palace and temple institutions served as a social safety net; the evidence for this function, however, is relatively restricted, consisting largely of references to the support of orphans and widows (Postgate 1992: 135; Westenholz 1999: 61). We know a lot about the conditions of institutional dependency in Mesopotamia (including, for example, tenancy, sharecropping, and debt slavery), but, to my knowledge, we do not know how dependents were treated in times of scarcity or crisis.

In a now-classic study of tenancy and taxation in Southeast Asia, however, James C. Scott has shown that this is precisely where our analyses should be focused (Scott 1976). From the perspective of peasants living near the edge of subsistence—especially those owing taxes or rent to the state or to a landlord— what matters most is what happens in lean years, when food is in short supply. In such circumstances, how were dependents treated? Were they guaranteed a minimum level of subsistence, even in a year of abnormally low harvests or during a time of environmental crisis? The detailed archaeological and written evidence available from Bronze Age Mesopotamia is well suited to an exploration of these questions concerning the effects of inequality, and these are questions that need to be investigated as a crucial counterpart to analyses focusing on resiliency, stability, and collapse at the system level.

In our own world, the issue of inequality is no less urgent. Although many environmental hazards are now of global concern, the impacts of these hazards and of related policy decisions are seldom experienced worldwide in a uniform fashion. As we work toward a more sustainable future for our planet in the context of an increasingly interconnected, globalized economy, we need to ensure that some people (or countries) do not benefit at the expense of others. In the same vein, there is a danger in treating resilience and sustainability *at the system level* as goals in themselves. What if scientific study demonstrates that the most resilient type of society is one built on extreme inequality and exploitation, one in which the system is resilient only at the cost of great suffering for large portions of the population? Would this be a system worth sustaining? Of course not. The goal is not simply resilience or sustainability but rather resilience and sustainability coupled with equality, justice, and other basic human rights.

*Acknowledgments.* I would like to thank Payson Sheets, Jago Cooper, Ben Fitzhugh, Andrew Dugmore, McGuire Gibson, Tony Wilkinson, Magnus Widell, and Kathryn Grossman for reading drafts of this chapter and providing helpful comments and criticism. I also thank members of the MASS Project for many stimulating discussions on the topics discussed here. The MASS Project has been supported by funding from the National Science Foundation (Grant no. 0216548). My own work has also been funded by a Research Fellowship from the American Academic Research Institute in Iraq (TAARII).

## NOTES

1. For an introduction to Mesopotamian history and archaeology, see, e.g., Pollock 1999; Postgate 1992; Roaf 1990; Van De Mieroop 2004. For the archaeology of Syria, see Akkermans and Schwartz 2003.

2. The term *Urban Revolution* was coined by V. Gordon Childe (1950) to describe the multifaceted process of urbanization and state formation initiated in Mesopotamia during the later part of the fourth millennium BC.

3. Since the beginning of the Gulf War in 1990, there has been a hiatus in fieldwork by foreign archaeological teams in Iraq, but some teams are beginning to resume work.

4. There is, however, the *Farmer's Instructions* (Civil 1994), a Sumerian text from the third millennium BC that provides a wealth of detail about agricultural practices and the annual agricultural cycle.

5. The chronicle does not actually cover the entire 600-year span (AD 600–1196) with the same level of comprehensiveness and accuracy. In fact, Widell (2007: 50–52) argues that the reliability of the account can only be assumed for 276 years within this period.

6. See, e.g., Pfälzner 2002 and my forthcoming PhD dissertation (University of Chicago, 2012).

7. The list of pests known from ancient Mesopotamia includes locusts, "spotty bugs," weevils, caterpillars, "eater"-pests, grubs, field mice, and granary mice, among others (George 1999: 291, 297–298).

8. The peak of the Akkadian state's power lasted from approximately 2340 to 2200 BC and that of the Ur III state from 2112 to 2004 BC.

9. For example, in the Lake Titicaca region of Bolivia, there have been efforts to reintroduce the raised-field farming system employed in the region during the first millennium AD (Kolata 1991).

## REFERENCES

Adams, Robert McC.
1965     *Land behind Baghdad.* University of Chicago Press, Chicago.

1978    Strategies of Maximization, Stability, and Resilience in Mesopotamian Society, Settlement, and Agriculture. *Proceedings of the American Philosophical Society* 122(5): 329–335.

1981    *Heartland of Cities: Surveys of Ancient Settlement and Land Use on the Central Floodplain of the Euphrates.* University of Chicago Press, Chicago.

Akkermans, Peter M.M.G., and Glenn M. Schwartz

2003    *The Archaeology of Syria: From Complex Hunter-Gatherers to Early Urban Societies (ca. 16,000–300 BC).* Cambridge University Press, Cambridge.

British Admiralty

1944    *Iraq and the Persian Gulf.* B.R. 524 (Restricted). Geographical Handbook Series. Naval Intelligence Division, Oxford.

Childe, V. Gordon

1950    The Urban Revolution. *Town Planning Review* 21: 3–17.

Civil, Miguel

1994    *The Farmer's Instructions: A Sumerian Agricultural Manual.* Aula Orientalis–Supplementa 5. Editorial AUSA, Sabadell, Spain.

Cole, Steven W., and Hermann Gasche

1998    Second- and First-Millennium BC Rivers in Northern Babylonia. In *Changing Watercourses in Babylonia: Towards a Reconstruction of the Ancient Environment in Lower Mesopotamia,* ed. Hermann Gasche and Michel Tanret. Mesopotamian History and Environment, Series II, Memoirs V, vol. 1. Oriental Institute of the University of Chicago, Chicago, and University of Ghent, Ghent, pp. 1–64.

Dalfes, H. Nüzhet, George Kukla, and Harvey Weiss, eds.

1997    *Third Millennium BC Climate Change and Old World Collapse.* Springer, Berlin.

Fernea, Robert A.

1970    *Shaykh and Effendi: Changing Patterns of Authority among the El Shabana of Southern Iraq.* Harvard Middle Eastern Studies 14. Harvard University Press, Cambridge, MA.

Gasche, Hermann

1989    *La Babylonie au 17ᵉ siècle avant notre ère: Approche archéologique, problèmes et perspectives.* Mesopotamian History and Environment, Series II, Memoirs I. University of Ghent, Ghent.

George, Andrew R.

1999    The Dogs of Ninkilim: Magic against Field Pests in Ancient Mesopotamia. In *Landwirtschaft im Alten Orient,* ed. Horst Klengel and Johannes Renger. Berliner Beiträge zum Vorderen Orient 18. Dietrich Reimer Verlag, Berlin, pp. 291–299.

Gibson, McGuire

1972    *The City and Area of Kish.* Field Research Reports, Coconut Grove, Miami.

1973    Population Shift and the Rise of Mesopotamian Civilization. In *The Explanation of Culture Change: Models in Prehistory,* ed. Colin Renfrew. Duckworth, London, pp. 447–463.

1974      Violation of Fallow and Engineered Disaster in Mesopotamian Civilization. In *Irrigation's Impact on Society,* ed. Theodore E. Downing and McGuire Gibson. University of Arizona Press, Tucson, pp. 7–19.

1980      Current Research at Nippur: Ecological, Anthropological and Documentary Interplay. In *L'archéologie de l'Iraq du début de l'époque néolithique à 333 avant notre ère,* ed. Marie-Thérèse Barrelet. Editions du Centre national de la recherche scientifique, Paris, pp. 193–206.

1992      The Origin and Development of Sumerian Civilization and Its Relation to Environment. In *Nature and Humankind in the Age of Environmental Crisis,* ed. Ito Shuntaro and Yasuda Yoshinori. International Research Center for Japanese Studies, Kyoto, Japan, pp. 1–27.

Halstead, Paul, and John O'Shea
1989      Introduction: Cultural Responses to Risk and Uncertainty. In *Bad Year Economics: Cultural Responses to Risk and Uncertainty,* ed. Paul Halstead and John O'Shea. Cambridge University Press, Cambridge, pp. 1–7.

Heimpel, Wolfgang
2003      *Letters to the King of Mari.* Eisenbrauns, Winona Lake, IN.

Jacobsen, Thorkild
1982      *Salinity and Irrigation Agriculture in Antiquity.* Bibliotheca Mesopotamica 14. Undena Publications, Malibu, CA.

Jacobsen, Thorkild, and Robert McC. Adams
1958      Salt and Silt in Ancient Mesopotamian Agriculture. *Science* 128(3334): 1251–1258.

Kolata, Alan L.
1991      The Technology and Organization of Agricultural Production in the Tiwanaku State. *Latin American Antiquity* 2(2): 99–125.

Kuzucuoglu, Catherine, and Catherine Marro, eds.
2007      *Sociétés humaines et changement climatique à la fin du troisième millénaire: une crise a-t-elle eu lieu en haute Mésopotamie? Actes du colloque de Lyon, 5–8 décembre 2005.* Varia Anatolica 19. Institut Français d'Études Anatoliennes–Georges Dumezil. DE BOCCARD Édition-Diffusion, Paris.

Liverani, Mario
1987      The Collapse of the Near Eastern Regional System at the End of the Bronze Age: The Case of Syria. In *Centre and Periphery in the Ancient World,* ed. Michael Rowlands, Mogens Larsen, and Kristian Kristiansen. Cambridge University Press, Cambridge, pp. 66–73.

Meyer, Jan-Waalke
2007      Town Planning in 3rd Millennium Tell Chuera. In *Power and Architecture: Monumental Public Architecture in the Bronze Age Near East and Aegean,* ed. Joachim Bretschneider, Jan Driessen, and Karel van Lerberghe. Orientalia Lovaniensia Analecta 156. Uitgeverij Peeters en Departement Oosterse Studies, Leuven, Belgium, pp. 129–142.

Neumann, J., and Simo Parpola
1987      Climatic Change and the Eleventh–Tenth-Century Eclipse of Assyria and Babylonia. *Journal of Near Eastern Studies* 46(3): 161–182.

Nissen, Hans J., Peter Damerow, and Robert K. Englund
  1993    *Archaic Bookkeeping: Writing and Techniques of Economic Administration in the Ancient Near East.* University of Chicago Press, Chicago.

Pfälzner, Peter
  2002    Modes of Storage and the Development of Economic Systems in the Early Jezireh-Period. In *Of Pots and Plans: Papers on the Archaeology and History of Mesopotamia and Syria Presented to David Oates in Honour of His 75th Birthday,* ed. Lamia Al-Gailani Werr, John Curtis, Harriet Martin, Augusta McMahon, Joan Oates, and Julian Reade. NABU Publications, London, pp. 259–286.

Pollock, Susan
  1999    *Ancient Mesopotamia: The Eden That Never Was.* Cambridge University Press, Cambridge.

Postgate, J. N.
  1992    *Early Mesopotamia: Society and Economy at the Dawn of History.* Routledge, London.

Powell, Marvin A.
  1985    Salt, Seed, and Yields in Sumerian Agriculture: A Critique of the Theory of Progressive Salinization. *Zeitschrift für Assyriologie und Vorderasiatische Archäologie* 75: 7–38.

Powell, Marvin A., ed.
  1987    *Labor in the Ancient Near East.* American Oriental Series 68. American Oriental Society, New Haven, CT.

Redman, Charles L.
  2005    Resilience Theory in Archaeology. *American Anthropologist* 107(1): 70–77.

Redman, Charles L., Margaret C. Nelson, and Ann P. Kinzig
  2009    The Resilience of Socioecological Landscapes: Lessons from the Hohokam. In *The Archaeology of Environmental Change: Socionatural Legacies of Degradation and Resilience,* ed. Christopher T. Fisher, J. Brett Hill, and Gary M. Feinman. University of Arizona Press, Tucson, pp. 15–39.

Richardson, Seth
  In prep    *On Babylon and Collapse.*

Roaf, Michael
  1990    *Cultural Atlas of Mesopotamia and the Ancient Near East.* Facts on File, New York.

Roberts, Neil, Warren J. Eastwood, Catherine Kuzucuoglu, Girolamo Fiorentino, and Valentina Caracuta
  2011    Climatic, Vegetation and Cultural Change in the Eastern Mediterranean during the Mid-Holocene Environmental Transition. *The Holocene* 21: 147–162.

Robertson, John F.
  2005    Social Tensions in the Ancient Near East. In *A Companion to the Ancient Near East,* ed. Daniel C. Snell. Blackwell, Oxford, pp. 196–210.

Scott, James C.
 1976    *The Moral Economy of the Peasant: Rebellion and Subsistence in Southeast Asia.* Yale University Press, New Haven, CT.

Stein, Gil
 2004    Structural Parameters and Sociocultural Factors in the Economic Organization of North Mesopotamian Urbanism in the Third Millennium B.C. In *Archaeological Perspectives on Political Economies,* ed. Gary M. Feinman and Linda M. Nicholas. University of Utah Press, Salt Lake City, pp. 61–78.

Stone, Elizabeth C.
 1977    Economic Crisis and Social Upheaval in Old Babylonian Nippur. In *Mountains and Lowlands: Essays in the Archaeology of Greater Mesopotamia,* ed. Louis D. Levine and T. Cuyler Young Jr. Bibliotheca Mesopotamica 7. Undena Publications, Malibu, CA, pp. 267–289.

 2007    The Mesopotamian Urban Experience. In *Settlement and Society: Essays Dedicated to Robert McCormick Adams,* ed. Elizabeth C. Stone. Ideas, Debates, and Perspectives 3. Cotsen Institute of Archaeology and the Oriental Institute of the University of Chicago, Chicago, pp. 213–234.

Ur, Jason
 2003    CORONA Satellite Photography and Ancient Road Networks: A Northern Mesopotamian Case Study. *Antiquity* 77: 102–115.

Van De Mieroop, Marc
 2004    *A History of the Ancient Near East ca. 3000–323 BC.* Blackwell, Oxford.

van Driel, G.
 1992    Weather: Between the Natural and the Unnatural in First Millennium Cuneiform Inscriptions. In *Natural Phenomena: Their Meaning, Depiction and Description in the Ancient Near East,* ed. Diederik J.W. Meijer. North-Holland, Amsterdam, pp. 39–52.

Verhoeven, Kris
 1998    Geomorphological Research in the Mesopotamian Flood Plain. In *Changing Watercourses in Babylonia: Towards a Reconstruction of the Ancient Environment in Lower Mesopotamia,* ed. Hermann Gasche and Michel Tanret. Mesopotamian History and Environment, Series II, Memoirs V, vol. 1. Oriental Institute of the University of Chicago, Chicago, and University of Ghent, Ghent, pp. 159–245.

Weiss, Harvey
 2000    Beyond the Younger Dryas: Collapse as Adaptation to Abrupt Climate Change in Ancient West Asia and the Eastern Mediterranean. In *Environmental Disaster and the Archaeology of Human Response,* ed. Garth Bawden and Richard Martin Reycraft. Anthropological Papers 7. Maxwell Museum of Anthropology, University of New Mexico, Albuquerque, pp. 75–95.

Weiss, Harvey, and Marie-Agnès Courty
 1993    The Genesis and Collapse of the Akkadian Empire: The Accidental Refraction of Historical Law. In *Akkad: The First World Empire. Struc-*

*ture, Ideology, Traditions,* ed. Mario Liverani. History of the Ancient Near East / Studies V. Sargon, Padova, Italy, pp. 131–155.

Weiss, Harvey, Marie-Agnès Courty, Wilma Wetterstrom, Francois Guichard, Louise Senior, Richard H. Meadow, and A. Curnow
1993    The Genesis and Collapse of Third Millennium North Mesopotamian Civilization. *Science* 261: 995–1004.

Westenholz, Aage
1999    The Old Akkadian Period: History and Culture. In *Mesopotamien: Akkade-Zeit und Ur III–Zeit,* ed. Walther Sallaberger and Aage Westenholz. Orbis Biblicus et Orientalis 160/3. Universitätsverlag Freiburg Schweiz and Vandenhoeck & Ruprecht Göttingen, Freiburg and Göttingen, pp. 17–117.

2002    The Sumerian City-State. In *A Comparative Study of Six City-State Cultures,* ed. Mogens Herman Hansen. C. A. Reitzels Forlag, Copenhagen, pp. 23–42.

Widell, Magnus
2007    Historical Evidence for Climate Instability and Environmental Catastrophes in Northern Syria and the Jazira: The Chronicle of Michael the Syrian. *Environment and History* 13: 47–70.

Wilkinson, Tony J.
1982    The Definition of Ancient Manured Zones by Means of Extensive Sherd-Sampling Techniques. *Journal of Field Archaeology* 9(3): 323–333.

1989    Extensive Sherd Scatters and Land-Use Intensity: Some Recent Results. *Journal of Field Archaeology* 16(1): 31–46.

1994    The Structure and Dynamics of Dry-Farming States in Upper Mesopotamia. *Current Anthropology* 35(5): 483–520.

1997    Environmental Fluctuations, Agricultural Production and Collapse: A View from Bronze Age Upper Mesopotamia. In *Third Millennium BC Climate Change and Old World Collapse,* ed. H. Nüzhet Dalfes, George Kukla, and Harvey Weiss. Springer-Verlag, Berlin, pp. 67–106.

2000a   Regional Approaches to Mesopotamian Archaeology: The Contribution of Archaeological Surveys. *Journal of Archaeological Research* 8: 219–267.

2000b   Settlement and Land Use in the Zone of Uncertainty in Upper Mesopotamia. In *Rainfall and Agriculture in Northern Mesopotamia,* ed. Remko M. Jas. MOS Studies 3. Publications de l'Institut historique-archéologique néerlandais de Stamboul 88. Nederlands Historisch–Archeologisch Instituut, Istanbul, Turkey, pp. 3–35.

2003    *Archaeological Landscapes of the Near East.* University of Arizona Press, Tucson.

Wilkinson, Tony J., John H. Christiansen, Jason A. Ur, Magnus Widell, and Mark Altaweel
2007a   Urbanization within a Dynamic Environment: Modeling Bronze Age Communities in Upper Mesopotamia. *American Anthropologist* 109(1): 52–68.

Wilkinson, Tony J., McGuire Gibson, John H. Christiansen, Magnus Widell, David Schloen, Nicholas Kouchoukos, Christopher Woods, John Sanders, Kathy-Lee Simunich, Mark Altaweel, Jason A. Ur, Carrie Hritz, Jacob Lauinger, Tate Paulette, and Jonathan Tenney
    2007b    Modeling Settlement Systems in a Dynamic Environment: Case Studies from Mesopotamia. In *The Model-Based Archaeology of Socionatural Systems,* ed. Timothy A. Kohler and Sander E. van der Leeuw. School for Advanced Research Press, Santa Fe, NM, pp. 175–208.

Willcocks, Sir W.
    1911    *The Irrigation of Mesopotamia.* E. and F. N. Spoon, Limited, London.

Yoffee, Norman
    1988    The Collapse of Ancient Mesopotamian States and Civilization. In *The Collapse of Ancient States and Civilizations,* ed. Norman Yoffee and George L. Cowgill. University of Arizona Press, Tucson, pp. 44–68.

## UNDERSTANDING HAZARDS, MITIGATING IMPACTS, AVOIDING DISASTERS

### Statement for Policy Makers and the Disaster Management Community

This chapter uses archaeological and written evidence to document the broad range of environmental hazards that confronted the inhabitants of Bronze Age Mesopotamia. Some of these hazards (e.g., droughts and locust attacks) could be expected to recur on a regular basis but could not be reliably predicted. Some (e.g., floods and river channel shifts) were more erratic, appearing suddenly and without warning. Others (e.g., salinization and soil degradation) took place gradually over much longer timescales. The impacts of these hazards varied widely, from short-term fluctuations in the food supply to declining soil fertility, settlement abandonment, and even large-scale political collapse.

Two key points—with direct relevance to the modern world—emerge from this study of Bronze Age Mesopotamia. First, it is vital that we pay careful attention to the effects and the effectiveness of different forms of institutional organization. In Mesopotamia, individual households and local communities used a variety of risk-buffering strategies to protect themselves from environmental hazards, but these households and communities were also tied into complex systems of institutional management. In some cases the centralized palace and temple institutions may have provided a degree of stability, insulating dependents from the worst effects of environmental hazards; in other cases, however, institutional practices appear to have triggered the onset of hazards or exacerbated their impacts. Second, the study of "resilience" must be combined with an analysis of the effects of inequality. In highly stratified societies, such as those of Bronze Age Mesopotamia, risks are seldom distributed evenly across the population. The impacts of environmental hazards will often be felt more deeply by some people than by others, and resilience may—but should not—come at the cost of inequality, exploitation, and suffering.

# EIGHT

# Long-Term Vulnerability and Resilience: Three Examples from Archaeological Study in the Southwestern United States and Northern Mexico

*Margaret C. Nelson, Michelle Hegmon, Keith W. Kintigh,*
*Ann P. Kinzig, Ben A. Nelson, John Marty Anderies, David A. Abbott,*
*Katherine A. Spielmann, Scott E. Ingram, Matthew A. Peeples,*
*Stephanie Kulow, Colleen A. Strawhacker, and Cathryn Meegan*

Events during the last several years—such as Hurricane Katrina, the earthquake in Haiti, the Southeast Asian tsunami, and continuing droughts in Africa—vividly illustrate the vulnerability of human society to environmental disturbances. That vulnerability lies in both the nature and magnitude of hazards in the environment and in the configurations (institutions, policies, practices) of human societies. We unintentionally play an essential role in creating our vulnerabilities. The concepts of resilience and vulnerability in coupled social-ecological systems have proved increasingly important for analyzing the human dimensions of environmental disturbance and change (Janssen and Ostrom 2006)—in the sense of this book, how people experience "hazards." For example, strong earthquakes in some regions of the world result in limited human suffering and infrastructure costs, while in others they are massively devastating in human life and property loss. The same can be said for disease, hurricane damage, and other occurrences we think of as "natural hazards." Human societies directly affect what a hazard is and how it is experienced.

In this chapter we illustrate the role analysis of archaeological data can play to inform our understanding of resilience and vulnerability in coupled social-ecological systems with a long-term view of the interaction between society and environment. Our research employs environmental and social information from six regions within the southwestern United States and northern

Mexico (figure 8.1) that collectively spans over a millennium. These examples address climate "hazards" directly, as well as the kinds of social pathways that can increase vulnerabilities to an array of conditions. It is the understanding of social and natural processes that can inform present decision-making, not the specific relationships evident in the past.

## CHALLENGES: DEFINING AND MEASURING RESILIENCE, VULNERABILITY, AND HAZARD

If we are to assess the hazards, delineate vulnerabilities, and move toward resilient systems, one of the greatest challenges we face is to understand the dynamics of social-ecological systems. To do that requires not only an understanding of contemporary systems but also an appreciation of how dynamics play out over very long time spans. We need to understand short-term and long-term processes as well as the short- and long-term solutions for addressing the impacts of "hazards." Our research addresses long time spans, focusing on vulnerabilities, resilience, and robustness. For this chapter we frame our work in terms of the experience of "hazards," focusing on the social and environmental contributions to that experience.

Before exploring three examples of our work, we define the key concepts. *Resilience* is the ability of a system to absorb disturbances (such as those described as hazards) without losing identity (Folke 2006) or the capacity to absorb perturbations while maintaining essential structures and functions (Holling, Gunderson, and Peterson 2002). Similar to resilience, *robustness* highlights the ability of systems to withstand change through both flexibility and resistance. Our version of robustness incorporates many of the features of resilience but emphasizes the role social and physical infrastructure can play in fostering both flexibility and inertia in dynamic social-ecological systems (Anderies, Janssen, and Ostrom 2004). In general, *vulnerability* is a function of the exposure and sensitivity of a system to a hazard and the adaptive capacity or resilience of the system to cope, adapt, or recover from the effects of the hazard (Adger 2006: 269; Smit et al. 2001: 893–895; Smit and Wandel 2006: 286; Turner et al. 2003). There are many specific definitions of vulnerability (see Cutter 1996: 531–532 for a summary), but it is commonly understood as the "potential for loss" (ibid.: 529), the "capacity to be wounded" (Kates 1985: 17), or the "potential for negative outcomes or consequences" (Meyer et al. 1998: 239). More specifically, it is "the degree to which a system [such as a human-environment system], subsystem, or system component is likely to experience harm due to exposure to a hazard, either a perturbation or stress/stressor" (Turner et al. 2003: 8074).

Scientific and policy forums on environmental change increasingly use a systems perspective to formulate policies that integrate the many dimensions

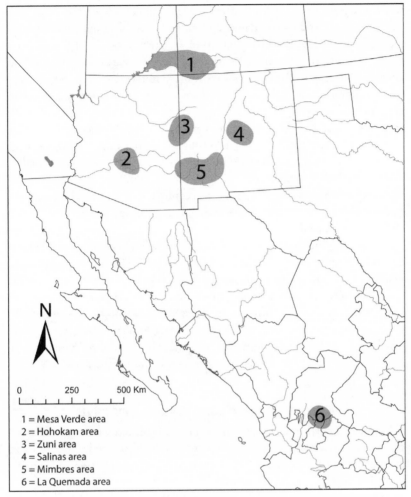

**8.1.** *Map of the southwestern United States and northern Mexico showing the areas encompassed by the six cases. Map by Matthew A. Peeples.*

of social-ecological systems (Adger 2006; Folke 2006; Janssen and Ostrom 2006; Janssen et al. 2006; Young et al. 2006). Resilience research explores multiple, open, interacting systems that move between states of stability and transformation (Holling 1973; Holling and Gunderson 2002). Vulnerability research, originating in geography and the study of natural hazards (Adger 2006), focuses on the attributes of people or groups that enable them to cope with the impact of disturbances.

Unfortunately, it is impossible to generate "absolute resilience or robustness" in social-ecological systems. Rather, we must ask, resilience of what to what (Carpenter et al. 2001)? Any strategies humans deploy to cope with disturbances introduce fundamental tradeoffs. To develop effective coping strategies in a rapidly changing world, we must recognize that a decision to increase resilience in one dimension is likely to increase vulnerabilities in another (Anderies et al. 2007). In two of the examples described in this chapter, we address human vulnerability to climatic variability and change, specifically focused on precipitation and stream flow, and we explore tradeoffs. We contribute to an emerging literature that focuses on robustness-vulnerability tradeoffs to understand how social-ecological systems organize, cope with variation, and change (Anderies 2006; Anderies et al. 2007; Anderies, Walker, and Kinzig 2006; Janssen, Anderies, and Ostrom 2007). In the third example we specifically focus on how human social configurations can create conditions of vulnerability that influence the way people experience disturbances, climatic changes, and variability.

Following the theme of this book, we view low precipitation and variable precipitation conditions as potential "hazards" within the southwestern United States and northern Mexico to which people may be or may become vulnerable. *Hazards* can be thought of as "threats to a system and the consequences they produce" (Turner et al. 2003: 8074). We outline features of climate conditions in the southwestern United States and northern Mexico that may be potential hazards, and we explore the role of social configurations in creating hazards and preventing people from responding effectively.

## ADVANTAGES OF A LONG-TERM PERSPECTIVE

We use data sequences that span millennium-long timescales in the southwestern United States and northern Mexico to assess how human societies and ecosystems interact. In this region of the world, low precipitation and variable precipitation are challenges or potential "hazards" for human occupation today and have been throughout human history. For farmers, the levels of precipitation in this region of the world are highly variable temporally and spatially and typically fall below the minimum needs of many domesticated crops (especially maize, the primary cultigen). The potential "hazards" of low precipitation and uncertain timing of precipitation can create conditions of famine whose timing can be uncertain. But the experience of potential hazards—whether they are realized and experienced as hazardous conditions—depends on a variety of social factors, from population size to the forms of physical infrastructure and social institutions. People address climatic challenges such as low and variable precipitation in various ways, from diversifying their use of resources and using a range of environmental settings, to building infrastructure (such as irrigation systems) to control the distribution of water, to settling in areas of high natural water table, which are rare (Spielmann et al. in press).

Sometimes humans build social systems that exacerbate rather than mitigate these potential "hazards" or that actually prevent people from responding to them effectively. In this chapter we examine three lessons to be learned from understanding long sequences of human-environment interaction. The first examines how diversity in food systems influences the vulnerability of human societies to food shortages as a result of low precipitation in this arid to semiarid region. The second examines how irrigation infrastructure both mitigates variability in the temporal and spatial patterns of precipitation and creates new vulnerabilities. The third emphasizes the role of social action in creating conditions of rigidity that exacerbate the potential for climate "hazards" to impact people. These studies are published fully elsewhere (Anderies, Nelson, and Kinzig 2008; Hegmon et al. 2008; Nelson et al. 2010). All have applications to the way we think about hazards in today's world, which we address in the final section of this chapter.

The archaeological cases we explore and compare in our studies are from the southwestern United States and northern Mexico. They include the Zuni area in northern New Mexico, the Salinas area in central New Mexico, the Mimbres area in southwestern New Mexico, the Mesa Verde area in the Four Corners of the southwestern United States, the Hohokam area in south-central Arizona, and the Malpaso Valley (occupation focused on the site of La Quemada) in Zacatecas, Mexico (figures 8.1, 8.2). All of these areas are in arid to semiarid settings* and, during the periods of study, are agriculturally based, non-state societies. They vary considerably in population size, social configurations, agricultural strategies, and social-environmental histories. Thus they provide a diverse set of cases, all situated in environmental settings that offer the same kinds of "hazards" of low and spatially unpredictable precipitation. In this chapter we discuss all except the Salinas case.

Although study of the past might appear divorced from contemporary concerns given globalization and the rapid technological change that characterize today's world, archaeology provides a long-term, historically contextualized view of many social-ecological changes, some more dramatic than others (Redman and Kinzig 2003; van der Leeuw and Redman 2002). While the cases do not help us predict the future, they do provide natural experiments by which we can come to better understand relationships between vulnerabilities and change and examine assumptions used to make contemporary decisions about managing for change versus managing for stability. Furthermore, most of the cases we explore are what archaeologists refer to as middle-range societies—

---

* Average annual precipitation levels range from a low of about 200 mm (8") in the Hohokam area to a high of about 450 mm (18") in the higher portions of the Mesa Verde area.

**8.2.** *Images that illustrate each case area. Compiled by Margaret Nelson.*

they have weakly developed institutionalized hierarchies. In the contemporary world, millions of people who live in what are effectively non-state societies are faced with a variety of "hazards"—from those such as earthquakes, whose causes are purely environmental, to those that are largely social, which is to say generated by human interactions (e.g., ethnic strife), to those in which human actions have environmental consequences. Our research is relevant to those experiences.

### CONTRIBUTION 1: DIVERSIFYING MAIZE-BASED SUBSISTENCE

The first example addresses the role of subsistence or dietary diversity in the capacity of systems to cope with climate "hazards" of low precipitation and variability in precipitation. This study is more fully developed in an article by John Anderies, Ben Nelson, and Ann Kinzig (2008).

The "common wisdom" or "rule of thumb" that diverse portfolios are advantageous in uncertain or variable environments is widespread. This strategy is certainly pervasive in today's stock market, where investors are advised to maintain a diverse set of stocks or mutual funds. It is also what drives the propensity to establish trade relationships between and among cultural groups residing in different bioclimatic zones, both in the past and the present. For investments and exchange networks, the nature of the diversity matters in

**8.3.** *Map of Mexico, with La Quemada indicated. Map by Will Russell.*

addressing vulnerabilities—elements of a portfolio should have a somewhat uncorrelated performance. The higher the probability that one element (crop, trading partner, mutual fund) of the portfolio will perform well when another is performing poorly, the higher the buffering against risk. On the other hand, it is well-known that in simple feedback systems there are consequences associated with a given choice of a portfolio aimed at coping with a particular range of variability; that choice can also reduce the capacity to cope with variability outside the target range (Anderies et al. 2007). As such, general "rules of thumb" might not be all that generalizable or transferable between different "experiments."

To explore this tradeoff, we analyzed the consequences of diversifying crops in prehispanic northern Mexico, focusing on conditions in the Malpaso Valley area around the prehispanic center of La Quemada (figures 8.1, 8.2, 8.3).

Specifically, we asked when and under what climatic circumstances would the addition of a second cultivated plant—agave—to a maize-based subsistence system allow farmers to persist in locations that might otherwise be untenable. By implication, we were interested in the conditions under which such diversification does not address the "hazard" of low and variable precipitation and may even increase vulnerability.

By 500 CE, inhabitants of the Malpaso Valley area (figure 8.3), within the modern state of Zacatecas, Mexico, subsisted on a classic Mesoamerican diet of maize, beans, and squash (Turkon 2004). If ethnographic equivalents shed light on the proportions of each, maize provided over 50 percent of the calories for this complement of crops (López Corral and Uruñuela y Ladón de Guevara 2005). During the period 500–900 CE, people spread north from population centers in central Mexico, aggregating at unprecedented scales in widely separated arable patches along the foothills of the Sierra Madre Occidental (Kelley 1971), including the Malpaso Valley. Various hypotheses have been advanced for these movements, including a diaspora following the breakup of the great city of Teotihuacan (Jiménez-Moreno 1959), climatic changes that allowed central Mexican lords to more profitably exploit the land and labor of northern Mexico (Armillas 1964), mutually beneficial alliances between the lords of central and northern Mexico (Jiménez-Betts and Darling 2000), or the pursuit of rare mineral resources (Weigand 1977). There are as yet no published paleoenvironmental data with which to evaluate these propositions.

Vulnerability to famine was almost certainly an issue for early northern Mexican maize farmers (Armillas 1964; Gunn and Adams 1981; Sauer 1963). The northern territories had lower annual precipitation, greater inter-annual variability in rainfall, and therefore greater probability of extended drought than the central regions of Mexico in which maize cultivation had originated. The abandonment of the northern regions in 900 CE has been attributed to this vulnerability to drought (Coe 1994); even today, farmers in the region report that they can only depend on good maize yields in two years out of ten (Nelson 1992).

Carl Sauer (1963) and Jeffrey P. Parsons and Mary P. Parsons (1990) point to agave cultivation as a potential buffer against famine events introduced by persistent drought, and we know agave was cultivated in prehispanic central and northern Mexican settlements (e.g., McClung de Tapia et al. 1992). This crop diversification is by no means the only possible risk-buffering strategy; other (not mutually exclusive) strategies include concentrating water resources through irrigation or terracing (e.g., Fisher, Pollard, and Frederick 1999; Howard 1993), food sharing (e.g., Hegmon 1996), mobility (e.g., Nelson and Anyon 1996), and crop storage (Seymour 1994). Moreover, agave may have been produced for reasons extending beyond subsistence—for instance, the alcoholic beverage *pulque*, produced from agave, was used in culturally important feasts (Clark and Blake 1994).

Given that agave is a perennial plant, with maturation times ranging from a few years to decades for the different species, and maize is an annual plant, the a priori arguments for cultivating agave in addition to maize as a risk reduction strategy in this arid and highly variable environment seem strong. But the general rule of thumb for diversifying in uncertain environments is unsatisfying. Climatic structures can vary significantly from place to place, with fundamentally different relationships between annual averages and inter-annual variability, for instance. Is agave equally useful in all variable environments? If not, when is it most useful? When is it least useful and potentially not worth the added costs of managing a diverse crop portfolio?

These are the questions we attempted to answer with simple models of maize and agave production and maize storage under diverse climatic conditions. Both maize and agave production are assumed to be water-limited. Variability in annual precipitation was taken to be either 20 percent or 50 percent of the mean precipitation. Mean annual precipitation ranged from levels at which maize crops would regularly fail to those at which maize yields would be maximized (yields would plateau with respect to increasing rainfall, likely because some other resource such as nitrogen or phosphorous becomes limiting). In a second set of simulations, mean annual rainfall was pegged at 70 percent of the level at which maximum yields would saturate, and inter-annual variability was allowed to range from 20 to 90 percent of this mean. Our measure of the risk-buffering potential of agave was the reduction in the experience of famine events, particularly those of long duration (three years or more) (see Anderies, Nelson, and Kinzig 2008 for further details of the model and results).

Our initial instinct, based on "common wisdom," was that agave would be most useful in relatively harsh environments (low rainfall, where maize would be expected to fail with some regularity) with high inter-annual variability in precipitation. Our results contradicted those instincts. Specifically, agave contributed most significantly to maize farmers' ability to survive drought (avoid famine events) when both the mean and variability of rainfall were "intermediate"—that is, rainfall was somewhere between levels that would guarantee either crop failure or maximum yields, with intermediate inter-annual variability. When variance was high, regardless of the mean rainfall, agave did not confer significant benefits. When variance was low, the most significant benefits to agave cultivation accrued in intermediate to high average rainfall conditions. Thus diversity is shown not to be an inherent good, regardless of local conditions, but rather is a conditional benefit that must be weighed against the cost of building that diversity. In this case, diversifying the cultivated resource base did not hedge against the vulnerability to famine resulting from low and variable precipitation, one of the primary hazards of farming in this area. As noted, agave may have been cultivated for entirely different reasons having to do with its value in making a fermented beverage for ceremonial use. If that motivation accounted for its cultivation, it would have been present in the rare circumstances when it might have contributed to reducing the risk of famine.

## CONTRIBUTION 2: THE ROLE OF IRRIGATION INFRASTRUCTURE IN VULNERABILITY TO CLIMATE CONDITIONS

The social benefits of technological innovations, especially those leading to increases in food production, are plainly evident in the short term. This second contribution takes the development of irrigation agriculture as an example to explore how the potential vulnerabilities that can accompany this innovation may play out in the very long term (intergenerationally).

In arid and semiarid environments, some form of irrigation is nearly always necessary for agriculture, and agriculture is necessary to support anything more than the extremely low population densities that can persist with a hunting-and-gathering adaptation. Irrigation agriculture enormously increases the number of people who can be supported in a given area and enhances the robustness of that population to high-frequency spatial and temporal variability in precipitation. It does this by delivering precipitation to fields that is captured over a much larger area and—in the case of irrigation from rivers fed by snowmelt—over a much longer time. That increase in robustness, however, is accompanied by potential vulnerabilities.

1.  The physical infrastructure of water-control systems may be vulnerable to destruction by rare climatic events, such as a major flood, which may make irrigation agriculture impossible for an extended period of time or render it useless when floods scour stream beds and become entrenched below the former floodplain.

2.  Residents of settlements that depend on irrigation may be resistant to relocation because of their material and labor investment in the irrigation infrastructure. These place-focused long-term occupations can severely deplete local resources such as soils, animals, and plants.

3.  Although productivity of irrigation agriculture makes population growth possible, long-term population growth may eventually outstrip the productive capacity of local resources, including those enhanced by the water-control infrastructure, leading to food shortages.

This second contribution (presented in more detail in Nelson et al. 2010) examines tradeoffs of robustness and vulnerability in the changing social, technological, and environmental contexts of three long-term prehispanic sequences in the US Southwest: the Mimbres area in southwestern New Mexico (650–1450 CE), the Zuni area in west-central New Mexico (850–1540 CE), and the Hohokam area in central Arizona (700–1450 CE) (see figures 8.1, 8.2).

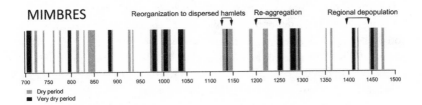

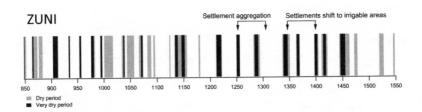

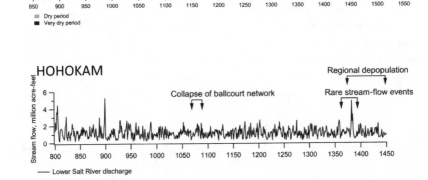

**8.4.** *Periods of extremely low precipitation in Mimbres and Zuni areas and stream-flow discharge patterns in the Lower Salt River in the Hohokam area. By Scott Ingram.*

In all three of these arid landscapes, people relied on agricultural systems that depended on physical and social infrastructure of irrigation to deliver adequate water to agricultural fields. Across the cases, the scale and the nature of the investments in infrastructure varied, as did local environmental conditions.

"Mimbres" refers to an archaeologically defined region in southwest New Mexico (see figures 8.1, 8.2). The subsistence economy of the Mimbres sequence is characterized by small-scale farming supplemented by hunting and gathering. Mimbres fields were primarily watered by small-scale canals feeding floodplain fields. This small-scale irrigation system increased the productivity of floodplain fields, as did the stone terracing systems on hill-slope and alluvial fan fields, ensuring more directed and abundant water and nutrient flow to field locales. Although many periods of severely low precipitation were experienced during the temporal interval discussed here, most were not associated with social transformations that are evident in the archaeological record (figure

207

8.4). However, an extended period of extremely low precipitation around 1130 CE coincides with the depopulation of nearly all the large villages, with emigration of the population to small settlements (Hegmon, Ennes, and Nelson 2000; Nelson 1999). Within a half-century, however, the local population and immigrants had again aggregated into new villages in the region (see "Contribution 3" below for more discussion of the Mimbres).

In the Mimbres case, the major transformation around 1130 CE was associated with a coincidence of all three vulnerabilities. Population had been growing for centuries, probably pushing (but not exceeding) the occupied areas' sustaining capacity by that time (Schollmeyer 2009). The investments in infrastructure and a focus on floodplain farming led to a place-focused residential pattern that, by the 1100s, resulted in depletion of soil (Sandor 1992), plant (Minnis 1985), and animal resources (Schollmeyer 2009). The increasing vulnerabilities associated with these long-term social and environmental processes were realized with the occurrence of a high-frequency event—an extended period of low precipitation about 1130 CE. In this case an agricultural strategy aimed at increasing robustness to high-frequency climatic variation eventually ran afoul of long-term vulnerabilities and thus engendered a transformation to a new phase of development. Vulnerabilities to resource depletion and low precipitation led to reorganization, but practices of managing fields in diverse settings may have tempered the changes brought on by those vulnerabilities.

Our examination of the Hohokam of central and southern Arizona (see figures 8.1, 8.2) focuses on the people who lived along the Lower Salt River in what is today the Phoenix metropolitan area (for more on the Hohokam, see "Contribution 3" below). The prehistoric residents flourished in the Phoenix basin for a millennium, occupying some of the largest and longest-lived settlements in the ancient US Southwest and developing the largest network of irrigation canals in Precolumbian North America (figure 8.5). The period 800–1450 CE encompassed a cultural florescence characterized by a regional system of ceremony and exchange, followed by a collapse of the regional networks and prevailing social institutions and a long slide toward total residential abandonment (Abbott 2003, 2006; Doelle and Wallace 1991; Doyel 2000).

The large-scale irrigation technology of the Hohokam was sustained for over a millennium. Its great capacity to supply agricultural surpluses contributed to the creation of a regional-scale economy that was highly robust to local fluctuations in rainfall. But this robustness came at the cost of increased vulnerability to social and ecological perturbations at specific localities, which, because of the crosscutting interdependencies, could be felt across the region. Although people were place-focused, for centuries they acquired a wide array of resources through an extensive regional exchange network. The ca. 1070 CE collapse of the regional system and the depopulation of much of the surrounding area resulted in a dramatic increase in the Phoenix basin population (Doelle,

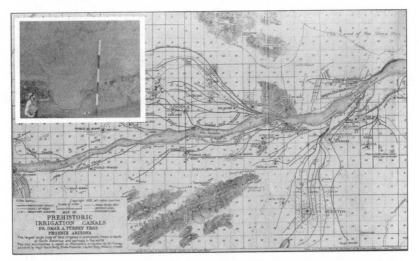

**8.5.** *The Hohokam irrigation system as mapped in the 1920s and a cross-section of an irrigation canal excavated by Jerry Howard. Map is from Omar Turney (1929).*

Gregory, and Wallace 1995; Doyel 1981; Teague 1984; Wilcox 1991) and a consequent depletion of local resources. With the replacement of the regional network with balkanized local networks, many exchanged resources were no longer available (Crown 1991) and the social relations that supported the canal systems were changed. Extreme climate events in the late 1300s—including two years of river flows higher than had been seen for 500 years (see figure 8.4)—were probably devastating to the irrigation infrastructure (Graybill et al. 2006: 117). Occurring in a context of population pressure, depleted resources, and institutional disarray, these events may well have contributed to the long-term slide toward near-total depopulation of the region; potential vulnerabilities were realized, people suffered, and institutions collapsed. We discuss this collapse more fully under "Contribution 3."

The Zuni area (see figures 8.1, 8.2), which spans the Arizona–New Mexico border along the southern margin of the Colorado Plateau, is one of only three areas in the Southwest continuously and densely occupied from the early centuries CE, through the Spanish Conquest, and up to the present (Ferguson and Hart 1985). From 850 to 1200 CE, settlements were relatively small and short-lived and the population was widely distributed (Peeples and Schachner 2007). By the end of the 1200s people had aggregated in large towns that, until the late 1300s, were concentrated in the eastern portion of the Zuni area (Kintigh 1985, 1996; Kintigh, Glowack, and Huntley 2004). As the long-term hydraulic conditions changed in the mid-1200s (see figure 8.4), an early reliance on small floodplain and sand-dune agricultural fields watered by groundwater and floodwater gave way to an agricultural strategy heavily reliant on small-scale runoff farming that, after 1300 CE, was augmented by ditch irrigation from large springs. By 1400 the entire population had moved to long-lived towns with canal-irrigated fields set on broad floodplains adjacent to the Zuni River (Kintigh 1985).

The Zuni case illustrates how social and physical changes together kept potential vulnerabilities from being realized. The water delivery infrastructure in the Zuni region was much smaller-scale and more dynamic. Farming strategies were altered with shifts in climate, hydrology, population density, and social institutions. Despite considerable investments in physical infrastructure (villages and fields), Zuni villagers did not become place-focused until the end of the prehistoric sequence when they had developed social institutions that could sustain the aggregated populations. The area's population seems to have leveled off by the late 1200s, and people in the proto-historic settlements evidently lived within their productive means. In this context, potential vulnerabilities to extended droughts seem not to have been realized.

For arid-land farmers, physical infrastructure that captures or directs water for agriculture ameliorates short-term temporal and spatial variability in precipitation and improves productivity. It makes town and village life possible in many places where it would not otherwise have been. Comparisons across these cases allow us to understand the interactions of social, technological, and environmental factors that promote the vulnerabilities that accompany irrigation agriculture and influence resilience in specific contexts. These comparisons help us understand, in social terms, why people experienced changes in climate in different ways. Looking across these cases, it is clear that any relatively short-term view (e.g., fifty years) would not allow us to understand the complex dynamics or predict their outcomes; a long-term view is essential.

## CONTRIBUTION 3: RIGIDITY TRAPS IN SOCIAL-ECOLOGICAL SYSTEMS

Intellectual traditions from Marxism to Buddhism understand a basic truth that is also central to resilience thinking: change is inevitable. Change is also the basic subject of historical inquiry, including archaeology; however, in studying many historical trajectories in the US Southwest, we are struck by the varied nature of changes. In some cases archaeologists and anthropologists document considerable continuity in traditions over long time spans in the context of other changes. In other cases, such as those discussed in this section, cultural traditions come to an end, sometimes with great loss of life. In this research we asked why some changes are so much more traumatic than others, why people do not address the disturbances that confront them. More specifically, we examined the hypothesis that resistance to change, described by a concept known as a *rigidity trap* in resilience thinking, contributes to severity of change when it (inevitably) comes. Rigidity traps prevent people from effectively responding to deteriorated conditions.

A rigidity trap is described by C. S. Holling and colleagues (2002: 96) as a situation in which there is a high degree of integration and the system can persist "even beyond the point where it is adaptive and creative . . . [with] efficient methods of social control whereby any novelty is either smothered or sees its inventor ejected." Did rigidity traps make change more difficult or traumatic among farming societies in the ancient Southwest? To answer this question, we undertook a comparative study of three cases of transformation—Mimbres, Mesa Verde, and Hohokam (see figures 8.1, 8.2). For each case we assessed:

1. The nature and severity of the transformations: How many people were affected and how were they affected? Did they leave their homeland? Is there any evidence of physical suffering?

2. The degree of rigidity: How integrated was the society? How hierarchical? Is there conformity, indicative of some kind of social control?

The original presentation of this research (Hegmon et al. 2008) details how these concepts were assessed in terms of a series of archaeologically measurable variables and describes the extensive data sources. Here we simply summarize each transformation and evidence for rigidity in each case.

The Mimbres region in southwest New Mexico is known for its beautiful pottery (figure 8.6), made mostly during the Mimbres Classic period (1000–1130 CE). The end of this period saw the end of this pottery tradition and the movement of many people out of their farming villages. Because archaeologists had defined the period as marked by village life with a certain type of pottery, its end had been interpreted as a collapse. But our research (see also Nelson et al. 2006) showed that the transformation itself was fairly mild. A few thousand people did leave their villages, moving both north and south of the Mimbres region, but some of them simply resettled a short distance from their former villages in what had been their temporary field houses, where they started importing and possibly making other kinds of pottery. It was a flexible strategy that exhibited no evidence of hierarchy, mild integration, and little rigidity overall.

The Mesa Verde region of southwest Colorado was occupied by tens of thousands of people in the early 1200s CE, and by 1300 CE it was virtually empty (Varien et al. 2007). After decades marked by competition and hostilities, including a village massacre (Kuckelman, Lightfoot, and Martin 2002), many of the people moved to northern New Mexico (Ortman 2009). This large-scale and traumatic transformation was associated with considerable rigidity, created in this context by increasingly aggregated settlements with large public architecture and some indications of hierarchy.

**8.6.** *A Classic Mimbres black-on-white painted bowl from 1000–1130 CE. Courtesy, Eastern Mimbres Archaeological Project, Arizona State University, Tempe.*

As discussed in the previous section, the Hohokam region in central and southern Arizona is known for the largest prehispanic canal irrigation system in North America (see figure 8.5). That system, which was enormously successful for centuries, went out of use sometime in the late fourteenth to the fifteenth century. Tens of thousands of people depended on it, but few were still in the area at the time of Spanish contact; the population seems to have died out, moved away, or both. This was an enormous and traumatic transformation, and it was preceded by a long period of rigidity, described in the book *Centuries of Decline* (Abbott 2003). There is evidence of social institutions that in this context were not responsive to changing conditions: hierarchy, public architecture that excluded many, and strongly aggregated settlements. In some settlements serious health problems were caused by poor diet, yet, unlike in the Mesa Verde region, people stayed and apparently suffered, possibly for generations. In the Hohokam case the irrigation that had worked so well to manage change and variability in precipitation and stream flow and to boost the productivity of this desert environment was part of a rigidity trap. People committed to this way of life were left with no options; their rigidity trap kept them in deteriorating conditions until the inevitable collapse that included tremendous population loss, in some cases through mortality resulting from poor health.

This research on rigidity in social systems demonstrates that humans unintentionally construct traps that both create vulnerabilities and prevent people from acting in their own interest to address changed conditions. These unintended consequences of development and commitment to stability have implications for the human experience of "hazards." The concept of a "hazard" is as much a product of human construction as of the conditions of the environment (e.g., Burton, Kates, and White 1993). One lesson from analysis of these cases is that the rigidity of social configurations, however they are constructed by people, can create conditions that exacerbate the influence of "hazards" of all sorts.

## FUTURE RESEARCH, LESSONS FOR THE PRESENT

This research has several important implications for resilience thinking with regard to vulnerability in social-ecological systems. It shows that resilience concepts can be assessed systematically in the archaeological record and thus pave the way for more research on long-term processes relevant to contemporary decisions about vulnerability and resilience. It shows how an understanding of relatively small-scale societies in the ancient past can provide insights relevant to our world today. Nuanced thinking about the costs and benefits of diversity, the tradeoffs in vulnerability resulting from investments in infrastructure, and the role of humans in constructing rigidity traps is important in managing toward reductions in the impacts of various disturbances or hazards. We offer a few specific thoughts for future consideration; they apply well beyond our thinking about the human experience of hazards.

1. Diversity has costs as well as benefits. In the subsistence realm it may be examined more productively in terms of the responsiveness of plants to varied climate conditions than as a simple function of the number of kinds of plants. What kind of diversity we promote in today's world may be more important than the simple value of diversity.

2. Addressing vulnerabilities in one domain or at one scale can create new vulnerabilities in other domains or at other scales. Absolute resilience is not a reasonable goal. Rather, the best we can do is seek to find a balance among vulnerabilities that reduces the cost of experiencing disturbances or disasters; in resilience terms, we must develop adaptive capacity to manage inevitable yet often unpredictable disturbances (including those that may be known hazards for which timing and intensity are unpredictable).

3. Isolation can contribute to rigidity and eventually to the severity of collapse and transformation. That is a lesson worth keeping in mind in today's world as we grapple with global connections.

Archaeologists have much to offer to modern policy making through explorations, over long timescales, of the key concepts employed in efforts to build resilience in modern social-ecological systems.

## REFERENCES

Abbott, David R.
2006　Hohokam Ritual and Economic Transformation: Ceramic Evidence from the Phoenix Basin, Arizona. *North American Archaeologist* 27: 285–310.

Abbott, David R., ed.
2003　*Centuries of Decline during the Hohokam Classic Period at Pueblo Grande.* University of Arizona Press, Tucson.

Adger, W. Neil
2006　Vulnerability. *Global Environmental Change* 16(3): 268–281.

Anderies, John M.
2006　Robustness, Institutions, and Large-Scale Change in Socio-Ecological Systems: The Hohokam of the Phoenix Basin. *Journal of Institutional Economics* 2(2): 133–155.

Anderies, John M., Marco A. Janssen, and Elinor Ostrom
2004　A Framework to Analyze the Robustness of Social-Ecological Systems from an Institutional Perspective. *Ecology and Society* 9(1):18. At http://www.ecologyandsociety.org/vol9/iss1/art18/.

Anderies, John M., Ben Nelson, and Ann P. Kinzig
2008　Analyzing the Impact of Agave Cultivation on Famine Risks in Arid Prehispanic Northern Mexico. *Human Ecology* 36(3): 409–422.

Anderies, John M., Armando Rodriguez, Marco Janssen, and Oguzhan Cifdaloz
2007　Panaceas, Uncertainty, and the Robust Control Framework in Sustainability Science. *PNAS* 104(39): 15194–15199.

Anderies, John M., Brian H. Walker, and Ann P. Kinzig
2006　Fifteen Weddings and a Funeral: Case Studies and Resilience-Based Management. *Ecology and Society* 11(1): 21. At http://www.ecologyandsociety.org/vol11/iss1/art21/.

Armillas, Pedro
1964　Condiciones Ambientales y Movimientos de Pueblos en la Frontera Septentrional de Mesoamerica. In *Publicaciones del Seminario de Antropología Americana,* ed. H. F. Marquez-Miranda. Universidades de Madrid, Seville, pp. 62–82.

Burton, Ian, Robert W. Kates, and Gilbert F. White
1993　*The Environment as Hazard,* 2nd ed. Guilford, New York.

Carpenter, Steve R., Brian H. Walker, John M. Anderies, and Nick Abel
2001    From Metaphor to Measurement: Resilience of What to What? *Ecosystems* 4: 765–781.

Clark, John E., and T. Michael Blake
1994    The Power of Prestige: Competitive Generosity and the Emergence of Rank Societies in Lowland Mesoamerica. In *Factional Competition and Political Development in the New World*, ed. Elizabeth E. Brumfiel and John W. Fox. Cambridge University Press, Cambridge, pp. 17–30.

Coe, Michael D.
1994    *Mexico*, 4th ed. Thames and Hudson, New York.

Crown, Patricia L.
1991    The Role of Exchange and Interaction in Salt–Gila Basin Hohokam Prehistory. In *Exploring the Hohokam: Prehistoric Desert Peoples of the American Southwest*, ed. George J. Gumerman. Amerind Foundation New World Studies Series 1. University of New Mexico Press, Albuquerque, pp. 383–416.

Cutter, Susan L.
1996    Vulnerability to Environmental Hazards. *Progress in Human Geography* 20(4): 529–539.

Doelle, William H., David A. Gregory, and Henry D. Wallace
1995    Classic Period Platform Mound Systems in Southern Arizona. In *The Roosevelt Community Development Study: New Perspectives on Tonto Basin Prehistory*, ed. Mark D. Elson, Mariam T. Stark, and David A. Gregory. Anthropological Papers 15. Center for Desert Archaeology, Tucson, pp. 385–440.

Doelle, William H., and Henry D. Wallace
1991    The Changing Role of the Tucson Basin in the Hohokam Regional System. In *Exploring the Hohokam: Prehistoric Desert Peoples of the American Southwest*, ed. George J. Gumerman. Amerind Foundation New World Studies Series 1. University of New Mexico Press, Albuquerque, pp. 279–346.

Doyel, David E.
1981    *Late Hohokam Prehistory in Southern Arizona*. Gila Press, Scottsdale, AZ.
2000    The Santan Phase in the Phoenix Basin. In *The Hohokam Village Revisited*, ed. David E. Doyel, Suzanne Fish, and Paul Fish. SWARM Division, American Association for the Advancement of Science, Fort Collins, CO, pp. 221–244.

Ferguson, T. J., and E. Richard Hart
1985    *A Zuni Atlas*. University of Oklahoma Press, Norman.

Fisher, Christopher T., Helen P. Pollard, and Charles Frederick
1999    Intensive Agriculture and Socio-Political Development in the Lake Pàtzcuaro Basin, Michoacán, Mexico. *Antiquity* 73: 642–649.

Folke, Carl
   2006      Resilience: The Emergence of a Perspective for Social-Ecological Systems
            Analysis. *Global Environmental Change* 16: 253–267.

Graybill, Donald A., David A. Gregory, Gary S. Funkhouser, and Fred Nials
   2006      Long-Term Streamflow Reconstructions, River Channel Morphology,
            and Aboriginal Irrigation Systems along the Salt and Gila Rivers. In *Environmental Change and Human Adaptation in the Ancient American Southwest*, ed. David E. Doyel and Jeffrey S. Dean. University of Utah Press, Salt
            Lake City, pp. 69–123.

Gunn, Joel, and Richard Adams
   1981      Climatic Change, Culture, and Civilization in North America. *World Archaeology* 13: 87–100.

Hegmon, Michelle
   1996      Variability in Food Production, Strategies of Storage and Sharing, and
            the Pit House to Pueblo Transition in the Northern Southwest. In *Evolving Complexity and Environmental Risk in the Prehistoric Southwest*, ed.
            Joseph Tainter and Bonnie Tainter. Studies in the Sciences of Complexity.
            Santa Fe Institute, Santa Fe, NM, pp. 223–250.

Hegmon, Michelle, Mark Ennes, and Margaret C. Nelson
   2000      Corrugated Pottery, Technological Style, and Population Movement in
            the Mimbres Region of the American Southwest. *Journal of Anthropological Research* 56: 217–240.

Hegmon, Michelle, Matthew A. Peeples, Ann P. Kinzig, Stephanie Kulow, Cathryn
   M. Meegan, and Margaret C. Nelson
   2008      Social Transformation and Its Human Costs in the Prehispanic U.S.
            Southwest. *American Anthropologist* 110: 313–324.

Holling, C. S.
   1973      Resilience and Stability of Ecological Systems. *Annual Review of Ecology and Systematics* 4: 1–23.

Holling, C. S., and Lance H. Gunderson
   2002      Resilience and Adaptive Cycles. In *Panarchy: Understanding Transformations in Human and Natural Systems*, ed. Lance H. Gunderson and C. S.
            Holling. Island Press, Washington, DC, pp. 25–62.

Holling, C. S., Lance H. Gunderson, and Gary D. Peterson
   2002      Sustainability and Panarchies. In *Panarchy: Understanding Transformations in Human and Natural Systems,* ed. Lance H. Gunderson and C. S.
            Holling. Island Press, Washington, DC, pp. 63–102.

Howard, Jerry B.
   1993      A Paleohydraulic Approach to Examining Agricultural Intensification in
            Hohokam Irrigation Systems. In *Research in Economic Anthropology,* ed. V.
            L. Scarborough and B. L. Isaac. JAI Press, Greenwich, CT, pp. 263–324.

Janssen, Marco A., John M. Anderies, and Elinor Ostrom
   2007      Robustness of Social-Ecological Systems to Spatial and Temporal Disturbance Regimes. *Society and Natural Resources* 20(4): 307–322.

Janssen, Marco A., and Elinor Ostrom
2006    Resilience, Vulnerability, and Adaptation: A Cross-Cutting Theme of the Human Dimensions of the Global Environmental Change Program. *Global Environmental Change* 16(3): 237–239.

Janssen, Marco A., Michael L. Schoon, Weimao Ke, and Katy Börner
2006    Scholarly Networks on Resilience, Vulnerability and Adaptation within the Human Dimensions of Global Environmental Change. *Global Environmental Change* 16(3): 240–252.

Jiménez-Betts, Peter F., and J. Andrew Darling
2000    Archaeology of Southern Zacatecas: The Malpaso, Juchipila, and Valparaiso-Bolaños Valleys. In *Greater Mesoamerica: The Archaeology of West and Northwest Mexico*, ed. Michael S. Foster and Shirley Gorenstein. University of Utah Press, Salt Lake City, pp. 155–180.

Jiménez-Moreno, Wigberto
1959    Síntesis de la Historia Pretolteca de Mesoamérica. In *El Esplendor del México Antiguo*, vol. 2. Centro de Investigaciones Antropológicos, México, DF, pp. 1109–1196.

Kates, Robert
1985    The Interaction of Climate and Society. In *Climate Impact Assessment: Studies of the Interaction of Climate and Society*, ed. Mimi Berberian and Robert W. Kates, with Jesse H. Ausubel. John Wiley, Chichester, England, pp. 3–36.

Kelley, J. Charles
1971    Archaeology of the Northern Frontier: Zacatecas and Durango. In *Archaeology of Northern Mesoamerica*, part 2, vol. 11, of *Handbook of Middle American Indians*, ed. Gordon F. Ekholm and Ignacio Bernal. University of Texas Press, Austin, pp. 768–804.

Kintigh, Keith W.
1985    *Settlement, Subsistence, and Society in Late Zuni Prehistory*. Anthropological Papers of the University of Arizona 44. University of Arizona Press, Tucson.
1996    The Cibola Region in the Post-Chacoan Era. In *The Prehistoric Pueblo World, A.D. 1150–1350*, ed. M. A. Adler. University of Arizona Press, Tucson, pp. 131–144.

Kintigh, Keith W., Donna M. Glowack, and Deborah L. Huntley
2004    Long-Term Settlement History and the Emergence of Towns in the Zuni Area. *American Antiquity* 69(3): 432–456.

Kuckelman, Kristen A., Ricky R. Lightfoot, and Debra L. Martin
2002    The Bioarchaeology and Taphonomy of Violence at Castle Rock and Sand Canyon Pueblos, Southwestern Colorado. *American Antiquity* 67: 486–513.

López Corral, Alonso, and Gabriela Uruñuela y Ladón de Guevara
2005    Capacidad de Almacenamiento en Pozos Troncocónicos de Cholula, Puebla. Paper presented at the conference Arqueologica del Almacenamiento en

Tiempos Prehispánicos desde el Norte de Mexico Hasta el Altiplano Cen-tralî, June 8–11, Mexico City.

McClung de Tapia, Emily, J. González Vázquez, J. Zurita-Noguera, and M. C. Serra Puche
1992    Evidencia Para el uso del Agave sp. Durante el Periodo Formativo en el Sur de la Cuenca de México. *Antropologí a y Técnica* 5: 99–114.

Meyer, W. B., Karl W. Butzer, Theodore E. Downing, Billie L. Turner II, G. W. Wenzel, and James L. Wescoat
1998    Reasoning by Analogy. In *Human Choice and Climate Change,* vol. 3: *The Tools for Policy Analysis,* ed. S. Rayner and E. L. Malone. Battelle, Colum-bus, OH, pp. 217–289.

Minnis, Paul E.
1985    *Social Adaptation to Food Stress: A Prehistoric Southwestern Example.* Uni-versity of Chicago Press, Chicago.

Nelson, Ben A.
1992    El Maguey y Nopal en la Economía de Subsistencia de La Quemada, Zacatecas. In *Origen y Desarollo de la Civilización en el Occidente de México,* ed. B. Boehm de Lameiras and Philip C. Weigand. Colegio de Michoacán 1115, Zamora, Michoacán, pp. 359–382.

Nelson, Ben A., and Roger Anyon
1996    Fallow Valleys: Asynchronous Occupations in Southwestern New Mexico. *Kiva* 61: 275–294.

Nelson, Margaret C.
1999    *Mimbres during the Twelfth Century: Abandonment, Continuity, and Reor-ganization.* University of Arizona Press, Tucson.

Nelson, Margaret C., Michelle Hegmon, Stephanie Kulow, and Karen G. Schollmeyer
2006    Archaeological and Ecological Perspectives on Reorganization: A Case Study from the Mimbres Region of the U.S. Southwest. *American Antiq-uity* 71: 403–432.

Nelson, Margaret C., Keith W. Kintigh, David R. Abbott, and John M. Anderies
2010    The Cross-Scale Interplay between Social and Biophysical Context and the Vulnerability of Irrigation-Dependent Societies: Archaeology's Long-Term Perspective. *Ecology and Society* 15(3): 31. At http://www.ecology andsociety.org/vol15/iss3/art31/.

Ortman, Scott G.
2009    Genes, Language and Culture in Tewa Ethnogenesis, A.D. 1150–1400. PhD dissertation in Anthropology, Arizona State University, Tempe.

Parsons, Jeffrey R., and Mary H. Parsons
1990    *Maguey Utilization in Highland Central Mexico: An Archaeological Eth-nography.* Anthropological Papers 82. Museum of Anthropology, Univer-sity of Michigan, Ann Arbor.

Peeples, Matthew, and Gregson Schachner
2007    Long-Term Patterns of Settlement Movement along the Zuni River Drain-age. At http://www.public.asu.edu/~mpeeple/swsposter.html.

Redman, C. L., and Ann P. Kinzig
    2003    Resilience of Past Landscapes: Resilience Theory, Society, and the *Longue Durée. Conservation Ecology* 7(1): 14. At http://www.consecol.org/vol7/iss1/art14.

Sandor, Jonathan A.
    1992    Long-Term Effects of Prehistoric Agriculture on Soils: Examples from New Mexico and Peru. In *Soils in Archaeology: Landscape Evolution and Human Occupation*, ed. Vance T. Holliday. Smithsonian Institution Press, Washington, DC, pp. 217–245.

Sauer, Carl O.
    1963    *Land and Life: A Selection from the Writing of C. O. Sauer.* University of California Press, Berkeley.

Schollmeyer, K. G.
    2009    Resource Stress and Settlement Pattern Change in the Eastern Mimbres Area, Southwest New Mexico. PhD dissertation, School of Human Evolution and Social Change, Arizona State University, Tempe.

Seymour, Deni J.
    1994    Peripheral Considerations: Defining the Spatial and Physical Correlates of Storage Behavior in Hohokam Structures. *Kiva* 59: 377–394.

Smit, Barry, and Olga Pilifosova
    2001    Adaptation to Climate Change in the Context of Sustainable Development and Equity. In *Contribution of the Working Group to the Third Assessment Report of the Intergovernmental Panel on Climate Change.* Cambridge University Press, Cambridge, pp. 879–912.

Smit, Barry, and Johanna Wandel
    2006    Adaptation, Adaptive Capacity and Vulnerability. *Global Environmental Change* 16: 282–292.

Spielmann, Katherine A., Margaret C. Nelson, Scott Ingram, and Matthew A. Peeples
    In press    Mitigating Environmental Risk in the US Southwest. In *Forces of Nature: Environmental Risk and Resilience as Long-Term Factors of Cultural Change*, ed. Naomi Miller, Katherine Moore, and K. Ryan.

Teague, Lynne S.
    1984    The Organization of Hohokam Economy. In *Hohokam Archaeology along the Salt-Gila Aqueduct, Central Arizona Project*, vol. 9: *Synthesis and Conclusions*, ed. Lynne S. Teague and Patricia L. Crown. Archaeological Series 150. Arizona State Museum, Tucson, pp. 141–154.

Turkon, Paula
    2004    Food and Status in the Prehispanic Malpaso Valley, Zacatecas, Mexico. *Journal of Anthropological Archaeology* 23: 225–251.

Turner, B. L., II, R. E. Kasperson, P. A. Matson, J. J. McCarthy, R. W. Corell, L. Christensen, N. Eckley, J. X. Kasperson, A. Luers, M. L. Martello, C. Polsky, A. Pulsipher, and A. Schiller
    2003    A Framework for Vulnerability Analysis in Sustainability Science. *Proceedings of the National Academy of Sciences* 100(14): 8074–8079.

Turney, Omar
    1929      Prehistoric Irrigation. *Arizona Historical Review* 2(2): 11–52.

van der Leeuw, S., and C. Redman
    2002      Placing Archaeology at the Center of Socio-Natural Studies. *American Antiquity* 674: 597–605.

Varien, Mark D., Scott G. Ortman, Timothy A. Kohler, Donna M. Glowacki, and C. David Johnson
    2007      Historical Ecology in the Mesa Verde Region: Results from the Village Ecodynamics Project. *American Antiquity* 72: 273–299.

Weigand, Philip C.
    1977      The Prehistory of the State of Zacatecas: An Interpretation. In *Anuario de Historia Zacatecana*, ed. C. Esperanza Sánchez. Universidad Autonoma de Zacatecas, Zacatecas, Mexico, pp. 1–39.

Wilcox, David R.
    1991      Hohokam Social Complexity. In *Chaco and Hohokam: Prehistoric Regional Systems in the American Southwest*, ed. P. L. Crown and W. J. Judge. School of American Research Press, Santa Fe, NM, pp. 253–275.

Young, O. R., F. Berkhout, G. C. Gallopin, M. A. Janssen, Elinor Ostrom, and S. van der Leeuw
    2006      The Globalization of Socio-Ecological Systems: An Agenda for Scientific Research. *Global Environmental Change* 16(3): 304–316.

## UNDERSTANDING HAZARDS, MITIGATING IMPACTS, AVOIDING DISASTERS

### Statement for Policy Makers and the Disaster Management Community

Humans sometimes build social systems that exacerbate rather than mitigate potential climate "hazards" or that actually prevent people from responding effectively to them. In this chapter we examine three lessons to be learned from understanding long sequences of human-environment interaction. The first examines how diversity in food systems influences the vulnerability of human societies to food shortages as a result of low precipitation in the arid to semiarid region of the southwestern United States and northern Mexico. The second examines how irrigation infrastructure both mitigates variability in the temporal and spatial patterns of precipitation and creates new vulnerabilities, emphasizing the reality that there is no "absolute resilience or robustness." The third emphasizes the role of social action in creating conditions of rigidity and the extent to which rigidity, however it emerges in modern systems, may exacerbate the potential for climate "hazards" to impact people. Decision-making about sustainable practice that can promote resilience requires nuanced thinking about the costs and benefits of diversity, the tradeoffs between resilience and vulnerability that can result from the nature of our investments in infrastructure, and the role of humans in constructing rigidity traps. These are important factors in managing toward reductions in the impacts of various disturbances or hazards.

# NINE

# Social Evolution, Hazards, and Resilience:
# Some Concluding Thoughts

*Timothy A. Kohler*

The study of accident in history implies that of necessity.
—LEROY LADURIE (1977: 115)

Hazards are everywhere. Somewhere in the world there is always some kind of environmental disaster at hand—and often many at once. Most of these disasters have an obvious social dimension: a forest fire in the suburbs gets a lot more attention than one in the wilderness.

Less obviously, the kinds of impacts a "natural" disaster has on a society depend not only on the nature of the disaster but also to some extent on how that society is organized, as several of the preceding chapters point out. In this chapter I provide a necessarily brief and selective review of the ways the organization of societies has changed over very long spans of time (I'm an archaeologist, after all!). The typical hazards societies confront probably affect these long-term processes of social and political evolution, since—over long enough periods of time—well-functioning societies tend to change in directions that neutralize the hazards they currently face.

Archaeologists and other anthropologists have long recognized that societies have become more complex in a variety of senses, as the majority of the earth's peoples moved from hunting-and-gathering ways of life in the Pleistocene (a 2.5-million-year epoch of repeated glaciations ending about 12,000 years ago) to become mostly farmers and herders in the Holocene and eventually the kings or slaves, craftswomen or shopkeepers, and priests or police of the highly differentiated societies that began to appear a little over 5,000 years ago.

Simply identifying these general trends was a major preoccupation of mid–twentieth-century anthropology, aided considerably by a worldwide increase in the quantity and quality of archaeological research fortified by the then-new chronological framework provided by radiocarbon dating. Archaeologists, especially in North America, began to see themselves as scientists. As various regional chronologies became firmly anchored in time and their gaps filled in, archaeologists could more clearly perceive regularities through time within the huge diversity of the worldwide human experience.

Their fellow anthropologists could also recognize some similarities between ethnographically known societies and various past societies investigated by archaeologists. This allowed them to propose models for the social and political organization of ancient societies, based on the organization of various small-scale societies that were still, or recently had been, in existence. Among the most widely used of these models were the stages proposed by Elman Service (1962, 1975) and Morton Fried (1967). Related influential work was also published by Leslie White (1959) and, more recently, by Allen Johnson and Timothy Earle (1987).

## THAT OLD-TIME CULTURAL EVOLUTION

Anthropologists in this "cultural evolutionary" or "neo-evolutionary" tradition saw their work as a way of putting social and political flesh on the bones and stones provided by the archaeological record. Elman Service, for example, suggested that during the long Paleolithic era the world was populated mainly by patrilocal bands made up of a few nuclear families—ordinarily fewer than 100 people overall—with no specialized occupational groups, economic institutions, or classes; no institutions governing political or legal affairs; and no religious system separate from the constituent families. (Since the mid–nineteenth century, archaeologists have used the term *Paleolithic* to describe the societies and technologies of humans during the Pleistocene epoch.)

In the post-Pleistocene world, where plant and animal domestication offered significantly higher productivity and perhaps a "much more stable, consistent productivity than [existed] at the hunting-gathering level" (Service 1962: 112), tribes that were several times larger than bands emerged from bands. Tribes, according to Service, could avoid disintegrating into bands because of the invention of integrating organizations—"pan-tribal sodalities" such as clans, age-grade associations, and societies for warfare, curing, and so forth. Because of these sodalities tribes had many more social statuses than bands, but these statuses were not marked by differences in influence or power except within very restricted spheres.

Next in this series of idealized social types, which Service unabashedly referred to as levels or stages in a progressive sense, are chiefdoms, which are larger social groups than tribes. They are marked, according to Service, by centers coordinating economic, social, and religious activities within the society. Service considered redistribution of goods and labor to be an especially important central activity of the chiefdom, and he thought the responsibility and judgment this activity required, in turn, gave rise to permanent leadership. Although chiefdoms are commonly larger (usually much larger) in numbers of people and possibly geographic area than tribes, what most importantly separates them from the fiercely egalitarian bands and tribes are the differences in social power within a chiefdom: "chiefdoms are profoundly inegalitarian" (1962: 150). Quite possibly, this was the most important single transition in the evolution of human societies.

Finally, states (whose appearance Service considered in detail in his 1975 book) are ordinarily larger again than chiefdoms, in terms of both population and the space they occupy. They differed from chiefdoms not only in size but more essentially, Service believed, in having increased institutionalization of the centralized leadership and, eventually, a hereditary aristocracy that grew out of that leadership.

In the 1980s and 1990s, stage theories such as those of Service came under criticism for a variety of reasons, including what some considered the implicitly Colonial placement of the Western European or American types of political organization at the apex of a long evolutionary ladder. Then, too, many of us recognized that some archaeologically known societies may be nothing like societies that still happened to exist in the nineteenth or twentieth century. It was widely felt that archaeologists had spent altogether too much time trying to classify their societies using these categories rather than figuring out how societies actually operated and why they changed. Around this time many archaeologists simply became more interested in other topics such as identity, symbols, and meanings. Even archaeologists who remained interested in evolutionary processes were moving on to different kinds of models and approaches (see reviews in Kohler 2008; Shennan 2008). Yet despite all this, some researchers retained (or are returning to) a focus on long-term, comparative social evolution while keeping 1960s-style stage theories suitably at arm's length. Examples include a recent book by Norman Yoffee (2005) and chapters in books edited by T. Douglas Price and Gary Feinman (1995) and Kevin Vaughn and his colleagues (2010).

Here I want to couple my own interest in long-term comparative social evolution with the materials presented so far in this book. What implications might sudden environmental change have for the long-term processes of increasing social scale identified by Service and many others?

## SOCIAL CONSTRUCTION PROCESSES

To answer this question, we have to dig some new foundations. I would like to replace the aged and ambiguous term *cultural evolution* with *social evolution*. Social evolution is the long-term tendency for the largest group with which people identify and regularly coordinate their activities (whether by choice or necessity) to become larger in both numbers of people and spatial scale. Everything important about social evolution centers on groups. I contend that the principal motor for increases in group size has usually been inter-group competition[1] and that those physical and cultural capacities that differentiate us from our various last common ancestors with related creatures, moving backward in time along our phylogenetic tree for at least the last 2 million years, are the result of selection within our lineage for the ability to live successfully in ever larger groups. Full defense of this thesis is not possible here; I outline some of my reasons for this position in Kohler (2004).[2] Consider briefly how exquisitely designed are just two of humanity's defining features—culture and language—for communicating knowledge and norms within groups but how, at the same time, both tend to create barriers between and variability among groups. Over the roughly 200,000 years modern humans have existed, our success has been such that our societies have grown in size from family units or bands to states and empires.

The long-term tendency for groups to increase in size is a result of the fact that (all other factors equal) when two groups are in conflict, the larger prevails. (This has been formalized as Lanchester's Square Law; see Lanchester 1916.) This is most obvious for the case of armed conflict and can result in cultural group selection: the replacement or absorption of one cultural group by another (Bowles, Choi, and Hopfensitz 2003). This is called *cultural* group selection because it refers to a process in which people do not necessarily perish but their culture disappears or changes profoundly. But larger *cultural* groups can also have more subtle advantages and need not be in armed conflict with other groups in order to prevail; larger *cultural* groups have an advantage over smaller *cultural* groups that would not be as true for, say, groups of other animals in which cultural traditions are of little or no importance. This is the case because larger human societies can accumulate and maintain more complex technologies and skills (Henrich 2004; Powell, Shennan, and Thomas 2009), including social technologies and skills; to the extent that these technologies and skills improve the group's quality of life, this in turn will make them a target for selective immigration from other groups (Boyd and Richerson 2009), further increasing their size. This process (also called payoff-biased migration, or voting with your feet) can even cause group-beneficial behaviors to spread so long as there is acculturation and certain other conditions are met. Cultural group selection probably explains why practices that should be discouraged by individual-level selection—such as young males' willingness to risk their lives for their social groups—can instead proliferate.

So if larger groups have such great advantages, why weren't there any Paleo-lithic empires? Of course, there are very important counterbalancing forces that prevent groups from becoming ever larger. Robert Carneiro (1987) and, more recently, Matthew Bandy (2008) have emphasized the strong tendency for groups to fission because of "scalar stress" (internal dissension) once they reach a certain size. Bandy, for example, suggests that "only the development of novel institutions of social integration at a suprahousehold level [Service's intra-tribal sodalities come to mind] could make possible the emergence of villages larger than [a] critical population threshold" (2008: 341). Small-scale human societies have a strong egalitarian ethos that also resists the develop-ment of internal inequalities, and they regularly employ public opinion and "punitive moral sanctioning to ensure that alpha-dominated hierarchies could not form" (Boehm 2000: 213). Also, large groups that are relatively sedentary may degrade their local environments more than did their less numerous, more mobile ancestors. Environmental degradation surrounding newly large and sedentary populations therefore presents another common barrier to growth, as Meredith Matthews and I (Kohler and Matthews 1988) argued for some early villages in the US Southwest.

I use the phrase *social construction work* for all those social and political processes that allow groups to grow larger, overcoming the probability of fission and the difficulties of cooperation and communication within ever larger groups and avoiding the environmental degradation that accompanies growth. Social construction processes are what people use to build and maintain groups.

What do these processes include? Very small groups can be built on the ancient biological (genetic) logic of inclusive fitness (or kin selection): we are genetically programmed to be biased toward helping those to whom we are related. But such motivations decay quickly as groups expand beyond just a few households; I'm much more likely to help my brother than help my third cousin. Kim Hill and colleagues (2011) have recently shown that contempo-rary hunter-gatherer bands are composed of mostly unrelated people, though they often include adult brothers and sisters. If this was also true of ancient foragers, then the logic of inclusive fitness plays only a very small part in the story of how we evolved to cooperate so efficiently.

As we move in size beyond the scale at which inclusive fitness can be effec-tive, myriad potential mechanisms for inducing and sustaining cooperation within groups have been suggested by economists, political scientists, physi-cists, and game theoreticians. A partial list includes mutualism, conditional rec-iprocity, indirect reciprocity, "strong reciprocity," and reputation management, including signaling. These mechanisms interact in complicated ways with levels of selection, for example, if they rely—as many do—on the existence of under-lying norms or institutions whose existence might depend on prior (cultural) group selection or if they tend to be effective in stabilizing those same norms.

So much work is being done in these areas that we are beginning to see a series of papers just trying to systematically define and classify the competing and often partially overlapping approaches and disentangle the difficult semantic issues that accompany them (e.g., West, Griffin, and Gardner 2007). I strongly suspect that this multiplicity of pathways represents real complication in the social world and that within-group cooperation can be achieved in a variety of ways.[3] It is also important to remember that all of these are mechanisms for bottom-up coordination and that they may play only minor roles in societies in which one subgroup has achieved an ability to coerce the behaviors of other subgroups. In what follows I refer to cooperation induced from the top down as *political coordination*, using *coordination* as a general term to include both bottom-up and top-down processes. Political coordination may be structured in a variety of ways, but in the early states most of interest to archaeologists, ritual, ceremony, and ideology (i.e., "symbolic capital" in Yoffee's [2005: 197] nice phrase) may have been especially important, though they must have been backed up by the possibility of coercion.

## SOCIAL EVOLUTION, HAZARDS, AND RESILIENCE

The mid–twentieth-century cultural evolutionists generally believed that greater productivity per unit land area and also stable, consistent productivity were important in creating conditions conducive to transitions between stages. This implies that a general absence of hazards or disasters might have been important. The foregoing chapters, however, suggest to me slightly different conclusions. First, the effects of hazards on social evolution depend on their spatial severity, areal scope, and predictability and the way these interact with the most prominent mechanisms stabilizing within-group coordination. Moreover, some kinds of hazards might have been more or less irrelevant. Finally and most significant, I argue here that the evolutionary tendency toward increase in scale and hierarchy is in itself a response to the hazard of being absorbed or displaced by neighboring groups.

Ben Fitzhugh (chapter 1) finds that the unpredictable and occasionally large but highly localized volcanic eruptions in the prehistoric Kurils had little discernible effect on the human societies in the area. More or less the same thing can apparently be said about earthquakes and tsunamis, although in that case site locations at higher-than-expected elevations may be attributable to a defense against these hazards. Perhaps this apparent lack of impact results from the fact that the spatial scope of these events was small compared to the size of areas across which specific groups would commonly range. It is interesting that Fitzhugh considers one of the greatest hazards for the small-scale societies in this area to have been incorporation into the states that eventually bordered them on both sides.

Fitzhugh's chapter left me wondering, though, whether the "failure" of Kuril inhabitants to develop the sort of complex hunter-gatherer societies evident on the North American Northwest Coast or in southwest Florida or even nearby on Honshu is a result of the relatively high periodicity of the disruptions he notes or whether it is more a matter of the relatively low productivity that limited human population sizes. Or, to put it another way, if the Kurils existed without volcanoes and tsunamis, would complex hunter-gatherer societies have developed there? A science of comparative human social evolution wants to know. I'll have more to say about such counterfactual speculations later.

Payson Sheets presents a well-developed framework for understanding the differential consequences of volcanic impacts on ancient societies of Central America and Mesoamerica. In my view it is particularly important to try to quantify the degree of disruption of various impacts—as he can do with volcanoes using the Smithsonian's Volcanic Explosivity Index—but, of course, such quantification is not the whole story, since small VEI events can still cause a great deal of damage locally and even large ones may have beneficial effects for people who are far enough away.

I also think Sheets is absolutely right to emphasize population density and carrying capacity considerations in his explanations for why some disruptions had no apparent effects and others did. About Arenal he says, "In spite of carefully examining the cultural inventory (artifacts, features, architecture, subsistence, economy, political organization, and pattern of settlement) for any evidence of volcanically induced change, we could find none. And that was not because of a paucity of eruptions." Sheets contrasts this with the (admittedly much larger) eruption of Ilopango, which brought down the entire Miraflores branch of Maya civilization. Presumably this was not only a result of the size of the event but also of its impact on all levels of the social and political hierarchy, not just on one corner of a polity.

In general, in assessing the effects of disasters, it would be helpful if we could predict what the population and settlement patterns in an area affected by such disasters might have been in the absence of these hazards. In the case of Arenal, for example, is the absence of change an effect of interest in a larger framework of comparative social change? Such questions are at present idle speculation, but it is not impossible that we will someday have the means to address them. Computer simulation models will be necessary to advance this strategy of investigating "counterfactuals." Margaret Nelson and her colleagues, in their chapter, discuss a model of "what might happen" in systems of mixed maize and agave cultivation as rainfall changes in its annual mean and variance. Similarly, with a group of colleagues, I have been developing models of subsistence and settlement for the northern US Southwest (e.g., Kohler et al. 2007) that ask, for example, what the population size through time in our

229

study area would have been if only high-frequency (annual and decadal) variability in temperature and precipitation affected productivity and people had no ability to immigrate into or emigrate from our study area.

I'll restrict my specific comments to one more chapter—the only one for which I can claim any specific expertise. Nelson and her colleagues present a number of provocative thoughts and suggestions in their discussion of potential hazards to ancient societies within the southwestern United States and northern Mexico and their differential vulnerability to those hazards. For example, they contrast the Mimbres and Hohokam, on one hand, and the Zuni, on the other, in their investigation of the role of irrigation infrastructure in vulnerability. The first two cases led to collapse, at least in some senses of that word, whereas the Zuni showed remarkable robustness and continuity. The authors suggest that these differences resulted from, at Zuni, a smaller-scale and "more dynamic" water-delivery system, an absence of population growth after the late AD 1200s, and what might have been in some sense a more appropriate pacing between the development of social institutions (what I'm calling *social construction*) and the appearance of large-scale aggregates (the late prehispanic towns).

This all seems plausible to me, but the points also beg for explanation. We know that one of the difficulties for the Hohokam system was the arrival between AD 1250 and 1350 of large numbers of Pueblo immigrants from the north, exacerbating social tensions and contributing to a shift to aggregation (Hill et al. 2010). The Zuni area appears to have grown across this century as well, but why were the ultimate results so different? Couching these questions in terms of "vulnerability" and "resilience" has the advantage of helping us identify interesting contrasts, but it doesn't necessarily get us any closer to explaining the differing underlying causal chains that appear to have different ultimate results.

Much the same can be said for the concept of *rigidity traps*. My own analysis of the causes for the depopulation of the thirteenth-century Mesa Verde region in southwestern Colorado (Kohler 2010) emphasizes the importance of high-frequency drought and low-frequency cold conditions in depressing maize production, as well as the generally depleted nature of the landscape after two centuries of very dense populations. But there are also important senses in which something like "rigidity traps" probably contributed to the depopulation (Bocinsky and Kohler in press). First, depletion of deer populations meant that most people were getting their high-quality (meat) protein from turkey, which was fed corn (Rawlings and Driver 2010), so populations were ultimately dependent on the success of maize farming for both their calories and their protein.

Second, Mesa Verde region societies appear to have been hanging on to a style of social organization in which households and lineages (or clans) retained a great deal of power, likely including landownership. Given the structure of potential production across these landscapes, the most consistently productive agricultural lands were likely monopolized by senior and more powerful lineages residing in some of the most advantageously placed villages. Despite this, walled, densely packed villages with new forms of ceremonial structures were constructed during the last three decades of occupation, suggesting that at the same time, increasing interdependence existed among lineages and sodalities within the largest villages. Such interdependence probably means that all the occupants of a village had to be pulling together to make a village work properly.

The regional context also needs to be considered: these societies were in contact and competition with societies in the northern Rio Grande, which were developing social organizations in which lineages and households apparently held less power. Some of this power seems instead to have been given up to pueblo (town) elders, and agricultural lands in particular may have been held and distributed at the level of the pueblo, as was common in the last century in these societies. The social chaos that Nelson and her colleagues allude to, which accompanied the final year(s) of occupation in the Mesa Verde region, probably pitted haves against have-nots, within villages but especially between them. Given the general untenability of local agriculture, especially in the suboptimal fields available to them, the have-nots were on their way south. I think they made sure that the haves weren't coming along; we know of at least two village-wide massacres from this period (Kuckelman 2010).

So, was the Mesa Verde area depopulated because of rigidity traps? If this analysis (which includes informed intuition and some speculation) is correct, that is indeed part of the story. And yet, while calling the particular binds confronting these societies "rigidity traps" may be useful as recognizing a class of problem, it is no more explanatory than calling a society a tribe. I am certainly not accusing Nelson and colleagues of mere taxonomizing; many explanatory details for the studies they summarize here are presented in other publications. I do worry, though, that just as past archaeologists reified the ideal types of the neo-evolutionary sequence a little too enthusiastically, thereby concealing their internal heterogeneity, future archaeologists may become so enamored of these concepts that their analyses stop with classification. (Paulette makes similar points in his chapter.)

## CONCLUSION

Societies grow in size in part to overcome hazards, and one of the principal ones—little discussed elsewhere in this volume—is the danger of being absorbed, displaced, or destroyed by neighboring societies. Inevitably, this growth requires social construction work, and new hazards then present themselves as a result of the greater populations now to be supported and the possibility that the new social roles will cause internal schisms to develop within the group along lines of contrasting interests.

In this chapter I emphasize how societies evolved toward larger sizes and increasing hierarchical control because in more hierarchical societies the effects of disasters seem to be related to which social and political levels are affected, as well as to how widespread destruction is within a territory. As Paulette demonstrates in his discussion of the world's first cities and states in Mesopotamia, it is not simply a matter of saying that states are more (or less) resilient than smaller-scale societies. States vary in their institutional forms and in their capacity (and willingness) to respond to suffering caused by disaster among segments of their populations. Polities may even exploit environmental disasters to spread or cement their control; for example, the rapid growth of Teotihuacan around AD 200 may be linked to the eruption of Popocatepetl (70 km to the south), as noted by Emily McClung de Tapia. Paulette demonstrates boom-and-bust cycles in early Near Eastern states, but Nelson and her colleagues demonstrate these cycles for the smaller-scale societies of the US Southwest as well.

Another reason these long-term trends in social evolution are important to a volume such as this is that they emerge precisely from the response to the hazard of being overtaken by one's neighbors. But this response eventually raises other kinds of hazards by requiring social construction work that may not be entirely successful in alleviating intra-group stress that, in turn, can be greatly magnified by disasters. At the same time, ignoring for the moment the way humans divide themselves into groups, regional populations also tended to grow as new and more productive subsistence systems were developed or in response to temporarily better production as a result of climatic variability. Population growth packs the landscape with ownership rights and therefore limits mobility, which was humanity's original and best response to local environmental downturns. Under these conditions a disaster—or even locally deleterious climatic variability—might lead to partial emigration if that is possible (which might look like collapse if the remaining, smaller groups abandon the social construction mechanisms they no longer need), complete emigration, or death.

As long as population levels were sufficiently low, death (by this mechanism at least) should have been rare and mobility common. Therefore, as Payson Sheets notes in chapter 2, population growth has been, and continues to be, one of humanity's greatest traps, since it quickly absorbs the fruits of previous technological advances and social construction efforts and hungrily demands new ones—which, in turn, invariably present new hazards whose spectra can be only dimly glimpsed.

Most of us archaeologists study periods when the world was inhabited by only a few million people. Even if there were hundreds of millions, they were so disconnected that effectively their numbers were much lower. Only archaeologists working on the nineteenth and twentieth centuries have had to think about the possible effects of 1 billion increasingly connected people. Today the world has nearly 7 billion people, and most estimates call for at least 2 billion more by 2050. Is anything archaeologists have learned about how societies work over long periods, in what today looks like an almost empty world, still valid for understanding the pressing issues we face today?

The fundamental things apply. There will always be competition between social and political groups. Humanity will never escape some limits on its numbers and its achievements, imposed by the natural world. But can archaeologists draw more precise lessons from the long sweep of history by finding the level of abstraction appropriate to that task? We need to try, and I hope that books like this are a step in that direction. More than three decades ago Emmanuel LeRoy Ladurie wrote of the dangers of doing social science without considering the effects and lessons of (pre)history:

> History . . . surprised the social sciences at the swimming hole and made off with their clothes, and the victims had not even noticed their nakedness . . . Everybody, by now, has been forced to admit the obvious: it is not possible to construct a science of man without a temporal dimension any more than it is possible to construct a science of astrophysics without knowing the age of the stars and the galaxies. (1977: 135–136)

*Acknowledgments.* Many thanks to Tom McGovern, Andy Dugmore, Astrid Ogilvie, and Sophia Perdikaris for their invitation to participate in the Global Long-Term Human Ecodynamics Conference at Eagle Hill, Maine, and to Jago Cooper and Payson Sheets and two anonymous reviewers for their comments on an earlier version of this chapter.

## NOTES

1. Since we have been discussing them, I should acknowledge that some neo-evolutionists recognized the centrality of inter-group competition. Service (1962: 113), for example, proposed that "the competition of societies in the neolithic phase of cultural development seems to have been the general factor which led to the development of integrating pan-tribal societies." Or: "The fact that there is frequently a contiguous belt of chiefdoms suggests the possibility that the cycle of expansion by incorporation and subsequent disintegration is a common cause of the origin and spread of many chiefdoms. It is also possible that just plain warfare between a chiefdom and adjacent tribes could lead tribes to remake themselves politically, copying the salient features of a chiefdom, in order to resist incorporation more effectively" (ibid.: 152).

2. This position implies that human groups themselves became important units of selection. For selection at this level to be important, however, these groups would also have had to have been fairly homogeneous internally but quite variable from group to group.

3. The relative underrepresentation of anthropologists in this literature has had the result that for groups of intermediate size, the role in social construction of one of our group's favorite topics—kinship—has been slighted. Early on, Marshall Sahlins (among many others) recognized that kinship provides the model for political relationships in small-scale societies (e.g., 1961: 333)—indeed, it *is* the political system. But kinship, too, eventually fails as a construction principle as groups increase in size.

## REFERENCES

Bandy, Matthew
    2008    Global Patterns of Early Village Development. In *The Neolithic Demographic Transition and Its Consequences*, ed. Jean-Pierre Bocquet-Appel and Ofer Bar-Yosef. Springer Science+Business Media B.V., Heidelberg, pp. 333–357.

Bocinsky, R. Kyle, and Timothy A. Kohler
    In press    Complexity, Rigidity, and Resilience in the Ancient Puebloan Southwest. In *Field to Table* (volume to be submitted to the University of South Carolina Press), ed. David Goldstein.

Boehm, Christopher
    2000    Group Selection in the Upper Paleolithic. *Journal of Consciousness Studies* 7: 211–215.

Bowles, Samuel, Jung-Kyoo Choi, and Astrid Hopfensitz
    2003    The Co-Evolution of Individual Behaviors and Social Institutions. *Journal of Theoretical Biology* 223: 135–147.

Boyd, Robert, and Peter J. Richerson
    2009    Voting with Your Feet: Payoff Biased Migration and the Evolution of Group Beneficial Behavior. *Journal of Theoretical Biology* 25: 331–339.

Carneiro, Robert
    1987    Village Splitting as a Function of Population Size. In *Themes in Ethnology and Culture History: Essays in Honor of David F. Aberle*, ed, Leland Donald. Archana, Meerut, India, pp. 94–124.

Fried, Morton H.
    1967    *The Evolution of Political Society: An Essay in Political Anthropology*. Random House, New York.

Henrich, Joseph
    2004    Demography and Cultural Evolution: How Adaptive Cultural Processes Can Produce Maladaptive Losses: The Tasmanian Case. *American Antiquity* 69: 197–214.

Hill, J. Brett, Jeffery J. Clark, William H. Doelle, and Patrick D. Lyons
    2010    Depopulation of the Northern Southwest: A Macro-Regional Perspective. In *Leaving Mesa Verde: Peril and Change in the Thirteenth-Century Southwest*, ed. Timothy A. Kohler, Mark D. Varien, and Aaron M. Wright. University of Arizona Press, Tucson, pp. 34–52.

Hill, Kim R., Robert S. Walker, Miran Božičević, James Eder, Thomas Headland, Barry Hewlett, A. Magdalena Hurtado, Frank Marlowe, Polly Wiessner, and Brian Wood
2011    Co-Residence Patterns in Hunter-Gatherer Societies Show Unique Human Social Structure. *Science* 331: 1286–1289.

Johnson, Allen W., and Timothy Earle
1987    *The Evolution of Human Societies: From Foraging Group to Agrarian State.* Stanford University Press, Stanford, CA.

Kohler, Timothy A.
2004    Population and Resources in Prehistory. In *The Archaeology of Global Change: The Impact of Humans on Their Environment*, ed. Charles L. Redman, Steven R. James, Paul R. Fish, and J. Daniel Rogers. Smithsonian Books, Washington, DC, pp. 257–270.

2008    Evolutionary Archaeology. In *Encyclopedia of Archaeology*, vol. 2, ed. Deborah Pearsall. Elsevier, San Diego, CA, pp. 1332–1338.

2010    A New Paleoproductivity Reconstruction for Southwestern Colorado, and Its Implications for Understanding Thirteenth-Century Depopulation. In *Leaving Mesa Verde: Peril and Change in the Thirteenth-Century Southwest*, ed. Timothy A. Kohler, Mark D. Varien, and Aaron M. Wright. University of Arizona Press, Tucson, pp. 103–127.

Kohler, Timothy A., C. David Johnson, Mark Varien, Scott Ortman, Robert Reynolds, Ziad Kobti, Jason Cowan, Kenneth Kolm, Schaun Smith, and Lorene Yap
2007    Settlement Ecodynamics in the Prehispanic Central Mesa Verde Region. In *The Model-Based Archaeology of Socionatural Systems*, ed. Timothy A. Kohler and Sander van der Leeuw. School of American Research Press, Santa Fe, NM, pp. 61–104.

Kohler, Timothy A., and Meredith H. Matthews
1988    Long-Term Anasazi Land-Use Patterns and Forest Reduction: A Case Study from Southwest Colorado. *American Antiquity* 53: 537–564.

Kuckelman, Kristin A.
2010    Catalysts of the Thirteenth-Century Depopulation of Sand Canyon Pueblo and the Central Mesa Verde Region. In *Leaving Mesa Verde: Peril and Change in the Thirteenth-Century Southwest*, ed. Timothy A. Kohler, Mark D. Varien, and Aaron M. Wright. University of Arizona Press, Tucson, pp. 180–199.

Lanchester, Frederick William
1916    *Aircraft in Warfare: The Dawn of the Fourth Arm.* Constable and Co., London.

LeRoy Ladurie, Emmanuel
1977    Motionless History. *Social Science History* 1: 115–136.

Powell, Adam, Stephen Shennan, and Mark G. Thomas
2009    Late Pleistocene Demography and the Appearance of Modern Human Behavior. *Science* 324: 1298–1301.

Price, T. Douglas, and Gary M. Feinman, eds.
　1995　*Foundations of Social Inequality*. Plenum, New York.

Rawlings, Tiffany A., and Jonathan C. Driver
　2010　Paleodiet of Domestic Turkey, Shields Pueblo (5MT3807), Colorado: Isotopic Analysis and Its Implications for Care of a Household Domesticate. *Journal of Archaeological Science* 37: 2433–2441.

Sahlins, Marshall D.
　1961　The Segmentary Lineage: An Organization of Predatory Expansion. *American Anthropologist* 63: 322–345.

Service, Elman R.
　1962　*Primitive Social Organization: An Evolutionary Perspective*. Random House, New York.
　1975　*Origins of the State and Civilization: The Process of Cultural Evolution*. W. W. Norton, New York.

Shennan, Stephen
　2008　Evolution in Archaeology. *Annual Review of Anthropology* 37: 75–91.

Vaughn, Kevin J., Jelmer W. Eerkens, and John Kanter, eds.
　2010　*The Evolution of Leadership: Transitions in Decision Making from Small-Scale to Middle-Range Societies*. School of Advanced Research Press, Santa Fe, NM.

West, Stuart A., Ashleigh S. Griffin, and Andy Gardner
　2007　Social Semantics: Altruism, Cooperation, Mutualism, Strong Reciprocity and Group Selection. *Journal of Evolutionary Biology* 20(2): 415–432.

White, Leslie
　1959　*The Evolution of Culture: The Development of Civilization to the Fall of Rome*. McGraw-Hill, New York.

Yoffee, Norman
　2005　*Myths of the Archaic State: Evolution of the Earliest Cities, States, and Civilizations*. Cambridge University Press, Cambridge.

# TEN

# Global Environmental Change, Resilience, and Sustainable Outcomes

*Charles L. Redman*

It is increasingly clear that change is as "normal" a condition as stability when considering the condition of social-ecological systems. It is equally clear that knowledge of those systems must rely not just on the characteristics of the elements of the systems but equally on an understanding of the interactions among those units and the interactions of that system with forces and entities external to it. Moreover, there is deepening recognition that the world is extremely complex, that even the best scientific research on it comes with great uncertainty, and that many processes that govern it behave in a nonlinear fashion. All of this makes understanding and managing the world around us and our place within it extremely challenging, yet doing so remains fundamentally important to our collective future. We all must face living with the dangers of sudden environmental change. The chapters in this volume provide a new perspective on this problem by analyzing how past societies attempted to understand the hazards they faced, mitigate their impacts, and each in its own way avoid disasters. Each chapter is an analysis of regional archaeological data to learn about social responses to the threat and actuality of environmental hazards engendered by sudden and not so sudden but significant environmental change. Despite their limitations, archaeological data provide a new and potentially useful source of insight into how human groups adapt to the threat of environmental changes and how they respond to environmental changes that do occur.

The new insights archaeological case studies offer are particularly welcome in that global environmental change is one of the primary threats to society in the twenty-first century. Because the impact of climate change can be expected to be a gradual process that, on average, may not change as much as inter-annual or interregional variability, most global changes will not be obvious to the casual observer. However, predictions are that we will best sense the effects of anthropogenic climate change through the occurrence of more frequent and extreme "natural events." For example, the gradual increase in atmospheric temperature will not be noticeable on a year-to-year basis (or at least separable from normal inter-annual fluctuations), yet it is likely that the frequency and intensity of heat waves impacting cities around the world will increase and significantly affect their populations. Heat waves are already the natural disaster responsible for the greatest number of fatalities worldwide, and we can expect that number to grow in the coming decades. Climate change will also alter regional precipitation patterns, leading to more frequent and intense flooding in some regions and more frequent and intense droughts in others. These changes, in turn, will exacerbate patterns of erosion and be responsible for mudslides, dust storms, and other hazards. It is expected that as ocean waters warm, storms such as hurricanes will increase in intensity, leading to greater wind damage and coastal flooding.

The impacts of global climate change will most likely be experienced as the kinds of natural hazards that have been happening regionally since pre-historic times, but they can be expected to occur more frequently and to be more intense. Hence, the way people have organized themselves in the face of regional natural hazards or sudden environmental changes in the past provides insight into what the key variables will be in organizing ourselves to recognize and deal with global environmental change in the future. Several observations reported in this volume's chapters have revealed patterns in the past that should help structure contemporary thinking. A theme that runs through almost all of the chapters is that environmental change and natural hazards are not disasters in themselves. As Jago Cooper points out, the recognition and impact of hazards on local societies are culturally contingent and are very much shaped by the ecological knowledge of members of the society. Several of the authors indicate that the way these hazards are culturally constructed and conveyed is directly related to their frequency of occurrence and impact in the recent past. More frequent and more sudden hazards are often prominently encoded in local knowledge and are more likely to be acted upon in precautionary ways Cooper and Payson Sheets describe in the volume's introduction.

Geography is also a key factor in understanding human attitudes and adaptations to potential natural hazards. Although volcanic activity is not usually associated with anthropogenically caused global environmental change, it is certainly a natural hazard and also an excellent "laboratory" for understanding human preparations and responses to sudden environmental change. As both Ben Fitzhugh and Sheets point out, the direct impact of each form of volcanic activity has a spatial signature that is different from others, depending on the distance and direction from the epicenter. In some areas destruction and fatalities are so complete that avoidance may be the only safe adaptation. In other situations there is a warning; serious impacts can be avoided through mobility, and the locality can be reoccupied relatively soon. Fitzhugh found that settlements were not in the locations that would have been most vulnerable to destruction from tsunamis, perhaps not because of recognition of that danger itself but more likely prompted by the more frequent and sometimes devastating ocean storms. This avoidance of vulnerable areas was more possible in the Kuril Islands because of their low population density and the relative mobility of their settlements, allowing residents to avoid and reoccupy areas relatively soon after hazards hit. In fact, in both regions (and in the US Southwest as well) the authors suggest that for some localities the long-term effect of volcanic activity is positive because it improves agricultural potential and even increases usable land surface in coastal or island situations.

Geography sometimes acts to draw settlements into vulnerable areas because of its potential advantages. As Margaret Nelson and colleagues suggest for the arid US Southwest, Daniel Sandweiss and Jeffrey Quilter for the deserts of coastal Peru, and Tate Paulette for Mesopotamia, settlement along river courses through otherwise arid terrain allows for irrigation agriculture that could have supported large populations and advanced societies. To take advantage of the potential of river water at the scale each of these societies did, major investments in infrastructure were required to divert the water from the rivers and distribute it across the fields. As Nelson and colleagues point out, this made these societies "place-restricted" so that moving their settlements was not easy to do; hence they were more or less "trapped" by their food-producing technology. This caused them to be vulnerable to floods that would periodically destroy much of the irrigation infrastructure, imposing a major reconstruction cost on society. Some major floods, as in the Peruvian case, carried such sediment loads that entire settlements could be destroyed; in extreme situations the actual course of the river would change, leaving many major settlements without their primary source of sustenance—as is hypothesized to have happened in early Mesopotamian history. In other situations, as Emily McClung de Tapia describes for Teotihuacan in central Mexico, the presence of a growing city whose residents were originally attracted by environmental resources often depletes those resources as its population and footprint grow. Hence the deforestation surrounding Teotihuacan made it more vulnerable to flooding and soil erosion, while at the same time the spread of the city itself consumed optimal agricultural land, leading to a dual vulnerability in the long term.

Just as geography may have acted as a positive attractor to settlements and, later, put the settlements at risk, so did social institutions develop that were designed to take advantage of the situation but eventually created a rigidity that stifled adaptive responses. Many of the authors report on situations that reflected this phenomenon. Andrew Dugmore and Orri Vésteinsson relate that the long-distance administration that had contributed to the establishment and periodic success of Icelandic society was also unresponsive to environmental changes and inhibited necessary restructuring of adaptations. Similarly, in Mesopotamia, hierarchically distant administrators had little awareness of or concern for the changing local conditions that undermined agricultural productivity. Both Sheets for Central America and Nelson and colleagues for the Southwest identified key cross-scale interactions in which the environmental changes gradually undermined the adaptive capabilities of the central government, stifling change and making it less able to cope with subsequent shocks.

Sheets and Cooper reflect the range of the chapter authors' ideas by suggesting in their introduction six "tools" prehistoric (and perhaps contemporary) societies used to cope with sudden environmental change: settlement location, household architecture, food procurement strategies, reciprocal social networks, education, and disaster management planning. I would like to generalize this one level further and consider these and other strategies as examples of four basic problem-solving strategies people have used to cope with all sorts of challenges they have faced. The four domains of adaptive strategies societies have employed throughout time can be summarized as follows (Redman 1999):

1. Locational flexibility and mobility

2. Ecosystem management

3. Built environment and other technologies

4. Social complexification

What makes many of the strategies in all of these domains so challenging to either endorse or condemn is that each of them appears to have emerged because it had very positive results for the communities involved. Yet many of the strategies introduced new vulnerabilities that, over time, may have undermined those same communities. For example, locational flexibility and mobility as a key element of a settlement system dominated much of early human prehistory. However, the advantages of sedentism in terms of investing in more substantial facilities and productive infrastructure led increasing numbers of communities to adopt a more place-restricted settlement pattern. Similarly, with ecosystem management, many immediate advantages would accrue by practicing deforestation to open landscapes for cereal production, introducing non-native species for food production, and redirecting local hydrology for irrigating fields.

However, each of these practices also introduces vulnerabilities that may not be apparent until a substantial period of time has passed or the region experiences what would not otherwise be a disastrous environmental stress.

Humans are probably best known as creators of new technologies and built environments to meet the challenges they face. Terraces to improve agriculture on slopes, levees to keep modest rises in river levels from flooding homes and fields, and the more recent use of chemicals to combat pests and competing plants all produce clear advantages but also lead to unintended consequences. For example, terraces require continual labor inputs and inhibit mobility, levees allow more construction in floodplains that may be disastrous in extreme events when the river overtops them, and the heavy use of formerly effective chemicals can either have deleterious side effects or cause the pests to evolve into chemical-resistant strains. This is an important lesson for those currently considering technological versus social solutions to the threats posed by accelerating climate change. Finally, what may be the most subtle contradictions arise from the establishment of social institutions—both informal rules and more formal organizations—to take advantage of, and continue to manage, environmental opportunities and threats. The case studies point out how various institutions that emerged to derive benefits from local environmental conditions often stagnated or were at an inappropriate scale to continue as a positive force once the environment and society had changed.

The objective of recategorizing these adaptive strategies is to situate the insights that have emerged from the case histories of particular human responses to sudden environmental changes as reflective of the more universal issue of human decision-making as it led to the success or failure of societies. There are any number of specific reasons societies have stagnated, diminished, or ceased to exist as a cultural unit; but, as Jared Diamond suggests, all of these cases had one common thread: a failure within the decision-making process. Diamond sees four basic reasons for these failures that can also be seen in the case studies reported here: failing to anticipate the problem, not recognizing the problem, not trying to solve it, and, if recognizing the problem and trying to solve it, not responding in a timely or appropriate manner (2005: 221).

From the case studies, two other insights can be added. First, many human responses to environmental changes are intended to introduce adjustments or buffering that allow the society to weather the more frequent smaller-scale and smaller-intensity events that must be confronted on decadal or more frequent timescales; by doing so the responses often introduce serious vulnerabilities to the less frequent but devastating extreme events. Second and related to the first, most human decision-making appears to be designed to enhance short-term opportunities and minimize risks to frequent or short-term threats, with little attention to the long-term implications of these actions or to how to deal with opportunities and threats that only become apparent after a long time. It is easy for an archaeologist who focuses on long-term phenomena to suggest that the panacea for a society is to reverse this priority or at least put long-term planning and management in the forefront. I would like to do this, but I also recognize that, in this competitive world, for a society to "reach" the long term it has to be successful in a series of short-term situations. Hence this is not a simple tradeoff; rather, one must discover long-term positive actions that are also positive in the short term. History has demonstrated that many societies are not able to find solutions that achieve both goals.

Diamond presents another way to conceptualize this fundamental trade-off. He sees many of these decisions coming down to a social group or a society having to decide in the face or threat of environmental change which of its normative beliefs, practices, and institutions to hold on to and which to give up. It is not a trivial matter that one should be expected to effectively "adapt" to the new conditions by giving up traditional ways of doing things because many of these traditional ways of doing things may be the essence of the group's social identity or other functioning. Diamond retells how the late Medieval Norse of Greenland held on to their agrarian ways instead of switching to their neighboring Inuits' mobile hunting strategies; this allowed them to retain their social identity but led to their complete demographic collapse (Diamond 2005: 248–276; McGovern et al. 1988). This is not just a historic issue, of little con-temporary significance. Thomas Friedman suggests in *The Lexus and the Olive Tree* (1999) that how to maintain traditional values while adopting efficient foreign practices is a basic conundrum facing much of the modern world.

We can go further in linking the insights from the case studies to two related conceptual frameworks: vulnerability and resilience theories. Nelson and colleagues and several other authors have already started this, and I am building on their foundations. A system's vulnerability is related to three primary factors: magnitude of the stress or shock, exposure of the system to the stress or shock, and the system's sensitivity to the stress or shock (Adger 2006; Turner et al. 2003). Concerning hazards such as volcanoes, hurri-canes, droughts, and floods, it is unlikely that action by the social group to be impacted could significantly change the external input of the hazard. This does not deny the long-term impact cumulative, local mitigation strategies might have on diminishing the level of anthropogenically induced global environ-mental change, only that the results of these effects will not be apparent in a short time. However, mitigation and adaptation strategies aimed at reducing the system's exposure to the stress and strategies aimed at reducing its sensitiv-ity to the stress can have significant effects on reducing the impact. Minimizing exposure through settlement location and mobility, enhanced architectural precautions, and a diversity of food sources can reduce the vulnerability to associated environmental changes. Equally important are efforts to strengthen the system against the adverse impacts of hazards it will be exposed to, such as building social networks to provide aid and shelter to those affected. We have also recognized in recent years that hazards differentially impact the weaker segments of society and that building their capacities would disproportionately lower the overall vulnerability of the system.

Related to efforts to reduce system vulnerability by lowering the sensitivity of the system is building its resilience to stresses and shocks. The resilience of a social-ecological system is defined as its ability to experience external stresses and shocks and maintain its core functioning and characteristics (Folke 2006; Holling and Gunderson 2002). Nelson and her colleagues as well as Paulette relate their case studies to ideas from resilience theory. Several key concepts resonate with the situations described in the case studies. First is that change is to be expected and welcomed rather than feared and resisted. The goal is to experience change in a "graceful" way that does not damage the system in an undesirable way. Resilience theorists have created a metaphor figure shaped like a figure 8 to represent the stages of the adaptive cycle of a system experiencing change (Holling and Gunderson 2002: figure 2.1). The adaptive cycle emphasizes the opportunity for positive growth to result from stress-induced system change.

F. Stuart Chapin and his colleagues (2009: 324–328) have suggested four domains of strategies that would enhance social-ecological resilience: fostering biological, economic, and cultural diversity; fostering a mix of stabilizing feedback and creative renewal; fostering social learning through experimentation and innovation; and adapting governance to changing conditions. Among the strategies they recommend, several are particularly appropriate here. Renew the functional diversity of degraded systems after the hazard or sudden change has occurred. Foster retention of stories that illustrate past patterns of adaptation to change (eco-knowledge as described in Cooper's chapter). Subsidize innovations that foster economic novelty and diversity. Foster stabilizing feedbacks that sustain natural and social capital. Allow modest disturbances that permit the system to adjust to changes in underlying controls. Broaden the problem definition by learning from multiple cultural and disciplinary perspectives and facilitating dialogue and knowledge coproduction among multiple groups of stakeholders. Provide an environment for leadership to emerge and trust to develop. Foster social networking that bridges communication and accountability among existing organizations.

Sudden environmental change has characteristically been viewed with horror. Its unpredictability, enormity, and devastating impact on numerous people contribute to its being seen as a terrible calamity. There is no question that both modern and ancient natural hazards have caused significant loss of life and property and adversely affected many people. Unfortunately, the course of modern history seems to have made these patterns worse, not better. Damage could be reduced and loss of life minimized, and in many cases positive results could emerge in the aftermath of many of these phenomena. It is laudable that this volume brings forward case studies from the past and endeavors to reanalyze them so that we might learn how to minimize our vulnerability to these hazards, build our social-ecological system's resilience against their unavoidable occurrence, and seek ways to gracefully experience them and emerge with newly reformed and, it is hoped, improved societies.

## REFERENCES CITED

Adger, W. Neil
    2006    Vulnerability. *Global Environmental Change* 16: 268–281.

Chapin, F. Stuart, III, Gary P. Kofinas, Carl Folke, Stephen R. Carpenter, Per Olsson, Nick Abel, Reinette Biggs, Rosamond L. Naylor, Evelyn Pinkerton, D. Mark Stafford Smith, Will Steffen, Brian Walker, and Oran R. Young
    2009    Resilience-Based Stewardship: Strategies for Navigating Sustainable Pathways in a Changing World. In *Principles of Ecosystem Stewardship: Resilience-Based Natural Resource Management in a Changing World*, ed. F. Stuart Chapin III, Gary P. Kofinas, and Carl Folke. Springer, New York, pp. 319–337.

Diamond, Jared
    2005    *Collapse: How Societies Choose to Fail or Succeed.* Viking, New York.

Folke, Carl
    2006    Resilience: The Emergence of a Perspective for Social-Ecological Systems Analyses. *Global Environmental Change* 16(3): 253–267.

Friedman, Thomas
    1999    *The Lexus and the Olive Tree.* Farrar, Straus and Giroux, New York.

Holling, C. S., and Lance H. Gunderson
    2002    Resilience and Adaptive Cycles. In *Panarchy*, ed. Lance H. Gunderson and C. S. Holling. Island, Washington, DC, pp. 2–62.

McGovern, Thomas H., Gerald Bigelow, Thomas Amorosi, and Daniel Russell
    1988    Northern Islands, Human Error, and Environmental Degradation: A View of Social and Ecological Change in the Medieval North Atlantic. *Human Ecology* 16(3): 225–270.

Redman, Charles L.
    1999    *Human Impact on Ancient Environments.* University of Arizona Press, Tucson.

Turner, Billie L., II, Pamela A. Matson, James J. McCarthy, Robert W. Corelli, Lindsey Christensen, Noelle Edkley, Grete K. Hovelsrud-Broda, Jeanne X. Kasperson, Roger E. Kasperson, Amy Luers, Marybeth L. Martello, Svein Mathiesen, Rosamond Naylor, Colin Polsky, Alexander Pulsipher, Andrew Schiller, Henrik Selin, and Nicholas Tyler
    2003    Illustrating the Coupled Human-Environment System for Vulnerability Analysis: Three Case Studies. *Proceedings of the National Academy of Sciences* 100(14): 8080–8085.

# Contributors

**David A. Abbott**
ARIZONA STATE UNIVERSITY
School of Human Evolution and
    Social Change
david.abbott@asu.edu

**John Marty Anderies**
ARIZONA STATE UNIVERSITY
School of Human Evolution and
    Social Change
School of Sustainability
m.anderies@asu.edu

**Jago Cooper**
UNIVERSITY COLLEGE, LONDON
Institute of Archaeology
jago.cooper@ucl.ac.uk

**Andrew Dugmore**
UNIVERSITY OF EDINBURGH
Geography, School of GeoSciences
andrew.dugmore@ed.ac.uk

**Ben Fitzhugh**
UNIVERSITY OF WASHINGTON
Department of Anthropology
fitzhugh@uw.edu

**Michelle Hegmon**
ARIZONA STATE UNIVERSITY
School of Human Evolution and
    Social Change
mhegmon@asu.edu

**Scott E. Ingram**
ARIZONA STATE UNIVERSITY
School of Human Evolution and
 Social Change
scott.ingram@asu.edu

**Keith W. Kintigh**
ARIZONA STATE UNIVERSITY
School of Human Evolution and
 Social Change
kintigh@asu.edu

**Ann P. Kinzig**
ARIZONA STATE UNIVERSITY
School of Life Sciences
School of Sustainability
ann.kinzig@asu.edu

**Timothy A. Kohler**
WASHINGTON STATE UNIVERSITY
Department of Anthropology
tako@wsu.edu

**Stephanie Kulow**
ARIZONA STATE UNIVERSITY
School of Human Evolution and
 Social Change
stephanie.kulow@asu.edu

**Emily McClung de Tapia**
UNIVERSIDAD NACIONAL AUTÓNOMA
 DE MÉXICO
Laboratorio de Paleoetnobotánica
 y Paleoambiente, Instituto de
 Investigaciones Antropológicas
mcclung@servidor.unam.mx

**Thomas H. McGovern**
CITY UNIVERSITY OF NEW YORK
Anthropology Program
nabo@voicenet.com

**Cathryn Meegan**
GRAND CANYON COLLEGE
Ken Blanchard College of Business
mecat@mainex1.asu.edu

**Ben A. Nelson**
ARIZONA STATE UNIVERSITY
School of Human Evolution and
 Social Change
bnelson@asu.edu

**Margaret C. Nelson**
ARIZONA STATE UNIVERSITY
School of Human Evolution and
 Social Change
School of Life Sciences
mnelson@asu.edu

**Tate Paulette**
UNIVERSITY OF CHICAGO
Near Eastern Languages and
 Civilizations
tate@uchicago.edu

**Matthew A. Peeples**
ARIZONA STATE UNIVERSITY
School of Human Evolution and
 Social Change
matthew.peeples@asu.edu

**Jeffrey Quilter**

HARVARD UNIVERSITY
Department of Anthropology
quilter@fas.harvard.edu


**Charles L. Redman**

ARIZONA STATE UNIVERSITY
School of Sustainability
charles.redman@asu.edu


**Daniel H. Sandweiss**

UNIVERSITY OF MAINE
Department of Anthropology
daniels@maine.edu


**Payson Sheets**

UNIVERSITY OF COLORADO,
BOULDER
Department of Anthropology
Payson.Sheets@colorado.edu


**Katherine A. Spielmann**

ARIZONA STATE UNIVERSITY
School of Human Evolution and
Social Change
School of Sustainability
kate.spielmann@asu.edu


**Colleen A. Strawhacker**

ARIZONA STATE UNIVERSITY
School of Human Evolution and
Social Change
colleen.strawhacker@asu.edu


**Orri Vésteinsson**

UNIVERSITY OF ICELAND
Department of Archaeology
orri@hi.is

# Index